YOU CAN'T GET MUCH CLOSER THAN THIS

YOU CAN'T GET MUCH CLOSER THAN THIS

*Combat with the 80th
"Blue Ridge" Division in
World War II Europe*

A.Z. ADKINS JR.
& ANDREW Z. ADKINS, III

CASEMATE
Philadelphia & Oxford

Published in the United States of America and Great Britain in 2015 by
CASEMATE PUBLISHERS
908 Darby Road, Havertown, PA 19083
and
10 Hythe Bridge Street, Oxford, OX1 2EW

ISBN 978-1-61200-310-8
Digital Edition: ISBN 978-1-61200-311-5

Cataloging-in-publication data is available from the Library of Congress
and the British Library.

10 9 8 7 6 5 4 3 2 1

Printed and bound in the United States of America.

For a complete list of Casemate titles please contact:

CASEMATE PUBLISHERS (US)
Telephone (610) 853-9131, Fax (610) 853-9146
E-mail: casemate@casematepublishing.com

CASEMATE PUBLISHERS (UK)
Telephone (01865) 241249, Fax (01865) 794449
E-mail: casemate-uk@casematepublishing.co.uk

This book is gratefully dedicated to all the veterans of World War II, their wives and husbands, and their children.

We are who we are because of what these brave men and women fought and died for.

CAPTAIN A. Z. ADKINS, JR.

CONTENTS

Contents (continued)

Maps

Illustrations

PREFACE

For Christmas 1984, my dad gave me a 200-page three-ring binder titled "A World War II Diary." I didn't know he had kept a diary of his service, so it came as something of a surprise. Of course, I knew he had served in the infantry during WWII, but little else. And then in 1984 I was holding a day-by-day account of the most tumultuous time of his life.

Like many sons of World War II veterans, I grew up hearing occasional "war" stories and learned enough to know what a good job our soldiers had done. But like so many other veterans, my father did not talk much about the blood, the death, and what hurt the most—the loss of his men and his buddies.

I think this diary helped him bring a little more closure in his personal struggle to put the war far behind him. He was proud of his service for his country and proud of his accomplishments. Although he was awarded the Bronze Star, he never considered himself a hero. "The heroes were the ones who didn't come home," he once told me. I've heard that same phrase time and time again from many veterans.

When my parents were first married, my mother placed all his medals in a display case. I remember asking my dad once about them.

"Which is your favorite?"

Without hesitation he pointed to the Combat Infantry Badge. "That one."

His answer surprised me. "Why that one and not the Bronze Star?"

"Because being in the infantry, on the front lines—you can't get much closer than that."

At the time I thought he meant closer to the war. But as I've grown older, with a family of my own, I know now what he really meant. He was telling me you can't get much closer to your buddies; you can't get much closer to your own fears; and you can't get much closer to God.

There are many people who contributed to helping me complete my dad's WWII journal. Without their help and encouragement, this would remain a memoir on my bookshelf forever.

I'd like to thank Eric Hammel, my first editor who found me and provided me with much needed patience and guidance with the first draft. I also owe a debt of gratitude to Theodore P. Savas, who continued the editorial process with suggestions and thoughts to help round out the story, and to my publisher, David Farnsworth, of Casemate Publishing.

Jane Yates, archivist at The Citadel, was instrumental in helping me research archives and news events at The Citadel during the Pearl Harbor attack, which allowed me to describe the culture and attitudes of cadets during my dad's years at the Citadel.

When I read James Bradley's book Flags of Our Fathers, I felt so many obvious parallels between his relationship with his dad and my relationship with mine—I knew I had to finish this project.

My deepest gratitude is due my patient, devoted, and loving wife Becky, who kept encouraging me to finish this labor of love; and to my own children, Evelyn and Jared, who keep my humble and down to earth. I also need to thank my sister, Anne, who provided me with a plethora of facts about our dad I had not previously known.

Finally, I think my dad would like me to thank his parents, A. Z. and Lois, and his sisters Hazel and Lois, who kept him close to their hearts and to the Almighty Creator who watched over him in battle. I know he'd also sincerely thank his 80th Infantry Division buddies who fought and died through those tumultuous months treading through the snow, the mud, and the blood, and enduring the most miserable conditions imaginable. And I know he would say, "God Bless America!"

Andrew Z. Adkins III
Gainesville, Florida

Chapter 1

THE MAKING OF A SOLDIER

December 7, 1941–August 5, 1944

December 7, 1941, began just like any other Sunday at The Citadel in Charleston, South Carolina. There was early morning reveille, followed by physical training and a good breakfast. Sunday service followed in the Summerall Chapel. Little did we know this would be the "day that shall live in infamy."

As part of our education in world politics, we were required to stay informed of current events around the world. But, like most other 20-year-olds in a military college, my main focus was on education and an eventual commission, not world politics. I was still eighteen months away from graduation.

We knew Europe was again engulfed in war with Hitler's blitzkrieg into Poland in 1939. In the early morning darkness of May 10, 1940, the Germans attacked Holland and Belgium. French and British troops rushed to the rescue but were caught in the retreat of refugees and slowly pushed back. The troops fought valiantly, but in vain; the German war machine continued to advance unperturbed. In England, Hitler's invasion forced the resignation of Prime Minister Neville Chamberlain; Winston Churchill took his place. The Germans skirted the French Maginot Line and slashed into France through Luxembourg and the Ardennes Forest. Hitler's tanks rushed straight to the sea, reached the English Channel on May 21, and cut off the Allied armies in the north. The Germans turned once again, fought their way into the heart of France, and entered Paris on June 14, 1940.

On the other side of the world, the Japanese military was engaged in the seemingly endless war it had started against China in 1931 and was in desperate need of oil and other raw materials. Commercial access was gradually curtailed as the Japanese conquests continued. Eighteen months earlier, President Franklin D. Roosevelt had transferred the U.S. Pacific Fleet to Pearl Harbor as a presumed deterrent to Japanese aggression. In July 1941, the Western powers effectively halted trade with Japan. Desperate, the Japanese schemed to seize the oil and mineral-rich Netherlands East Indies and Southeast Asia; a Pacific war was now virtually inevitable. By late November 1941, with peace negotiations clearly approaching an end, American officials expected a Japanese attack into the Indies, Malaya, and probably the Philippines. No one expected an attack on Hawaii.

I think I first learned of the attack on Pearl Harbor late in the afternoon. Most cadets were sleeping or listening to the music on the radio when the reports started coming in. "Pearl Harbor bombed" and "Japanese attack the Philippines." Word traveled fast through The Citadel. At first we thought the stories were rumors or somebody's idea of a joke. Soon, our worst fears proved to be true: Japan *had* attacked Pearl Harbor. The first of two waves of attacks hit its target beginning at 7:53 a.m. Hawaii time; 366 Japanese fighters and bombers struck the airfields and battleships. The second wave of 168 planes attacked other ships and shipyard facilities at 8:55 a.m. It was all over by 9:55. By 1:00 p.m., the carriers that had launched the planes from 274 miles off the coast of Oahu were heading back to Japan.

The Citadel cadets received the news with surprising calmness, almost as if it had been expected. Later, we learned that 2,403 men had died in the unprovoked attack, and another 1,178 had been wounded. The strike destroyed 188 planes and crippled a Pacific Fleet that now included eight damaged or destroyed battleships. Nearly half of the dead were aboard the USS *Arizona*. Innocent men and women lost their lives protecting our country. That night we marched to supper chanting "Beat Japan" to the rhythm of the old Bulldog cadence.

On Monday, December 8, 1941, President Roosevelt signed the declaration of war granted by Congress. In the most historic speech of modern times, he stated the goal of the country would be the "absolute abolishment" of Japan, no matter what the cost. "The rising sun has risen; and it must now set never to rise again" was the opinion of one congressional observer. The next day, Germany and Italy, as partners of Japan in the Tripartite Pact, declared war on the United States. The shock of these declarations of war changed the entire future for most of us. It was then that we knew, deep down inside, that we were destined to be The Citadel's second war class.

My first instinct, like that of most cadets at The Citadel, was to drop out of college, join the Army, and fight those cowardly bastards who had murdered innocent Americans. In fact, some of my Citadel buddies did just that. In a letter dated December 9, 1941, I wrote my dad: "All of the cadets, just like everybody else, are gravely concerned with matters. None of us want to sit still, but we all realize that is the only thing to do. So we will just continue our regular schedule." My father's advice was solid: "Finish school, son. This will be a long war and you'll have your chance to serve your country and fight." He was right, as usual.

The Citadel, like many other American institutions, began planning for possible repercussions by unknown enemies. General Charles Pelot Summerall, president of The Citadel, issued General Order No. 14 on December 12, 1941, giving precise instructions to cadets, faculty, and administration in case The Citadel was attacked:

> 1. At the sounding of the City Siren for the air raid alarm, all members of the faculty and their families will remain in their houses until the alarm ceases.

> 2. The Commandant of Cadets will issue orders to carry out the instructions of the President as to the formation and security of the Corps of Cadets.

> 3. The employees in the mess and the laundry will remain indoors.

> 4. The Commandant of Cadets will appoint a fire marshal and will organize the companies into fire fighting units with assignments to all buildings on the campus. Requisitions will be submitted for all equipment needed.

5. The Commandant of Cadets will cooperate with the aircraft warning service in operating a warning station. He will secure the necessary equipment and have the Officer-in-Charge turn off the current at the master switch when the blackout is ordered.

6. All persons will turn out all lights immediately when the air raid alarm sounds at night.

7. The Commandant of Cadets will order practice alarms and practice the Corps of Cadets in the alert, the blackout and in fighting fire.

By Command of General Summerall

I continued my studies in political science, but with a renewed sense of strength, courage, and focus. When I first entered The Citadel in September 1939, I was eighteen years old, full of exuberance and young foolishness. My father was a lawyer and I was a spoiled brat, or so my two older sisters told me. My father insisted I attend The Citadel and become a man. After the bombing at Pearl Harbor, it meant more to me than ever to be an American, a feeling that would surface again and again in my years in the U.S. Army and continue throughout the rest of my life.

February 16, 1942, was another important day in the life of a cadet at The Citadel. Several hundred cadets who had turned twenty on or before December 31, 1942, and who were not in the Reserve Officers Training Corps or the Naval Reserve, registered for the draft. They were now eligible for service in the armed forces of the United States. Although they didn't expect to be called into service before the end of the present college term, they were subject to immediate call if they were needed.

"There were Citadel men at Pearl Harbor when the enemy struck so violently and unsuspectingly," exclaimed *The Sphinx*, the 1943 Citadel yearbook. It continued:

> There were sons of The Citadel on Bataan and Corregidor. They fought and some of them died though the task was hopeless, and only then did the survivors submit in body as prisoners of war. They are now present in Africa, India, China, Australia, Persia, and Iceland; in short, wherever the American flag is flying as a symbol of freedom and liberty, there are Citadel men there to guard it. In all

parts of the world, in every climate, they have fought as they were taught, that right is might and that a free people with the love of God and mankind firmly embedded in their hearts could never be crushed or moved from the pedestal on which they stand as living symbols of truth and freedom.

Those words echoed in my mind and heart every day. I graduated from The Citadel on Saturday, May 29, 1943. Four years earlier we had started out with 501 entering cadets and had been whittled down to 218. Chief Justice George W. Maxey, of the Supreme Court of Pennsylvania, told the survivors of the 1943 graduating class, "You young men are now going forth to fight for civilization against barbarism. Whenever the armies of Germany and Japan have exercised their furious and brutal power they have trodden under every decency of life and established new landmarks of infamy. . . . America accepts the challenge and answers 'present' when the roll is called of nations which love liberty and the right enough to fight for them."

My class would be the last graduating class for the duration of the war. Underclassmen, as well as graduating seniors, had also received orders to report for active duty. Besides a diploma, it was also customary for graduating seniors to receive graduation rings. Realizing that there would be no senior class the following year, the Class of 1943 voted that the Class of 1944 also be given rings as departing juniors, bearing the numerals "44."

It was an exciting time for me. I'll admit, I was a little nervous because I didn't know where I might end up fighting what was now known as World War II. I reported to Fort Benning, Georgia—Officer Candidate School—on July 25, 1943.

Fort Benning

Fort Benning, Georgia, was an astonishing military facility. Much larger than The Citadel, it housed tens of thousands of men and women. It was the training ground for the Army's officers. In a letter to my mother and father dated July 28, 1943, I wrote, "We have about 200 men in our company—63 from The Citadel, 124 from Texas A&M, and a few regular Army men. If things go O.K. I'll be here until the latter part of November."

Fort Benning was no picnic. The routine was dawn-to-dusk studies and physical work, followed by more studying and never enough sleep. Not everyone made it. "The school board met last week and kicked out 40 men in my company of 200, so you can see this place isn't easy," I wrote home that September. "Bob Roper left because his eyes were weak. He was sent to a finance school. My old roommate, Fred Fuller, was kicked out by the board—he has a growth on his lungs and is just waiting around for orders. He thinks he'll get a medical discharge from the Army."

The problem at Fort Benning was there were too many officer candidates. The "school board" was composed of high ranking and company officers who met periodically to interview men who had fallen behind. Fort Benning was hard on a man, and the fact that the Army had too many second lieutenants made matters worse, because they could run you into the ground and weed out those who couldn't make it.

"We went on our bivouac a week ago last Thursday and stayed until the following Monday. We slept on the ground in little tents like the one dad gave me when I was a little boy," I wrote my parents. "We were studying problems of scouting and patrolling and technique of rifle fire. It was hot in the daytime and cold at night. It's a hard life, but I [am] learning a lot."

After four months of grueling officer training I finally graduated November 23, 1943. I was now a fully commissioned second lieutenant in the United States Army. I have to admit, there were times when I didn't think I'd make it, whether it was the physical training or the continuous studying and testing. But I was determined to enter this war as an officer in the U.S. Army.

I was finally able to proudly wear my new officer's uniform, tailor-made, with my single gold bar. Several weeks prior to graduation we had a uniform display and I selected several officer uniforms. With all those who were dropping out (the school board continued to drop officer candidates because there were still too many), I wasn't sure if I'd ever be able to wear my new uniforms.

I was proud of myself. I had gone from an 18-year-old high school graduate of Bradford County High School in Starke, Florida, to a graduate of The Citadel in Charleston, South Carolina, and now a graduate and commissioned officer of Fort Benning, Georgia. My orders now read, "Report to the 80th Infantry

Division, California–Arizona Maneuver Area, Camp Laguna." Now just where in the hell is Yuma, Arizona?

California–Arizona Maneuver Area: Camp Laguna

In the early days of World War II, it became apparent the United States would need to meet the challenges of engaging the enemy in the deserts of North Africa. On March 1, 1942, Major General George S. Patton, Jr., commanding general of the I Armored Corps, himself a native of southern California, opened the Desert Training Center (DTC) in the Mojave Desert. Patton chose the town of Desert Center, population 19, as his headquarters. On October 20, the DTC was expanded to include maneuver areas and became the California–Arizona Maneuver Area (CAMA).

From 1942 to 1944, the facility served as the largest military training facility and a place to toughen the infantry for the rigors of combat in the forthcoming invasion of North Africa. In addition, it was a fertile testing ground to develop suitable equipment for harsh desert conditions. General Patton commanded the facility in its early years, followed by General Walton Walker.

The DTC/CAMA encompassed about 18,000 square miles (more than 12 million acres) in California, Arizona, and Nevada, stretching from Indio, California, eastward to Prescott, Arizona, and from Yuma, Arizona, northward to Searchlight, Nevada—roughly 350 miles wide and 250 miles deep. Patton and his team of advisors designated various locations within the area where temporary tent camps would be built to house individual units. The camps were situated so each unit could train individually without interfering with others. As each individual unit reached the end of its training period, it would join one or more units to train in corps operations.

Due to its hasty construction, expected short duration, and the U.S. Army's desire to train men in sparse conditions, the DTC/CAMA contained few permanent structures and was quite basic compared to other military bases. The Laguna Maneuver Area, one of eleven divisional camps in the CAMA, consisted of large valleys tucked between a series of mountain ranges.

I traveled by train to Yuma, Arizona, stopping in New Orleans to pick up the majority of my buddies from Fort Benning, Georgia. We got into Yuma on a Sunday afternoon, December 5, 1943. After several days on the train, I was hungry for some good chow. A few of us decided to go into town for some supper. I'd never been to Arizona before, so I didn't really know what to expect. I loved fried seafood though, so I ordered a big platter of fried oysters. Imagine my surprise when they came and I found out the restaurant didn't have any catsup. Here I was a fresh lieutenant, straight from officer training, lean and mean to the bone, facing a plate of big juicy fried oysters without any catsup! I just about gagged myself to death trying to choke down those awful slimy things and still keep a straight face in front of my buddies.

I was assigned to Company H, the heavy weapons company in the 2d Battalion, 317th Infantry Regiment, 80th Infantry Division. Eventually, I would be assigned as a mortar section leader. I would soon learn everything there was to know about the 81mm medium mortar, including range firing and tactics. I soon wished I'd paid more attention in my math classes at The Citadel, because firing the mortar involved a lot of angles, calculations, and math.

The heavy weapons company was one of four companies in a battalion. My company's mission was to provide support to the three rifle companies (Companies E, F, and G) in the 2d Battalion. The heavy weapons company was equipped with 81mm mortars and water-cooled .30-caliber medium machine guns. The mortar platoon was composed of three mortar sections with two squads each, which gave the company a total of six mortars. Each mortar squad consisted of six men: a squad leader (usually a staff sergeant), the #1 gunner (usually a corporal), the assistant gunner, and three ammunition bearers. At least, that's how it was described in the U.S. Army Table of Organization and Equipment (TO&E).

The 81mm (3.2 inches) mortar consisted of a 49.5-inch-long smooth-bore tube with a fixed firing pin at the bottom. The tube fit into a base plate that rested on the ground; the plate also helped to dissipate the recoil shock. A bipod, which was used to adjust for elevation, also supported the front end of the tube. The mortar was carried in three sections: the tube, the base-plate, and the bipod. The total weight of the 81mm mortar was about 135 pounds, and it was usually carried by two men.

The 81mm mortar had a range of 100 to 3,290 yards (almost two miles) and could be fired at a rate of 30 to 35 rounds per minute, with a normal rate of fire of 18 rounds per minute. There were two types of rounds used in the mortar: a high explosive (HE) round, weighing between seven and ten pounds was used to destroy enemy antitank guns, automatic weapons, mortars, and personnel; and a smoke round to screen the movement of troops during an attack.

My initial training in the desert began with the field artillery. I was temporarily assigned to Battery B, 313th Field Artillery Battalion, as the liaison officer from the 2d Battalion, 317th Infantry. It was a big title, but my job was to observe and learn as much as I could about field artillery.

My "home" was a tent I shared with two other officers. As you can imagine, there was sand everywhere and in everything. One of the nice things about being an officer in the desert was that each tent was assigned an orderly who did most of the manual work, including cleaning our tent, shining our shoes, and bringing water. I stayed with the artillery for about a month. One of the most important artillery lessons I learned from a seasoned veteran during this training period was this: "When the enemy is in range, so are you."

Several times during training in the desert I was able to take a few days leave and head down to Mexico, usually a little border town called Mexicali, about twenty miles from El Centro, California. We were allowed to bring back up to $7.50 worth of merchandise without paying duty fees; anything over $7.50 would cost an additional 60 percent! Most of the time I brought back some silk stockings for my mother in Starke, Florida. One of my buddies let me in on a little secret: if you tie the stockings around your waist, they won't be noticed when crossing the border. At the time, an American dollar was worth about 4.8 Mexican pesos. My Spanish was nonexistent, and most of the shopkeepers could only speak broken English, so I had quite a time trying to wheel and deal with those guys.

Training in the desert varied from week to week. Some weeks we would go on long, grueling hikes over the blistering sand. Temperatures would sometimes reach 125 degrees with little or no shade. Water was always in short supply. I found out later that part of the training included purposefully cutting back on rations, something we would experience time and time again during the Battle of the Bulge. Training under these conditions not only built us up physically but demonstrated how we would fight as teams: squads, platoons, companies, battalions, regiments, and divisions. We learned to fight both the enemy and the elements.

It was during these heavy training days that I learned most about soldiering from my company sergeants. Sergeant Ralph Freeman and Sgt John Quinn, who had been with the company since the 80th Infantry Division was reactivated in Camp Forrest, Tennessee, were seasoned soldiers, hard as a rock, and held the respect of every man in the company. I learned quickly that a good sergeant is worth his weight in gold.

Lieutenant Doug Brown and Lt. Bob Strutz, rifle platoon leaders in Company G, became good friends during training. Lieutenant Doug Cox was a mortar section leader in Company H, as was I. We constantly traded information and ideas about mortar tactics, as well as leading our men into battle. Lieutenant Bill Butz, a tall, good-looking Texan, was a machine gun platoon leader in Company H. Lieutenant Charlie Raymond was my mortar platoon leader. He and I became close friends, even though he was senior to me. Captain Jim Farrell, a red-headed fellow from North Carolina, was our company commander who led by example. Wherever his men were ordered to go, Captain Farrell was right there with them leading the way. You learn to count on your buddies; you watch their back, they watch your back. You put your life in their hands and you trust them and their instincts. You can't get much closer than that.

We left CAMA the early part of April 1944. The 80th Division's next stop was Camp Dix, New Jersey. The train ride carried us through El Paso, Kansas City, Chicago, and Pittsburgh. We knew by now we were headed to the European Theater of Operations (ETO) rather than the Pacific Theater. Divisions heading to the Pacific trained in the Louisiana jungle training center.

Camp Dix and the Atlantic Crossing

When we arrived at Camp Dix, New Jersey, we were issued new clothing and in some cases new weapons. We also received numerous inoculations. Preparations for overseas movement (POM) would last about a month. Camp Dix wasn't the greatest place in the world, but it sure beat the hell out of the tents we had been living in for the past four months. I was able to get home to visit my mom and dad during this time. It was really swell to see them, let them know what I'd been up to, and to eat some of my mom's home cooking. Those eight days went by really fast.

Word came soon that we would be moving out. We didn't know where, but we knew it would be overseas, most likely Europe. We had heard through the grapevine that the United States was planning something big, but we didn't have a clue as to how we would be involved. We also began a more stringent censorship on all outgoing mail.

The news of June 6, 1944, or D-Day as it would become forever known, hit us without any warning. The Army had done a good job planning Operation Overlord. We followed the war news through *Stars & Stripes*, reading everything we could lay our hands on. Most of us thought we would be heading over there very soon.

On July 4, 1944, the 80th Division boarded the *Queen Mary* after a three-day troop train ride. Very few of us had ever been on a ship and this was a huge one, complete with camouflaged paint. There were about 28,000 troops onboard and hardly any room to move about. I don't remember much about the crossing other than it seemed like we stood in lines for everything. Just as soon as we finished standing in line for breakfast, we started standing in line for supper. The food was worse than what we had had in the desert. Breakfast consisted of fried kippers or kidneys, served with God know what else. We also received boiled meat and potatoes. Fortunately, I still had a few candy bars my mom had sent me.

We had heard stories of ships being sunk by German submarines when they crossed the Atlantic, but for some reason I wasn't worried. Someone later told me that the *Queen Mary* could do 40 knots while the German subs could only do about 15 knots. There was no way they could catch up to us.

I was at peace with myself, even though I knew we were headed for war and possible death. Maybe it was my training; maybe it was my strong religious upbringing. I don't know. I pondered over where I'd been the past few years. From a high school football all-county center (it so happened I was the only center in the county) to The Citadel. The Citadel built character through discipline and camaraderie, as well as a well-rounded education. Fort Benning taught me the ins and outs of being an officer and how to lead men. But I think Camp Laguna taught me the most. That was where I learned how to lead men through example, and understand and appreciate practical battlefield strategies. We had trained there as a unit; these were the men I would go to war with. I had made many good friends over the past few months.

I was 22. Many of my men weren't even out of their teens. Many of the noncoms were only a few years older. I thought then I was prepared for anything and everything. The things I would learn on the battlefield that couldn't be taught anywhere were fear and death. Nothing could prepare you for that.

A few days after leaving the United States we landed at Greenock, Firth of Clyde, Scotland, and were greeted by a performing group of bagpipes. It was cool and misty, a typical Scottish day. The country was beautiful at this time of the year. Fields of heather and flowers all over the hills shined brightly. All of the houses were built of stone and brick and seemed like they'd been there forever. The people were nice and couldn't seem to do enough for us. We weren't there long. Later that evening, the 317th boarded a train and traveled south to Ashton, England.

We trained more intensely, even though there didn't seem to be room enough for what we needed to do. But we made do, because we knew that we would be joining the war soon. Our training included learning how to waterproof equipment in preparation for crossing the English Channel.

We also learned about hedgerows and hedgerow fighting, something we were not quite prepared for. A hedgerow was actually a fence made half of earth and half of hedge. It stood anywhere from a few feet to more than fifteen feet high. The hedgerow was several feet thick with a hedge of bramble, hawthorn, vines, and trees. Many of the Norman farmers had used these for centuries to enclose their plots of land, protect their crops and cattle from the ocean winds, and occasionally for firewood. Hedgerows did not follow any set pattern other than land plots; they were irregular in shape. Wagon trails and small roads wound among the hedgerows with sunken lanes that were often damp and dreary.[1]

We invited officers from one of the nearby hospitals to visit with us and tell us about the types of fighting men we would soon come up against. There were several disheartening stories of men who had been blown to pieces by mortar shells and died instantly on the battlefield. One thing we did realize, though, was that we had trained as a unit and we would fight as a unit. No man would be left behind.

In late July we prepared for our trip across the English Channel. The beachhead at Normandy had grown substantially since D-Day. We boarded trains at night, pulled the curtains down over the windows and eventually arrived at Southampton, England, where we boarded ships for a channel crossing that would take twenty-one hours. When we got close to the beach, we climbed over the ship's rail and down a cargo net onto a landing craft. We all huddled down as we headed over the last few hundred yards to the beach. When we grounded on the beach, the ramp went down and we waded in water above our knees to cover the short distance to the beach. I stepped ashore at Utah Beach on August 5, 1944, at three in the afternoon. It was D-Day plus 60.

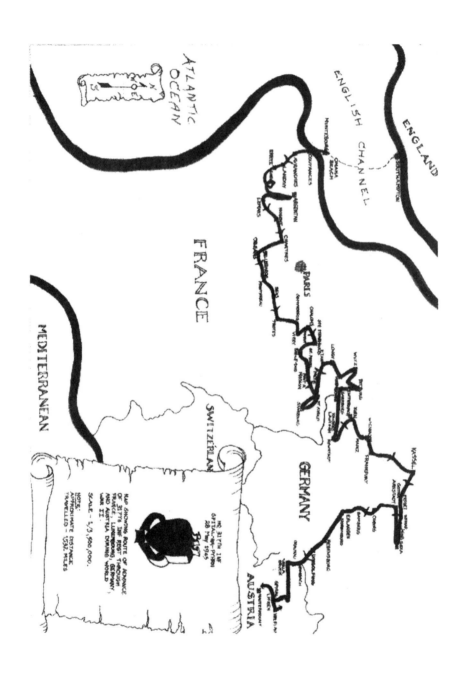

Chapter 2

FIRST TASTE OF BATTLE

August 5, 1944–September 4, 1944

We reached the regimental assembly area, about five hundred yards from the beach, and climbed aboard trucks for a ride to our bivouac area near Vareville, France. We noticed that the assembly area had a peculiar and unforgettable odor: dead men who had begun to decay. Once smelled, the stench of a decaying corpse is never forgotten.

We inspected and cleaned our weapons while we waited for the rest of the division to arrive. We were tense, but ready. On August 6, we climbed aboard trucks once more and rode to the vicinity of Coigny, France. We were close to combat, but not yet in battle. Everybody was on the alert. Any fast-moving jeep, command car, or truck meant the division was moving out. The unexpected appearance of a high-ranking official meant the same thing.[1] Rumors flew all over the place, and I admit I found myself caught up in the chaos.

We had been assigned to the XX Corps of General George Patton's Third Army. Not far to the south of us the Germans were in trouble. Patton's VIII Corps had smashed through the German Army at Avranches, crossed the Selune River at Pontaubault, and was driving into Brittany. The Germans had been thrown into confusion, but had plenty of fight left in them.

On August 6, the Germans counterattacked from Mortain. Their aim was to slice the Third Army supply lines near Avranches and cut off part of Patton's army from the rest of the Allied forces. The 80th Infantry Division received its battle orders the very next day: Help stop the German counterattack.

On August 8, we moved by truck forty miles to Pain D' Vaine, on to LeMans, and then to the vicinity of St. Hilaire, which was literally in shambles. Little shops and houses were smashed and gutted, their walls stood jagged and roofless. The roads were shell pocked from artillery and littered with battle debris. Nearby fields were strewn with the bloated, stinking corpses of men and animals. Charred enemy vehicles lined the route.[2] This was our first glimpse of the killing power of artillery.

We reached the assembly area north of Evron and received orders at 7:00 p.m. to attack and seize Evron. The 1st and 3d battalions attacked in echelon, with my battalion held in reserve. The objective of this attack was to seize Evron and gain the high ground to the northeast. The 317th occupied the town by ten the next morning. This was our first taste of battle. Even though I wasn't in the middle of it, I certainly heard from those who were. We had a few casualties, and some were even caused by our own forces.

Over the next few days we marched and rode in trucks through several small towns with very little resistance. In the middle of August, we moved into an assembly area in the vicinity of Argentan, the town through which the German Army intended to escape to the east from the Falaise Pocket. This pocket was caused by the closing up of the Canadian forces coming from the north and the American forces coming from the south. This was to be our first major encounter with the Germans, our "baptism by fire."

On the morning of August 20, the 3d Battalion attacked Argentan, contacted Canadian units, and sealed the fate of the German Seventh Army, which was completely smashed in the closing of the Argentan-Falaise gap. Ten thousand Germans died and another 50,000 were captured. "It was literary possible to walk for hundreds of yards at a time, stepping on nothing but dead and decaying flesh," wrote Eisenhower after visiting the site. Thereafter, Falaise was known as "The Killing Grounds."

During the attack, PFC Hoyt Rowell, a medic assigned to the 317th Infantry Regiment, was rendering aid to wounded riflemen under a hail of shells and bullets. When friendly artillery began to fall close, he raced across an open field to an artillery observer and lifted the fire. Returning across the same hazardous route, he continued to aid the wounded. For this display of heroism, Rowell earned the first Distinguished Service Cross (DSC) awarded to a member of the 80th Infantry Division in the war.[3]

This was our first real test in battle. Our orders were to seize the high ground northeast of Argentan, then swing southwest to take the city. We tried to as we had been trained, but it was much different when the stakes were real. No one at Camp Laguna had shot back at us, let alone dropped mortar shells all around us. Adrenaline kicks in during times like this, and it affects men in different ways. Some were exhilarated; others simply fell apart from fear. A few good men became "shell-shocked."[4] We also lost communications between our forward observation posts (OP), most likely because of the constant shelling or tank movements over the telephone wires.

My battalion attacked straight up the south slope of Hill 244, which was our objective. The high ground controlled Argentan from the north and the Argentan–Trun highway in the Foret de Gouffern. The ground north of Argentan sloped upward to form two smaller hills, 180 and 181, then dipped sharply and rose again to form the heavily forested Hill 244.[5] Enemy resistance was strong, and machine gun fire slashed into Companies E and G, which suffered seventeen casualties. One was PFC Earl Goins, Company E, a North Carolinian, who earned the Distinguished Service Cross when he rushed ahead through deadly fire and silenced a machine gun that blocked the advance of his company. Goins's heroism allowed his fellow GIs to outflank the remaining enemy gunners, who eventually withdrew. By noon, both companies were atop Hill 244.[6]

There was confusion everywhere. American and British warplanes roamed the skies and bombed and strafed German tanks, trucks, and infantry columns. Hundreds of German soldiers dropped their weapons and raised their hands, looking to surrender to the nearest Allied force. Others seemed too afraid to fight or flee and huddled near their stalled vehicles.[7]

By nightfall on August 20, the 80th Division had won Argentan. In the three-day battle, the 80th destroyed fourteen enemy tanks and captured about 1,000 German soldiers. Huge quantities of enemy equipment and supplies were captured or destroyed, including a dump with

27,000 tons of ammunition and a map depot. But our victory did not come easily. More than 400 80th Infantry Division soldiers had been killed or wounded.

I was deeply shaken by the experience, but came through it ok. The first moment I could, I wrote a letter to my mom and dad. It was Thursday, August 24, 1944. "Mom & Dad, I have been doing a little fighting lately, and have been in one major battle," I began. "You [will] probably read about it in the papers. I came through it without a scratch. I have been 'baptized' to fire, so now I know all the tricks. Therefore, there is absolutely nothing to worry about. I am a good soldier, love and believe in my God and my family and therefore I will be home before very long. All you have to do is pray for me and everything will be alright."

What I didn't tell them was I had killed my first German. While I'm sure my mortar fire had dropped on the enemy several times and killed and wounded some of them, this was the first time I had taken a life with my rifle. There wasn't much to it, as I think about it. We had been trained to think of the German soldiers as "the enemy" who had been killing innocent men, women, and children as they marched through invasion after invasion. In fact, we were told enough of these horror stories that the enemy was dehumanized in our minds. These Germans would stop at nothing to kill American soldiers, too.

I was moving slowly through the wood with a squad of riflemen from Company F, looking for a place to dig in my mortars. Suddenly, the lead scout dropped down and signaled that he had seen movement to our right front. We all froze in our position, dropped down to our knees, and strained to see any movement through the trees. We spotted a small party of German soldiers moving quietly from our right to the left, about thirty yards in front of us. The riflemen waited until they had the enemy in their sights, then the lead scout shouted "Halt." The Germans spun around and fired in our direction. All of us fired back. I took carefully aim at one of them and slowly squeezed the trigger on my M-1 carbine. It was almost like slow motion. Through the small sights, I saw his head open up as the bullet passed through the left side of his face. It was a sickening sight, but as I was caught up in the heat of battle, I didn't have a reaction other than feeling I had saved my own life. No one in the squad was hit. We wiped out the entire 8-man Kraut reconnaissance patrol.

We checked them over to see if any were alive and searched their bodies for their soldbuch. The soldbuch was the main form of identification carried by members of the Wehrmacht. Inside was each soldier's individual service record, which might contain information about his movements as well as personal data. Finding nothing of military value, I took the liberty of removing a German infantry patch, one of many souvenirs I would take during this war.

* * *

A few days later, I ran into a lieutenant who had been in command of the 80th Reconnaissance Troop after the Battle of Argentan. We started shooting the breeze and our conversation turned to Martincourt, a quiet, sleepy little French village with about two hundred and fifty people. The Germans were in and around the town. A small group of FFI (French Forces of the Interior) men had attacked the Germans near the town. In reprisal, the Germans moved into Martincourt through the town's two streets with tanks and infantry, killing everybody they saw. When they finished, they burned the town to the ground.

My battalion had started moving cross-country at dawn one morning and was still going at midnight. We were so tired some of the men fell to the side of the road and had to be prodded back in line. A little after midnight we spotted a big fire ahead. As we got closer, we could tell a village was burning. We didn't see a living thing as we entered the town.

Suddenly, an old woman emerged out of the rubble and in a frightened voice asked, "American? American?"

"Yes, we're American," one of us answered.

The woman was silent for a moment and then as if she suddenly realized that we were Americans and not Germans, cried into the burning rubble, "Les Americans ici, Les Americans, ici!" ("The Americans are here!)

Soon people, or rather human wrecks, began peeking out from behind the piles of smoldering rubble. Their eyes were hollow, bloodshot, and full of fear. They were crying and could hardly talk. One of our men who could speak a little French tried to soothe them and learn what had happened. An old man led us to the remains of a little church and showed us the charred body of a little boy. Most of his head had been blown away. The old man said the little boy had been in bed with a broken leg when the Germans arrived. One of the Krauts had killed him with a pistol. I felt sick and my stomach tightened in both disgust and anger.

All over the town were dead, charred bodies lying alongside burned carcasses of pigs and chickens. The partially burned body of an old man was in a small orchard on the edge of town. This old grandfather had been picking apples in his orchard when a tank shell blew away half his back and an incendiary grenade burned what was left. This was the first evidence we had seen of a German atrocity. It would not be the last.

The colonel assured the townspeople of Martincourt that the Germans would not be back, and urged them to do the best they could until we could send for help. With tear-stained eyes, they lined either side of the road and sang the French national anthem, *L'Marseille*, as we moved on.

Chapter 3

CROSSING THE MOSELLE

September 5, 1944–September 12, 1944

We had crossed the English Channel in ships. Now we had to cross rivers in small boats. We knew the drill, but we had yet to cross a major river under fire.

The Army dictated several different doctrines for crossing rivers and establishing a bridgehead once over. In situations where heavy resistance was expected, such as at the Moselle River, infantry divisions forced crossings on a wide front with several determined attacks at separate locations. This was our plan.

To transport our infantry across the Moselle, engineers used a standard M2 assault boat, which carried a crew of three engineers and a twelve-man rifle squad complete with weapons and equipment. Seventeen boats would be required to carry an entire rifle company of 193 officers and men.[1]

Crossing a major river was planned in four phases, and the crossing was usually done under the cover of darkness. First, we would meet in assembly areas to complete preparations for the crossing. Next, we would move into attack positions close to the river. The engineers would guide us to the riverbank to board the assault boats. We would load twelve men to a boat and the engineers would ferry us across in successive waves. Once across the river, we would try to

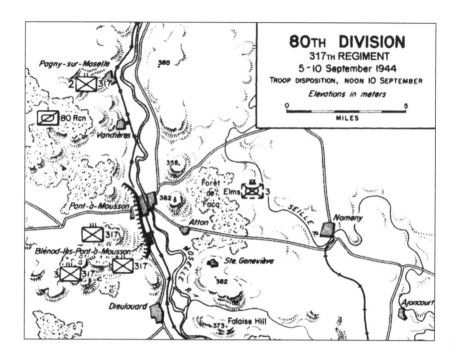

capture the area around the crossing sites. When these crossing sites were secure and free from enemy small arms fire, the engineers would build foot bridges, and then larger tread way bridges, to allow more troops and equipment to cross the river and expand the beachhead. At least, that was the plan on paper.

My battalion (2d Battalion, 317th Infantry Regiment, 80th Infantry Division) first tried to cross the Moselle on September 5, 1944. The 2d Battalion's task was to ford the river near Pagny-sur-Moselle, take Hill 385, and continue to attack southward to secure Hill 358. The 1st Battalion was to cross in assault boats near Blenód-les-Pont-a- Mousson, then maneuver to capture Hill 382 across from Pont-a- Mousson. The 3d Battalion was in reserve and was ordered to follow the 1st Battalion to help expand the bridgehead and allow our follow-on troops, artillery, and supplies to cross.

For two days officers and certain noncoms of the battalion had worked their way to an old chateau on top of a hill overlooking the town of Pagny-sur-Moselle, France, the Rhine–Marne Canal, and the Moselle River. To cross the river at this point, it was necessary to go through Pagny. The French told us there were Germans in the town and that they were well supplied with artillery, mortars, and heavy and light machine guns.

To take the town of Pagny, Lt. Col. Russell Murray, our battalion commander, ordered us to attack in a column of companies. Company G was to lead the attack with Lt. Doug Brown's rifle platoon in the lead, followed by Company E, then Company H. Doug thought perhaps he might need some mortar support in his attack, and since I was a mortar section leader in Company H, he requested I go along with him as an observer.

Before sending the first squad to attack, Doug, his squad leaders, and I went to a small knoll about three hundred yards from the edge of town. To our immediate front was an open field with a row of houses on the opposite side. A small farm enclosed within a stone fence was on our right. At the edge of the fence was a ditch. Doug's first objective was to clear the houses across the field.

It was about 11:00 a.m. The sky was clear and the temperature a comfortable 70 degrees. Doug ordered two squads abreast, led by their scouts. As usual, the lieutenant was up front with his scouts. A sniper opened up on them from the center house when they were about a hundred and fifty yards away. Everybody hugged the ground. The fire momentarily pinned down Doug and his platoon. The lieutenant signaled for his men to move again, and as they did another sniper opened up from a barn in the small farm yard to our right. In order not to hold up the advance, Lieutenant Cox brought up a section of 81mm mortars from Company H to take care of the nuisance in the farmyard.

Just as we thought we would be able to continue our advance, the Krauts started to throw in artillery from the hill east of Pagny-sur-Moselle—105s and 88s. The artillery caught me and Charlie Raymond, my mortar platoon leader, as we tried to lay telephone wire from our guns to the little knoll we were using as our OP. Although we had been under artillery fire before, we were still not used to it. I don't think you ever got used to it. The first few rounds landed in open fields well to our front. The next barrage landed in the woods behind us, where our battalion was concentrated. This caused a little temporary disorganization, not to mention a few casualties.

One of the shells had landed near Brown. Although there was not a scratch on him, the concussion had thrown him in the air and knocked him unconscious. His runner carried him to a barn in the farmyard on our right. The sudden artillery barrage disorganized his platoon, so Lt. Jim Bob Simmons brought his rifle platoon through Brown's, cleared the row of houses, and crossed the Rhine–Marne Canal, all under heavy fire.

While we were waiting to figure out what had happened and what to do next, I went to the barn to check on the lieutenant. His pulse was strong and he regained consciousness after a little cold water was thrown on him. His runner and I got some Frenchmen to carry him back to the medics.

Wondering about the delay, I went to look for Capt. Jim Farrell, my company commander, to find out more about our situation. I found him leaning against a railroad embankment on our side of the Rhine–Marne Canal, nonchalantly nibbling a chocolate bar.

"Captain, what's holding us up?"

"I don't know. Simmons got across the canal and was headed for the river when he got orders to pull back on this side."

A few minutes later, Capt. Jim Morgan, commander of Company G, arrived to tell us we were moving a little farther south to try another crossing there after dark. We still didn't know what was keeping us from crossing the Moselle.

It was about 6:00 p.m. when we started moving cross-country about a mile to our south toward a small town called Vandiéres. Company G's Lieutenant Bob Strutz had taken his rifle platoon to a little town on the edge of the canal area to reconnoiter and build a bridge across the canal where the Germans had blown out the original structure. Bob leaned his rifle against a tree in order to help his men move two barges they needed to build the bridge. That's when a small Kraut patrol showed up. A German hollered, "Halt!" In true western style, Bob whirled around, drew the .38 Colt he always carried on his right hip, and fired at the Kraut. The bullet missed. The stunned Kraut returned fire but it was wide of the mark. He withdrew quickly. The other Germans also managed a few shots, but they must have been stunned by Strutz's willingness to draw a pistol and stand there firing, because the whole patrol withdrew. The whole episode took just a handful of seconds. When it was over, Bob had a neat little hole in his raincoat where the first bullet went right between his legs.

The rest of the battalion reached the Rhine–Marne Canal about 2:00 a.m. on September 6, 1944. The canal was about fifty feet wide at this point. The barges they had tied together made a nice foot bridge, and with Company E in the lead, we walked across single file and reorganized on the opposite bank in a column of twos. It took about two hours for the entire battalion to cross. I had no idea what we were supposed to do once we were over that canal.

The battalion moved south along the edge of the canal for about a thousand yards until we came to the river's edge. There was my first close-up view of a little creek they called a river. Usually, the Moselle was about six to eight feet deep and had an average width of 150 feet. Because of recent heavy rains and opened dams upstream, the current was very swift, about five to six knots. To make matters worse, the Moselle's flat flood plain varied in width from four hundred to one thousand yards. We knew the Germans were observing everything from the high hills on the eastern bank.[2] We didn't know it at the time, but because of the delay in getting supplies to the Third Army on the front lines, the Germans had been able to stock up on supplies of their own, as well as reinforcements and artillery.

We turned left and followed the bank of the winding Moselle, heading north. The rain had ceased, the night was bright and clear, and the only noise was the sound of infantrymen walking. We continued for about a thousand yards. When I looked to my right, I could see the river was only about a hundred yards wide in this sector. Our column was stretched in a horse-shoe manner, bending to the south, then to the north, alongside the river. One of the gunners behind me was griping about having to carry "this damned heavy mortar base plate all over this godforsaken country." As he was grumbling and I was chuckling under my breath we all heard the word "Halt!" yelled out from across the river. We instinctively hit the ground—and not a moment too soon. The Krauts opened up an intense machine gun fire that swept the spot where we had just been standing. The rounds whizzed their way past just inches above our heads. Initially only one gun had opened, but within a few seconds there were four or five of them stuttering and clacking in their effort to cut us down.

My platoon was close enough to see the muzzle blast, hear the Krauts work the bolt when the gun jammed, and hear them talking. As always, they fired not in bursts of six, but in bursts of belts. Some of us fired back even though they could not see the enemy. One of Lieutenant Brown's light machine guns was brought up and the gunner opened fire from his hip. I only managed to fire a single magazine from my carbine before the damn thing jammed on me.

The machine gun across the river from us jammed as well. We could hear the Krauts bitching and yelling and working the bolt. We noticed early on that the gun was beside a large tree silhouetted against the sky. Sergeant Freeman had a bazooka he wanted to fire into the base of the tree. There was no one around to sling any lead to support us, so I told him not to fire. Firing a bazooka at night produced a bright white flash that would certainly give away our position. It would have been suicide unless we had plenty of suppressing fire to keep the Krauts busy. And we didn't.

These Krauts knew what they were doing. One gun fired tracers about four or five feet above the ground while another squeezed off grazing fire with ball ammunition parallel with the gun that fired tracers. We knew this because we could hear the bullets cutting the grass around us and yet see tracers going over our heads. We lay there for a few minutes, trying to catch our breath and figure what to do next. We were completely pinned down. And then the Krauts fired a red flare. I knew then we were in trouble.

Within a short time mortar shells began dropping all around us. We were in a tight spot, completely disorganized and pinned down without any artillery support. The Moselle was to our front and the Rhine–Marne Canal was behind us. After what seemed like hours word finally arrived to withdraw to the canal; everyone started back immediately. Only Sgt. Ralph Freeman, Sgt. John Quinn, Cpl. John Binnig, and I were left in our sector.

The four of us started back to the canal, which was about three hundred yards to our rear. I crawled for a time and then got up and ran like hell. The Krauts had slowed up a little on their firing. They had been caught with their pants down, too. Lieutenant Raymond was waiting for us at a small opening in the thin woods next to the canal. A railroad embankment stood between the tree line and our canal, and we crouched behind the embankment with part of our bodies in the water. A few mortar shells arced their way through the night in our direction and the machine guns fired interdiction fire. There was nothing we could do but lay there until daylight, and it was one miserable long night. The bridge we had come over was eight hundred yards to my left. Like every other stationary object in the area, the Germans had zeroed their artillery in on this bridge and had it covered well. It was impossible to do much of anything until sunrise. I don't know why, but just then I got sleepy. It was just one of those things. Freeman and Quinn were pissed because at that inopportune moment, both had to take a crap. They fought the urge.

At daylight, we pulled out our smokes that we had wanted for so long. Freeman and Quinn crawled up over the railroad behind trees and relieved themselves. We reorganized and waited for word to come down on what to do next. Some of the men had dropped their equipment, including mortar and machine gun parts, near the river. To this day it remains a mystery to me why the entire battalion—a battalion in a column of twos caught in the crossfire of four machine guns—hadn't been wiped out.

Bob Strutz told me later that two of his men had been trapped in a hole near the river and could not move. They couldn't even reach for their canteens. When the sun rose the jig was up, so they raised a white handkerchief. The Krauts told them to come out and walk to the river. When they reached the water the Krauts told them to swim across. One of the men had sense enough to tell the Krauts they could not swim, so the Krauts told them to move downstream a short distance and ford the river at a shallow spot. The men walked a little downstream and then ran like hell. Both made it safely back.

Daylight brought with it danger in the form of artillery shells—105s and 88s. As we clung desperately to the side of the embankment, the shells whizzed overhead and exploded all around us. Some of the men began to panic and started to run and swim the canal. Shell fragments from the large shells killed several of them. The canal was only about forty or fifty feet wide, but it was deep. Anyone who could dog-paddle could have made it, but some of the men who tried it couldn't swim a stroke. They drowned before anyone could get there to help them.

I later heard that a sergeant went after one of his men who couldn't swim. He got the man ashore, but he drowned in the effort. A few troops who lose their nerve can spread panic throughout an entire battalion. Captain Jim Morgan hollered to the men around us that if anyone else tried to swim the canal, he would shoot them down himself. I believed he would have, too. He waved his carbine to show them he meant what he said. That seemed to quiet things down a little.

Word came down that we were to work our way toward the blown-out bridge. We were going to try to get back across the canal. Everyone was anxious to get out of that place. When we reached the bridge, Lieutenants Raymond and Cox went across the canal first. I was ordered to direct the men from our platoon to them. We were really disorganized at this time and it was all we could do to prevent an "every man for himself" situation. All during this time, medics were trying to get the wounded back across the canal using small boats.

Our platoon assembled in an orchard in town. It wasn't long before artillery started to fall in the orchard. One of the rounds landed close by and exploded with a terrible concussion that shook the ground like an earthquake and threw shrapnel in every direction. One of the pieces struck Pvt. John Concini. As a medic attended to him, I ran farther into town and found a gutter behind a stone wall to house the platoon. Lieutenant Raymond fed the platoon to me. I reorganized the men while he and Cox went to look for a gun position to position our mortars. Company F, with Bill Butz's machine gun platoon, stayed in position along the canal while the rest of the battalion took up position in the town and on the high ground behind the town.

The men crouched there in the gutter with a few shells falling around while we reorganized. Everyone was dazed and tired. We had been in caught a death trap and knew it, and the fact that so many of us got out at all was a miracle. This was the first really hot spot we had been in. Some of the men were missing, but most came straggling in later. Sergeant Freeman, the platoon sergeant, came up and told us the news: Concini was dead. That really hurt his buddies. He was the first to go.

My company had crossed the canal with five complete mortars, but we had only three and a couple of pieces left over. A heavy weapons company normally carries a complement of six 81mm mortars.

Raymond's runner, Private Haraksin (affectionately called Junior), reached me about this time. "Lieutenant Raymond wants I should take you up on a hill he is on." Junior always spoke slowly and with a drawl. How a Pennsylvania Yankee acquired a Southern accent, I will never know.

"What hill, Junior?"

"Over that a way," he answered. We followed Junior south along the street for about five hundred yards, turned west, and headed through another orchard in which Company E was digging in. Then we headed southwest about a thousand yards. We were gradually walking up a slope that broke on top of a long hill about eight hundred yards wide. Near the top was an open spot. Lieutenant Raymond was sitting and waiting for us there. No matter which way you looked—north, south, east, or west—it was eight hundred yards of open flat ground. The Moselle River valley was a flat flood plain without cover or concealment. The Germans had excellent fields of fire. The river and canal formed a double obstacle to our troops. I couldn't remember reading anything in the field manual about how to place mortar on terrain like this. While we were deciding what to do, I heard a cry from the orchard below. It was Pvt. Jay Miller, one of our runners. He had been hit by shrapnel and was calling for a medic.

We dug our mortars in on our flat hill. Company G was to our right along a deep wooded draw. Down to our left front was Company E, digging in inside an apple orchard. Still farther to our left front was Company F, with Bill Butz's machine gun platoon, digging in along the blown bridge and the barges we had tied together.

Down in front in the valley, we could see the Rhine–Marne Canal. It was glass smooth. Behind the canal was the snakelike Moselle, and behind the Moselle the terrain rose to high rolling hills. Lieutenant Raymond and I searched the high ground across the Moselle. We looked through our glasses hoping to find something to shoot at. It would be good for morale if we could fire at the Krauts for Concini. Although we looked for what seemed like hours, we didn't see anything move. The Krauts were continuously throwing artillery and mortar our way, but most of it was landing on the canal near Bill Butz's position. I am sure the Texan was not pleased about that.

By now much of the adrenaline had worn off and we were hungry and thirsty. There was no food to speak of, and we had last filled our canteens thirty-six hours earlier. Most were now bone dry. We were on our own, scrounging whatever we could for food and water. Someone discovered some plums in the orchard and we ate them. I still remember how good they tasted.

Lieutenant Raymond headed down into town to see what was cooking. He sent word back to bring the platoon to a road junction northwest of our present position. We couldn't get there by going down the hill the way we had come up because the Krauts had the roads and orchards well covered with artillery, and they delighted in laying it down heavy when they saw even just two or three people moving. We got ourselves organized and headed out about 3:00 p.m.

Shaultz, one of the ammunition bearers, came in from the south and said Captain Morgan and Lt. George McDonell, Company G's executive officer, were there and that there was a big wooded draw to the south where we might be able to get out. We looked it over. It was a regular jungle and it would have taken us hours to get around the series of hills to where we were supposed to go. That left but one thing; go west approximately a thousand yards across exposed ground and then northwest down the hill to the river junction, where we were to meet up with Lieutenant Raymond.

We moved along on the hill and didn't know what was to our south beyond Company G. Captain Morgan later told me he had seen a German antitank gun, which he thought was an 88, looking down over the low ground we started moving through.

As we stood there by the guns trying to decide which way to go (the long way or the short exposed way), an artillery observation plane flew low over us. As the pilot leaned over the side we could see him point to the northwest. We didn't realize then what he was trying to tell us. Later, when I talked with Captain Morgan, it became apparent the pilot had also spotted the antitank gun and was trying to tell us not to go that way.

It was getting late and we had to hurry. I started infiltrating the men west across that long stretch of open ground where the Krauts could look down our throats. We maintained five or six hundred feet between men just in case the shells started falling. I told them to run, but they were very tired and carrying heavy equipment, so they couldn't run fast or far. I got the men started and then set out myself to find Lieutenant Raymond. Sergeant Freeman was bringing up the rear. It was about three quarters of a mile to Lieutenant Raymond's location, in a draw to the north of the river junction. I was tired as hell. I looked back at the men as they came stumbling down off the hill. It was good to see them. They were really spread out. I heaved a sigh of relief; artillery couldn't hurt them now.

As I was watching a Frenchman drive a herd of cows across the river junction, the Krauts laid down an artillery barrage on the help-less animals. I guess they were either bored or re-sighting their guns. We moved out in a hurry and headed toward a hill north of us, so I never learned what became of the Frenchman and his herd. Captain Jerry Sheehan, the battalion S-3 (operations officer) met us there to guide us to the battalion assembly area. Company G and Bill Butz's machine gun platoon were to stay on the high ground overlooking the town. We walked until about 10:00 p.m. Private Karol Jaworski, one of our ammunition bearers, couldn't keep up and fell out, so I carried his ammunition for him the rest of the way.

Our kitchen personnel had K-rations and oranges for us when we reached the battalion assembly area. Chow tasted good, especially in that it had been a while since we had eaten. Without any real rest they piled us into trucks and jeeps and hauled us to another assembly area about ten to fifteen miles to the southwest. We got ourselves straightened out as best we could, posted our security, and bedded down for the night. I don't recall much about that night except that one of the battalion ammunition trucks caught fire and exploded. The mighty "boom!" and pyrotechnical display scared the hell out of all of us. It rained that night, but we didn't care; we were dog tired.

The country around us was rolling with wooded hills. As we discovered, we were just west of Blénod-les-Pont-a-Mousson, a feature known as Foret de Puvenelle. We stayed there a couple of days to rest, draw equipment, reorganize, and train the newly arrived replacements.

Division staff tried to determine the best way to cross the Moselle River—in a different location and in a different manner from our first attempt. Reconnaissance patrols were sent out many times during these two days. Two Red Cross girls brought up their trucks and served us coffee and doughnuts, which was a real treat. We always appreciated the Red Cross and the efforts they made to help comfort us during these times.

On Sunday, Chaplain Graff held services in a small draw. A large number of men were there, and I wondered if the previous day's events could have anything to do with the larger-than-usual attendance. The chaplain prayed,

> Almighty Father, lift up our hearts and minds that we may serve You. Give us the courage to do the things that come to us to do. Keep us from downheartedness. Give us the wisdom and the joy to keep the hearts of those around us lifted. Give us willingness to share in the common responsibilities.
>
> Wherever we may be, let us never lose sight of Your presence. Though we stand surrounded by fear and peril, sustain us. We shall not be afraid when we know that You are there.
>
> To You we entrust our lives, our country, and our ideals. We are but trying to fulfill Your will the best we know how. We work not to

destroy but to preserve the good, not to enslave others but to liberate the enslaved in all lands. The victory for which we pray, which we try to serve, is the victory of all humanity.

Let us not fail in our faith in the dignity of the human spirit Let us not falter in the vision of a nobler, kinder way of life. Let not the love of freedom fade from our hearts.

Lord, lead us on to the tasks that lie ahead of us, to the labor of uniting the nations of the earth, to the peace founded not on force but on the mutual respect of free men. Amen.

It was on one of these rare quiet days that one of the men came into camp rolling something that resembled a cylindrical block of manure. We gathered around to see what he had. He said that it was French cheese, but we didn't believe him. To prove it, he pulled out his trench knife and peeled off a thick outer-layer, which resembled pressed manure. Beneath was a hard yellow substance: cheese. We all whipped out our knives and tore into it. It was the best cheese I had ever eaten.

After a few days we moved north to another and better bivouac area about a mile away to the southern edge of Bois Le Pretre. We used the woods to keep the movement concealed so the Germans would not be able to ascertain that we were concentrating troops for a river crossing. Word came around that we would try to cross the Moselle again shortly. Come hell, high water, or Germans, this time there would be no turning back. Any officer who led his men back across the river once we had crossed it would be court-martialed. We knew other outfits had also caught hell trying to cross the Moselle.

By this time most of the men who had been missing since our first attempt to cross the Moselle on September 6 had been accounted for. Three were still missing: Private Novak, Private First Class Sebra, and "The Frenchman."

Several Frenchmen had joined us in northern France when we were fighting in the hedgerows. During one of our movements by convoy, three had come to us and said they wanted to fight with the Americans. At that time we were riding in jeeps and trucks, and they happily climbed aboard. Soon thereafter we had to leave our trucks and start cross-country on foot. After several hours of marching over the broken terrain, the two older Frenchmen decided they could best serve their country by going back and joining a group of armed French we had recently passed. But the youngest of the three, whom we naturally named "Frenchie," decided he would stay with us. He had a French submachine gun that he said he had buried during the German occupation. We could not persuade him to trade it for a more reliable M-1 carbine.

I explained to him that, as much as we would like to have him fight with us, the U.S. Army could not take responsibility for him. We could not give him any pay, nor could we draw any equipment for him. That didn't seem to faze him a bit. All he said he wanted to do was to kill Germans. That was fine by us. The men took him under their wings, outfitted him in a G.I. uniform, and saw to it that he ate when they ate.

Company G had also acquired a couple of young French boys. They not only proved to be good scouts, but great foragers as well, and kept us well supplied with eggs and bread from the French farmers to supplement our diet of K- and C-rations..

The missing "Frenchie" finally found us after we moved into our new area and filled us in with information. Private Novak, he explained, was put on guard duty by another outfit and shot in the leg. Novak wrote some of the men later and said that he didn't want any misunderstanding, and that he had not shot himself. Sebra had simply been on the front too long. According to several of the guys, he just lost it and ended up back at the regimental aid station.

The artillery around us pounded the Krauts across the river night and day. We tried to relax but we knew elaborate plans were being made for the river crossing. My battalion was selected to spearhead the division across, with Company G leading the way, followed by Companies E and F; various attachments would follow. On several occasions the officers went to OPs overlooking our prospective crossing point. They also scouted the high ground across the river that was our objective. It looked like we had rough business ahead. The Germans had a great view and field of fire of every prospective crossing point. On one of these scouting trips, Captain Morgan was accidentally shot through the knee by a Frenchman and had to be evacuated. The Frenchman said he thought the captain was a German.

We were in Alsace-Lorraine now. The people were different here than they had been in Normandy. The Normans were very glad to see us and kept us supplied with bread, wine, champagne, and eggs. Here, they more or less took us for granted and were very cool toward us. These were the kind of people, as a prisoner later told us, who would yell, "Vive l'Amerique!" if the Americans came marching into their town. And if the Germans came in, they'd yell "Vive Germany!" We would quickly dispose of them if they interfered with our plans or turned on us.

Division staff finally completed plans for the river crossing. The plan was to place some fifty heavy machine guns on the high ground near Bois de Cuite, on the west side of the river, to give us overhead fire. Eight battalions of artillery were available to cover the crossing. The engineers would ferry us across the river in assault boats. There was only one hitch in the plan: in order to cross the Moselle, we first had to cross the Rhine–Marne Canal again.

Our first attempt to cross the Moselle had been a failure. In our mad dash across France, we reached the river before the Army was ready to properly support us. When we got to the river, we didn't have enough time for proper reconnaissance or sufficient supplies of food and ammunition. Intelligence information, usually gathered from reliable sources, underestimated the enemy strength, both in men and in artillery. We had no air support and very little artillery support. Besides that, we had tried to cross in broad daylight. We would be better prepared for our next attempt.[3]

For security reasons, the date and hour of the crossing were not disclosed until the last minute. At 6:00 p.m. on September 11, word came around to be prepared to move out at dark. This was it. Everyone was tense, but we were ready and determined to succeed. We were going to cross the river and stay across. We moved under cover of darkness to our LD (line of departure), a wooded hill overlooking the river north of the town of Dieulouard, about five miles south by southeast of Pont-à- Mousson.

The plan was for the artillery to lay down a fifteen-minute concentration of fire beginning at 4:30 a.m., after which Company G would spearhead the river crossing. We had about a two-hour wait when we reached our LD. The routes from the assembly area down to the boats had been well marked by the engineers. The markers were supplemented by the men tasked to lead the columns to the assault boats.

According to Regimental S-2 (intelligence), some five to six thousand enemy combat troops were waiting for us on the other side of the Moselle. They belonged to the 29th Panzer Grenadier Regiment and the 3d Motorized Division. They also had great observation points from the hills, automatic weapons, and an unknown quantity of artillery. We had our orders and we had learned some tricks from our previous attempt to cross the river.

The night was pitch black. Trying to keep contact with one another was very difficult, even though each man had a strip of luminous tape stuck on his back. Company E followed Company G. Each had a machine gun platoon from Company H with it. The 81mm mortars were to follow Company E across the canal and then take up the rear in crossing the river.

Our artillery opened up right on time—4:30 a.m. Tracer bullets from the .50-caliber machine guns arched through the night sky. It sounded good going the other way. We pulled out a few minutes later. 2d Battalion was on the left, and 3d Battalion was on the right; 1st Battalion was in reserve behind 2d.

Our mission was to cross the Moselle and take Genevieve Hill (Hill 382), the high ground east of Dieulouard. Somewhere along the line someone from Company E lost contact with the man in front of him and, as a result, everyone behind him was led down the wrong way. Lieutenant Raymond was mad as hell. He found a guide to show us the right way down. When we reached the road, our artillery opened up again. We lay down to wait for it to lift, then headed for the canal about six hundred yards away. Guides directed us to the pontoon bridge that Lt. Jim Bob Simmons had built earlier. We had to jump across a shattered twisted body on one end of the bridge, where one of Simmons' men had gotten it while helping to build the structure.

The crossing of the canal itself was anti-climatic. We had not known exactly what to expect, but the heavy greeting by the Krauts many were waiting for failed to materialize. We all breathed a sigh of relief as we assembled in a draw to reorganize and find out which way to go. That guy who lost contact with Company E really caused us hell! We had to be real careful, too. We knew the Germans had placed antipersonnel mines all over the place, and we could only hope the engineers had cleared all of them. A few days later we learned the 305th Engineer Combat Battalion had removed forty-four booby traps. The mines were blown in place by exploding the charges on top. God, I love those guys!

We were in the draw only a few minutes when the first Kraut shells started coming in. Several landed in the draw with us. We didn't hear them until they were right on top of us. As usual, we hit the ground as fast as we could. Standing up, even tens of yards away from the blast, was almost always fatal or nearly so. Several of my men were hit nonetheless. One of the shell fragments split open Cpl. Sidney Folmsbee's arm. I was going to try and help him when a small piece of shrapnel hit me in the butt, which hurt like hell! I reached around and felt blood. I thought for sure that my ass had been shot off, but I could walk and yell, so I knew it wasn't too bad.

The shellfire moved about in search of Allied soldiers to kill, and Lieutenants Raymond and Cox left to find the rest of the battalion. It was almost daylight now, and we still hadn't crossed the river, even though most of the battalion was already across. I decided to look for Lieutenant Raymond. I met him on the way back from the river. His messenger had "gotten lost." The engineers were there and had rubber-and-plywood assault boats to carry us across.

We put fifteen men into each assault boat—three engineers and twelve riflemen. The men paddled while one of the engineers in the stern guided the boat with a paddle. Seventeen boats were usually sufficient to carry a rifle company across a river. Sergeant Freeman and I stayed to take up the rear of the platoon. I remember taking furtive looks into the eastern sky. Daylight was coming quickly. That was bad.

Our artillery barrage, however, had done some good. The heavy pounding had pulverized the German defenders and driven most of them out of our way. The few who remained fired machine guns and 88s at the boats. The air was filled with zipping bullets and screaming shells, some of which struck boats loaded with soldiers. When we discovered the current was stronger than any of us expected, we all grabbed a paddle and pushed hard for the eastern bank. I knew that wherever we landed, Krauts would be waiting for us. Were they are nervous as I was? I looked at my watch. It was 6:30 a.m.

Chapter 4

HILL 382 (ST. GENEVIÈVE)

September 12, 1944–September 24, 1944

We reassembled after crossing the Moselle River. The 1st Battalion was to follow us across the Moselle, then the 3d Battalion, then the 318th Infantry Regiment. Part of the 2d Battalion had already reached the top of Hill 382.

Company G's objective was St. Geneviève, a small town on the north end of the hill. I'll never forget it. We started up the hill. It was about a mile to the top and tough going all the way. We reached the crest about 8:00 a.m. Things had quieted down somewhat, so the battalion worked to consolidate its position. We had to hurry because we knew the Germans would counterattack at the first good opportunity. They had lost their hill, but they would come back and try to retake it.

Hill 382 was a long, kidney-shaped hill running north and south. As we looked to the east, we could see to our immediate front a clear open space with splotches of trees. To our left front were thick woods known as Foret de Facq. To our right front were more thick woods. On the north end of our hill was the little village of St. Geneviève. The side of the hill to the east was steep and covered with brush. To the west, we could see the winding Moselle River in the valley far below.

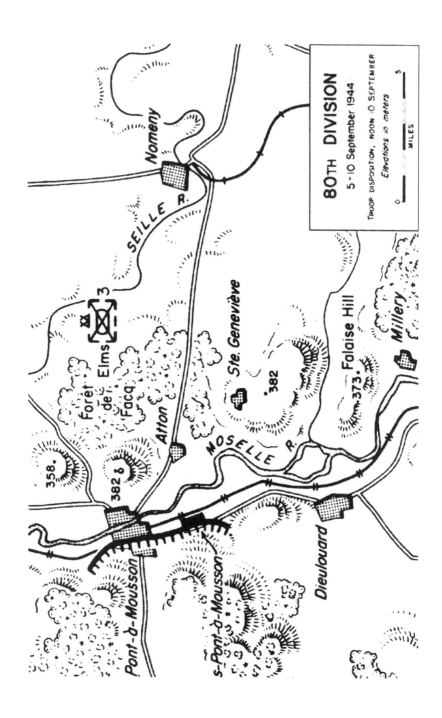

Company G was ordered to hold St. Geneviève with two rifle platoons supported by Bill Butz's machine gun platoon. The other rifle platoon of Company G extended to the south on the forward slope of the hill and tied in with Company F, whose lines extended farther south. Company E was in support, echeloned to the right rear of Company F, and the 1st Battalion was on our right flank. The beachhead was formed. The plan now was to hold the high ground until the 318th Infantry crossed over under the cover of darkness, fanned out to our left front, and took the Fortress Pont-a-Mousson about two miles north of us.

The hill we were on was full of natural crevices and World War I emplacements. It also had a few trees on it, so we took advantage of them. We put two sections of mortars in a huge natural cut about 150 yards to the right rear of the two other sections. We set up two OPs. One was to the left front of the mortar positions and the other was farther to the left front, near Company F. To our immediate front was low ground, some of it open, some thickly wooded. We could see Krauts all day long and, of course, we dropped mortar shells on them throughout the day. Occasional small arms rounds would zip over our heads or through our position. Everyone was tense, waiting for something big to happen.

I was with Company F overlooking our left front. As soon as my mortars were set up, we fired to establish a base point. I selected a small group of trees in the front of Company F's area and fired a round, adjusted my mortars, and fired again. My mortars were ready to go. To the left of my base point was a large wooded area where the Krauts were active. Around the middle of the afternoon we counted thirty Krauts moving from the woods to the small stand of trees I had earlier established as my base point. I could feel the adrenaline tingling my scalp as the enemy unwittingly moved into my killing zone. When the time was right, I ordered my two mortars to fire. Each let go six rounds. WHOMP . . . BOOM! The shells landed right in the middle of them. Those that were still able got out of there in a hurry! We counted the Germans as they fled. One . . . two . . . three . . . we stopped counting at seven, because that was it. Seven men. About twenty-three had been killed or wounded within a few seconds. We slapped each other on the back and offered one another congratulations. Colonel Murray, our battalion commander, was there with me. He liked it, too.

That night we put Sergeant Popejoy, Private Suggs, Private Windsor, Private First Class Herman, and Private Stanley at a combination OP/LP five hundred yards to our left flank to keep an eye on things. Lieutenants Raymond and Cox stayed with two sections of mortars, and Sergeant Freeman, Corporal Binnig, and I stayed with my section of mortars. I had each of my guns in a hole about thirty feet in diameter and about seven or eight feet deep at the center. The men had dug themselves foxholes inside this hole. Freeman, Binnig, and I stayed with Sergeant Zinn's gun. Two men per squad were on guard at a time.

We settled down for the night. I lit a cigarette and lay in the bottom of my foxhole, dragging deeply on the butt as I looked up into the beautiful night sky. With the exception of the rumbling of artillery in the distance, everything seemed so peaceful. My thoughts turned to home, my mom and dad and my sisters. I hoped they would sleep well this night. I knew I wouldn't be getting much sleep.

The Germans started their counterattack about 5:00 a.m. on the morning of September 13. We didn't know it at the time, but two battalions of the 29th Panzer Grenadier Regiment, reinforced with artillery and tanks, were engaged in the assault. They attacked us from the north, from Foret de Facq, through St. Geneviève and Bezaumont, then eastward toward Ville-au-Val. At first all the shooting was against Company G down in the town of St. Geneviève. The heavy combined arms fire inflicted numerous casualties and drove the company back. It reformed with Company E and Company F.

Everybody in my hole was awake in an instant. I crawled up on the edge to look and listen. It was a foggy morning. The Krauts were firing something I had never seen before from the east. It was a green tracer about 20mm size and it was time fused. That is, it exploded above the ground. The eerie green light caused by the exploding shells cast a nauseating glow over our sector. Every object became a moving green phantom in my mind. I tried to call Lieutenant Raymond over the phone, but there was no response. Either Charlie wasn't there, or the line was out.

We hugged the ground. Several shells landed in the hole with us, showering us with dirt and debris. I was dazed for a little while and had to shake my head to regain my senses. Someone was yelling. It took me a few seconds to realize it was Private Jaworski, one of our ammunition bearers. He was screaming in pain. Sergeant Freeman was dazed but unwounded. Sergeant Zinn was okay, calm as ever. A damn good soldier that Zinn. We hollered to see if anybody else was hit. Binnig had been Struck in the back and couldn't move at first. Jaworski's yelling prompted me to crawl toward his steaming foxhole. I was almost afraid to look inside. He was hit really badly. Both of his legs were mangled and bloody.

"Don't worry, Jaworski, you'll be ok," I told him. "I have to get you out of there to stop the bleeding."

He looked at me with his face screwed up in agony and nodded. I tried to lift him from his hole, but he cried out, "Oh, God, I can't stand it, I can't stand it!" I let him go for a few seconds and tried again. Again he screamed in pain. With the help of a couple other guys, we finally lifted him out and laid him on the ground. His pain was beyond description. He kept saying, "For God's sake, put a bullet through my head, Lieutenant! I can't stand it. Please, Lieutenant, put a bullet through my head!"

As others tried to patch his wounds I set off to find Company E to get a medic. I didn't know exactly where Company E was, so I ran to the left rear in the direction I thought would lead me to it. A voice cried out, "Halt, goddamn you, or you're a dead son of a bitch!"

"Don't shoot. It's Lieutenant Adkins from Company H. Don't shoot, I'm Lieutenant Adkins! I need a medic badly! My men are hurt and I can't find my platoon!" I yelled.

"Lieutenant, you almost got shot! What the hell's going on?" the soldier yelled back.

"The Krauts are pouring in against Company G," I replied.

"They're coming in on our rear, too. Our support platoon has already fallen back to our main line and everybody is turning around in their holes to shoot to the rear," said another voice from the dugout. "I think we are surrounded, or nearly so."

A white helmet with a red cross on it popped up. "Lieutenant! You say you need a medic? Let's go." It was Raul. He came with me without question even though the Krauts were walking artillery shells across our position. When we arrived, Raul gave Jaworski a shot of morphine and patched him up as best he could. It was obvious if he did not get serious help he would die soon. Binnig's back wound was not as bad as we first though, and he could hobble about under his own power. During the excitement I had forgotten all about Mazoney, a 35-year-old replacement who had been with us for just a few days. He was still in his hole. "Medic," he said calmly, "when you get through with him I wish you'd take a look at me. I think I've been hit in the back." Mazoney had been hit almost as badly as Jaworski. When Raul got him out and turned him over, he discovered that some shrapnel had cut a deep long furrow across his torso.

I told Binnig and Freeman to help Mazoney and themselves over to Company E and try and get back to the battalion aid station. Freeman was still dizzy as hell. I wanted someone to stay with Jaworski while I went to the platoon to get a litter for him. We had to get him to a doctor soon or he would die. Zinn said he would stay.

After I got back, I went to Sergeant Reinecke's hole. Private Cecil Roberts was the only one there. The rest had gone to the platoon (I had told them to leave if things got too hot.) Charlie Raymond, my platoon leader, was okay. He was setting up an all-round defense. Herman and Stanley had come back and told us the Krauts were coming in on Company G and Company F.

One of our men hollered to us. A group of twenty to thirty men was heading for our hole. We couldn't tell who they were. When they were a few yards away, Charlie shouted, "American?" They didn't seem to understand. It was then we recognized their helmets as German. One of them shouted to us. They didn't know what the hell the score was either. They had no idea where they were, or whether we were Germans or Americans. Charlie shouted for them to surrender. They kept shouting in German (I imagine they were asking us who and what the hell we were.) They didn't throw down their weapons, so we opened up. All we had were carbines, pistols, and M-1s. We killed a few, but the others ran off south toward 1st Battalion's position. We could hear the 1st Battalion shooting and shouting. Those they didn't kill, they took prisoner. Those Krauts were tired as hell. They were too tired to run, and they had to drag themselves along.

It began to quiet down at daybreak. I went back to see Zinn. Jaworski, despite his bad wounds, was sleeping. Thank god for morphine. We got him out soon afterward. Sergeant Freeman was there, even though I had told him to go to the battalion aid station. He wasn't going to leave his men. Some of the Krauts we had seen earlier had tried to come in the hole with him and Zinn. They showed me a grenade dud that had landed in one of the vacated foxholes. On the bank above them were three dead Krauts. They had been shooting back-to-back, had gotten one Kraut apiece and one together. Freeman's carbine jammed, but he was able to fix it. At one point Jaworski woke up and cried out, "Is anyone with me?" About that time Freeman shot his Kraut. If Freeman and Zinn hadn't stayed with Jaworski, the Germans would have gotten in the hole and killed him. Freeman and Zinn both got the Silver Star for that. Freeman's shot was a beauty. It caught the Kraut under the chin and went out through the top of his helmet. We looked at the hole Jaworski had been in. One shell had landed four feet to his left and another about six feet to his right. His foxhole wasn't deep enough; he could get his body in but not his feet. That's why his legs were mangled. Of course, we didn't learn the details of all this until later.

There was still a little shooting to our left flank. We had had no contact with Popejoy for several hours. We hoped that he, Windsor, and Suggs were still in the OP. I followed the phone line out to their OP and carried a telephone with me. When I was about six hundred yards out, I ran into some men from Company B who had been sent over to us to help out. They told me I better not go on, because the Krauts were firing a machine gun from that direction. I plugged my telephone into the line extending out from the mortars and told this to Charlie Raymond. He decided to come out and join us so as not to miss the fun. That guy took great delight in getting into the thick of it. He wasn't scared of a damn thing!

Charlie was only with us for a few minutes when things quieted down quite a bit. It was about this time when I spotted someone without a helmet sitting on the edge of the OP hole. I looked through my binoculars. It was John Windsor.

Jesus Christ! Why in the hell was he sitting up on the side of a hole without his helmet on while all the shooting was going on? I determined to chew his ass out when I reached him. As I ran toward him, I noticed another GI hovering over a hole with his rifle pointing at a Kraut. The enemy soldier was lying on the ground moaning. He was wounded.

"Come out, you bastard!" shouted the soldier. He paused a couple seconds. "I said get the hell up!"

The Kraut was pretending to get up, but was really trying to pull the pin on a hand grenade. When the GI realized this, he emptied his M-1 into the Kraut, whose body danced a bit before lying still. Why the hell didn't that son of a bitch surrender?

A few seconds later I reached Windsor. "Damn it, Windsor, what are you . . ." I stopped mid-sentence when I saw he had been hit. He had two slugs in his left shoulder and was in a lot of pain.

"Medic!" I screamed at the top of my lungs. I did what I could until a medic arrived a few minutes later.

I later learned what had happened at the OP. When the Krauts started their attack, Sergeant Popejoy sent Herman and Stanley back to tell us because they couldn't reach us by telephone. When we got there, we found that the Krauts had cut the phone wire. Popejoy, Suggs, and Windsor stayed in the hole. They could see the Germans moving around and could hear them talking. They exchanged fire. The Germans were obviously trying to get to the high ground around the OP. If they had gotten it, they would have had excellent fields of fire and good commanding terrain.

The Krauts had thrown hand grenades that landed all around the OP hole, but none got in. Windsor was shooting with his shoulders and head exposed. A Kraut about thirty feet away opened up on him with an automatic weapon. Every time Popejoy tried to get Windsor to duck, Windsor would say, "I ain't scared of the SOBs." After two rounds hit him, Popejoy whipped around and clipped the Kraut. When the ordeal finally ended, we found five dead Germans and two wounded. We also found four Kraut machine guns and two Panzerfausts. One dead Kraut officer had tried to crawl up a little into the hole. He made it to within six feet when Windsor killed him. If the Krauts had been able to take this high ground, they surely would have been able to raise hell with our battalion.

A number of prisoners had been taken by the battalion. I saw a German medic tending to his wounded. Popejoy said they saw him crawling around carrying a Geneva Cross flag during the little scrap.

Here's the big picture of what had happened: The Krauts had come around both ends of Hill 382. A fairly large force made their way through St. Geneviève. They attacked with tanks and infantry supported by artillery and drove Company G out. The 318th Infantry was crossing the Rhine–Marne Canal and Moselle River at the time, so it wasn't in position or organized to fight a defensive battle. German tanks raised hell with them. The 318th regimental CP was knocked out and some men were captured. The regimental commander was seriously wounded. My battalion CP caught a little hell, too. We lost more than one hundred men in that battle.

The Germans we faced were SS, elements of the 17th SS Panzer Grenadier Division. They wore camouflage suits over their regular uniforms and civilian clothing underneath. They wore enough stuff to be equivalent to our full field pack. It was apparent that they had come with the intention of staying on "our" hill. I guess we disappointed them.

Our regimental Intelligence and Reconnaissance (I&R) platoon leader had come up near Popejoy's OP during the night. He and some of his men were missing. Bill Butz had caught hell with Company G in the town of St. Geneviève. He and Lou Cox had also lost a few men.

This was the morning of September 13. We spent the rest of the day consolidating and strengthening our positions. Someone up the line must have smartened up and realized we needed a little help if they expected us to hold our hill. About noon, tank destroyers (TDs) and towed 76mm antitank (AT) guns came up the hill to join us. Two of the armored halftracks towing the AT guns parked on top of the hill near our hole. They had been parked there only a few minutes when the Krauts started to concentrate their artillery on them. As a result the shrapnel flew around like raindrops. Charlie Raymond shouted to the drivers, "For God's sake, put those things under cover. We want a little peace and quiet for a while."

When things quieted down a little, the men dug the mortars and themselves in deeper. My section moved into the big hole with the rest of the mortar platoon. I found a guy going to Regiment who promised to send a cablegram to my folks.

During the night when the Krauts had tried to come in our hole, we did not have any automatic weapons. We were not about to get caught in that situation again, so we set out to rearm ourselves. Charlie got a Thompson submachine gun. One of the men got his hands on a couple of .45-caliber M-3 "grease guns" and gave one of them to me. We sent carrying parties to the base of the hill to get food, water, and ammunition, and bring it back to us; we would be here for a while. Sergeant Freeman wasn't doing very well, so we sent him back to the medics.

In the early part of the night, Capt. Jim Farrell sent for Doug Cox and me. The company CP was about a half mile from our guns. We made our way through absolute darkness, with no moon or stars to light or guide our way.

"Do you know where we're going?" I asked Cox. When he answered yes, I just followed him. After we were challenged a couple of times by pickets from Company E, we continued on.

"Doug, I think we should have been challenged by Company F, right? Are you sure you know where you are going?

"Well, I think so." He hesitated. "How about you?"

"I'm not sure. I thought we should bear to the right a little more."

We came to some small woods I did not remember ever having seen. We went into the woods a little way and saw a group of men standing around. We felt relieved. They were probably part of Company E's light machine gun section, which was supposed to be in some woods. They didn't say anything, so we walked up to them.

I tapped one on the shoulder. "Hey, buddy, where is Company F?"

Just as I said that I saw the outline of a German helmet. My heart was racing and I couldn't breathe. When they heard the foreign tongue, one Kraut whirled around with a burp gun held at waist level. Doug grabbed the gun just as the Kraut pulled the trigger, spraying rounds all over the place. I think I fell on the ground. Doug dove in the other direction.

They must have thought I was dead or dying, and I am not sure they ever figured out there were two of us. The Germans started going through my pockets. If he had put his hand in my left breast pocket, the pounding of my heart would have knocked him ten feet! Some of our boys, whom we later learned were from Company F, heard the shooting and came to see what was happening. Luckily, the Krauts were a reconnaissance patrol and the last thing they wanted was a serious fight. As soon as they heard our boys approaching, they moved out as fast as they could. Doug's hand was singed, but I don't think he was as scared as I was. After it was all over, and for the rest of my Army career, every time my friends saw me they would say: "Hey Andy, did you ever find Company F?"

* * *

The Krauts attacked again early on the morning of September 14. Charlie Raymond and I were with the platoon, and Doug Cox was at the new OP near Company F. It was broiling by 8:00 a.m. It was also foggy, and we could barely make out silhouettes at one hundred yards out. Most of the action seemed to be down in St. Geneviève, where

Company G was dug in. Those boys were catching hell. We thought we had set up good communications to guard against confusion, but none of our phones worked. We had lost contact with everybody. We set up a perimeter defense in our hole while Charlie set off to find out what was going on.

It was getting hot as hell, and I had my hands full. The hole we were in was really large, with a cave in one side and a smaller hole on the other side. I sent Sergeant Volk to the smaller hole to take charge of the men there. A few minutes later I heard him yell, "Lieutenant, there ain't nobody here!" I didn't know what had happened, so I sent him some men. I found out later that Charlie had sent word back for everyone to clear out and go down to the 1st Battalion, on our right. Somehow, in the heat of things, that word only got as far as the men in the small hole. The rest of us had no idea.

By this time there was fighting going on all around us. We didn't know what to do except hold on and pray as the bullets whizzed above our heads and shells exploded almost everywhere. We couldn't get anyone on the phone. A guy from a tank destroyer outfit tumbled into our hole. He was crazed with fear. All he could do was lie on the ground and try to get his breath. He had no helmet and no weapon.

"Soldier!" I yelled at him. "Get yourself together! What's going on?"

"Lieutenant, for God's sake, get your men out of here!" he shouted back. "The Germans are all over the place! They've knocked out my gun and killed my buddies. They had me for a while. I lost my gun. Can you give me one? Give me a gun. Please, give me a gun!"

Whitwell was not about to take this sort of crap, and he reached over and knocked the hell out of him. Whitwell was one of the best— always cool as a cucumber. His actions quieted the TD man down some, and to his credit, he later apologized for his actions. We were all scared as hell, and his carrying on like that didn't help us any. He still wanted a gun, so I threw him my pistol.

The ground started moving and a terrible rumbling sound flooded our hole. Tanks! Voices shouting commands were heard next, but they were muted and distant. Were they German or American? Heavy shooting broke out about three or four hundred yards north of us. We crouched there on the side of the hole, waiting and praying. As the enemy moved closer we breathed a sigh of relief. They were our men! They saw us through the heavy fog about the same time, and one of them yelled out, "There are the bastards. Let them have it!"

I recognized that voice. It belonged to Lt. Ray Wadsinski, one of the rifle platoon leaders in Company G. He and twenty men were the only ones who got out of St. Geneviève. They opened up on us with light machine guns mounted on tanks. We ducked back into our hole and kept yelling, "Cut out the damn shooting, we're Americans!" It took quite a while, but they finally heard us and stopped shooting. Thankfully, no one was hurt by the friendly-fire.

Ray and I tried to find out from one another what was going on and where everybody was, but neither of us knew much of anything. Neither did the captain with the tanks. About that time we spotted a group of Krauts heading for our hole from the same direction they attacked the night before. The tanks pulled up closer and opened up with their machine guns. They just mowed the bastards down. There was so much noise we couldn't hear ourselves think.

The tank captain (whose name I no longer remember), Ray, and I were leaning against one of the tanks, trying to figure out what to do, when an 88 shell slammed into the tank. All I recall was picking myself up off the ground several yards away and scrambling like a madman for the big hole as the tank's ammunition exploded in a giant fireball. How we escaped being killed or seriously hurt I will never know, but a couple other tankers remained with the tank and were not as lucky. No one knew where the 88 came from, and how they could have zeroed in on us in this weather I will never know. Maybe it was just a lucky shot, but the tank captain decided to move south toward the 1st Battalion on our right flank. Ray wanted me to come with him, but I decided to stay in our hole.

Private Cecil Roberts and his bazooka (we only had two in the platoon), together with a couple of other men, were keeping a lookout on the west side of our hole. He called for me, so I crawled up beside him. We could hear a tank and some talking to our west, but we couldn't see anything because of the fog. I asked Roberts if his bazooka was ready to fire. He nodded in reply. We waited. The sounds came closer. It sounded like a German tank to me, with squeaky ball bearings. I looked through my binoculars and spotted through the haze the silhouette of a tank. The hatch on the turret was open. From the stabilizer on the muzzle I could tell it was a Tiger. A soldier was standing in front directing it. The tank looked as if it was slowly working its way toward us, although I didn't think it had spotted us. In all honesty I was scared to death. Roberts was scared, too, but he said, "I'm ready, sir."

The tank kept coming until it was only fifty yards away. I could hear my heart pounding over all the other noise, and the blood was pumping in my temples. I prayed to God not to let the tank come any closer toward us. I think I said out loud, "God, turn it the other way." Five seconds later the tank turned north and disappeared into the fog. Roberts and I sighed out loud, and he looked at me sort of funny, as if my prayer had worked. I just shrugged.

Men from other companies, some tankers and some TD guys, had gathered in the hole with us. They seemed more dazed and scared than we were.

"Look guys, if you are going to stay here, get off your dead butts and help my men defend the hole."

"We ain't going to run out on you, Lieutenant. We'll do what you say," answered one of them.

Crying was heard from the knocked-out tank. The guys we thought had been killed for certain were still alive! Some of the ammunition within the tank was still exploding, but some of the men risked their lives to get to the wounded. The men dragged and carried back two tankers to the hole. They were in bad shape, with terrible shrapnel wounds and burns. Doc Tillman, our platoon medic, fixed them up the best he could and shot them full of morphine. One of them died a few minutes later.

Later in the morning the other wounded tanker called for me. He was a good-looking young man about twenty. His legs were badly mangled and his hair and eyebrows had been singed off.

"Do you have any water?" he whispered. I unscrewed my canteen and held it to his lips while he drank. He was in a lot of pain, but the morphine Doc Tillman had given him helped.

"Where are you from?" he asked.

"Florida. I'm from Florida."

"Did you see my leg? How is it?"

"Yes. Well, it looks kinda messy." I don't know why I told him that.

"No, it's not bad at all," he answered.

"Where are you from?" I asked, trying as best I could to talk about anything other than his wounds.

"Indiana," he answered, dozing off to sleep. Thank god for morphine. I never learned his name.

About that time Doc Tillman came walking into the hole with a man on his back who had been shot through both feet. A little while later some medic jeeps came up to the hole. We sent the wounded out on them.

Some of the men were examining Private First Class McQuain's helmet. It looked like a sieve. When Ray Wadsinski and the tanks he rolled up with had opened up on us, a few of the slugs had ripped through McQuain's helmet. All McQuain had received was a scratched neck, ear, and hand. His luck had been incredible. When we had first tried to cross the Moselle, a stray bullet had pierced through the right side of his helmet and stopped between his helmet and liner. We decided he needed a new helmet.

As we were laughing about McQuain's luck, Charlie Raymond came marching back with eight prisoners, one of whom was wounded. "Where the hell have you been?" I asked.

He grinned and said, "I have been playing peek-a-boo with these cute little bastards. Ain't they pretty?"

"Why didn't you get all of us when you took the boys and pulled out last night?"

He looked surprised. "Didn't you get word to come?"

"Hell No!"

Charlie grinned. "You're alive, ain't you? What in the hell are you bitching about?"

The prisoners he had captured were perfect specimens of manhood. They were SS troops—all hand-picked men. We stripped them to the waist in order to search them. Their bodies were sleek and rippled with muscles. They weren't scared of a damn thing. We tried to get them to tell us how many German troops were to our front, but they wouldn't say anything, not even when we ground burning cigarette butts into their necks.

Lieutenant Lou Cox, a machine gun platoon leader in Company H, stormed into our hole, mad as a wet hen because Charlie had taken prisoners. "What in the hell do you mean by taking these bastards alive," he yelled. Captain Farrell came up and quieted Lou down. Charlie got some more men and hand grenades and went out again to get some Krauts he had cornered in a small patch of woods. They didn't want to surrender, so he sprayed the woods with his tommy gun and threw in a few hand grenades. That did the track, and the Krauts decided it was smarter to surrender than be killed.

I walked into St. Geneviève to see Bill Butz. As I approached the edge of town, I could see that the boys there had had a rough time.

I found Bill lying in a cellar dazed and unfocused, leaving his runner to explain to me what had happened. Bill had to abandon his machine guns when the German tanks rumbled into town. Corporal Richhart, Bill's platoon sergeant, had grabbed a bazooka to try and stop the Kraut armor. Bill loaded for him. They hit one tank and were reloading to fire at the other when the second tank rotated its turret and fired. The shell exploded beside them, blowing Richhart to pieces and throwing Bill against a wall.

Lieutenant George McDonell, 1st Sergeant John Geste, and several others were missing, explained Bill's runner. Bob Strutz was dead. He got it as he was running toward a tank to climb on its side and drop a grenade down the hatch. His head was completely gone. We looked for it, but could not find even a piece of it. One of Bill's best gunners had also been killed. His corpse was slumped against his gun, his head riddled with holes. Lieutenant Jim Bob Simmons was one of the lucky ones; he escaped the slaughter of St. Geneviève with half of his foot blown off.

The rest of the day was relatively quiet, except, of course, for the artillery that was always falling on some part of the hill we were on. We spent most of our time trying to rest and clean our equipment.

The 318th Infantry was still trying desperately to take Fortress Pont-A-Mousson. Atop that mountain were the ruins of an old castle. Pont-A-Mousson was a couple of miles away to our northwest, which made it to the left rear of our hill if we faced east. It was an excellent OP for German artillery observers. Not only could they open fire on the 318th, but also on us.

* * *

It was my night to stay at the OP near Company F. It was a quiet night except that it rained and we were all miserable. This was the night of September 14–15. September 15 was also fairly quiet. A steady rain continued to soak us. Whitwell and I stayed with Company F on the night of 15–16. There was more rain. We were having trouble with our light telephone wire being cut by tanks, so we got some heavy wire from the communications platoon. It wasn't much better. We did have SCR536 field radios to use when our wire went out, but sometimes they didn't work either.

Our dead lay everywhere, mixed with dead Germans. We didn't have time to move their bodies, nor did we dare to venture out into the open knowing the Germans were breathing down the back of our necks. It was hot during the day and their swollen bodies were beginning to stink. When a man is killed, he turns a chalky white. After a little while, he turns blue, then black, and begins to swell and stink. His features become distorted and grotesque. It's a sickening sight. It touches your soul to know these black stinking bodies were once your men, let alone your buddies. It tears you up inside when you think these rotting pieces of meat were once the men you had taught how to fight. The one comforting thought in this hell world was knowing these men would never suffer again and were no longer in pain.

* * *

It was still raining and foggy on the morning of September 16. I was with Lt. Jess Barton. Krauts had been trying to come up the hill all night long. It was so foggy we couldn't see anything, but we could hear them moving and we could hear vehicles to our front. Jess's hand was bandaged where he had been nicked by a sniper bullet. Lieutenant Omar Bergdal was trying to adjust artillery on the foggy area to our front. Because of the hill we were on, it was necessary for Bergdal to fire farther out and bring the rounds closer in. That did not suit Jess one bit. He wanted artillery, and he wanted it in a hurry.

"You're too damn slow," griped Jess.

Bergdal replied. "I have to go slow to clear the hill we are on."

"To hell with clearing us! Bring the damn stuff down on top of us and then move it out!" Jess retorted. I'm not sure I liked the sound of that!

We could still hear the Krauts in the foggy recesses across our front. We tossed hand grenades over the side of the hill to discourage any of the bastards who might want to come up. I was in a hole with a BAR man from Bob Strutz' rifle platoon. He was cleaning his BAR in the rain. He worshiped Lieutenant Strutz.

"I won't be satisfied until I kill a hundred Krauts for that swell guy lying up there." He pointed to Bob's body, which lay on the ledge in front of us. "You know, Lieutenant," the BAR man continued. "That guy had more guts than anybody I have ever known. He couldn't do enough for his men. He never asked us to do anything he himself wouldn't do."

Bob Strutz had no business being in the Army, much less in the infantry. He had a bad leg and had had to lie his way through his physical examination when he volunteered. But like most of the rest of us, he had pure American blood in his veins. He had loads of money and a beautiful wife. I think his father made corncob pipes.

Almost like a curtain in a play, the fog suddenly lifted a little. I could see three or four Krauts walking up the road leading into St. Geneviève. They were about four hundred yards away, and had no idea we could see them. The BAR man opened up on them and the Krauts scattered. I don't know whether he hit any of them, but it sure was good to see them jump around for their lives.

Krauts had been going in and out of the big woods to our left front. They were becoming more active. It looked as if they were trying to set up mortars at the edge of the woods. I fired our mortars at the maximum range, but the rounds fell short. I called back to Sergeant Zinn at the guns and explained the situation. He said, "Give me a minute, Lieutenant." If anyone could make these guns shoot farther, Zinn could. The field manual stated the maximum range of a high explosive (HE) mortar round is about 3,290 yards, but I knew Zinn would figure out a way. He added charges to the shells and spread the bipods. The rounds really went out. After a few of them found the range, the Kraut mortar crews decided their position was not so good after all and pulled back.

Soon after they left a German armored car drove around the south edge of the big woods. It was flying two huge Geneva Cross flags. Colonel Murray was there and gave orders not to fire. We passed it up the line. The vehicle went into St. Geneviève and about fifteen minutes later came out and went back into the woods. A few minutes later Kraut shells fell right on top of us. They had been falling all morning, but none this close. Those damn Krauts had brought an observer into the town under cover of the Geneva Cross. They had been known to do that.

We had been expecting some tanks from the 4th Armored Division to come in from the east to help us out. The recognition was to be a yellow flare. About the middle of the morning we saw some tanks coming toward us. We recognized them when they came in closer. A Company F man who had been up all night fired his flare and the tanks answered. They had the 2d Battalion, 318th Infantry, with them.

As usual, I was in the wrong place at the wrong time. Colonel Murray asked me if I thought I could deliver a message to the tank commander that he had just received over the radio. What could a shave-tail say to his battalion commander except, "Yes, sir." The message was from Division: the tanks and infantry were ordered to move to a wooded hill in the Foret de Facq between St. Geneviève and Pont-A-Mousson.

I asked Jess Barton for a man to go with me. The soldier's name was Meggins. He borrowed a BAR from my old friends, and I took my grease gun. On the way down we noticed fresh tracks in the mud. The Krauts had tried to come up during the night. It was a good thing Company F had been dropping those grenades over the side. I delivered the message to the tank commander. It was beginning to rain as we gathered around a torn-up house. I became dizzy and had to sit down for a while. It was then I realized I had forgotten to eat for the last couple of days.

As Meggins and I were getting ready to go back up the hill, our tanks started raising hell They had cornered a German tank, and finally nailed it on the way up. I looked up to where our positions were, but nothing could be seen. Everything looked natural, as if no one had been there at all. Our positions were excellent and well camouflaged. That is, of course, if the Krauts had wanted to come up the same way I did.

It was quiet the night of September 16–17. It was also quiet on the 17th, though it was cloudy and foggy weather with light rains. Toward the middle of the afternoon we heard that we were going to be relieved and sent into division reserve. I was with Company F with Maj. Karlton Warmbrod, the battalion executive officer, and Lou Cox. We were all tired and anxious to leave this hill. "Major, when are we going to pull out of here?" asked Lou. The major shot back, "What do you mean pull out? We're not pulling out of anywhere. We're being relieved!"

Rumor had it that we were going to guard a road block. We knew it didn't take a battalion to guard a road block, so we thought we might get a little rest. Lieutenant Saul Kadison, a new officer for Company H, joined us the next day about noon. It was still raining. About 2:00 p.m. on September 18, the 319th Infantry relieved us. We marched down off the hill, cold and wet in the drizzling rain—but damn glad to get off that hell hill.

On our way down, we ran into Lt. George McDonell and 1st Sgt. John Geste. They had been taken prisoner a few days earlier when the Germans had launched their first counterattack, but had managed to escape. We were damn glad to see them, but not nearly as happy as they were to see us.

* * *

Much to our disappointment, when we reached the river we were ordered to take Hill 351. Our weapons were on the carrier, so we had to load up and go off carrier.

Company F led the battalion toward the hill We could see it in the distance. It looked like a small, black, dirty knoll to me, with holes scattered about its surface. It was called "The Volcano" because it has similar features to one. We took the hill about six that evening without a shot being fired. About a dozen Krauts were there and they just surrendered. We thought we would stay for the night and then maybe get some rest. How wrong we were! The past few days had been a picnic compared to what we were about to go through.

The size of the hill was what a platoon would normally defend, yet we had a depleted battalion on it. It was rainy and misty. The hill was bald with a few crevices here and there. We started to dig in with Company F on the forward slope, Company G on the right, and Company E in the rear. The 81s were about three hundred yards to the rear of Company F. We tried to dig them in just as the hill sloped to the rear. There was a deep draw in front of our hill, and when the mist occasionally lifted we could see a thickly wooded hill to our front. We could also hear Krauts talking, and it sounded as if they were trying to come up on our positions. It was creepy. We dug faster.

Captain Talcot, the coolest artillery observer I've ever seen, set up his radio and prepared to barrage the wooded hill in front. Artillery forward observers had to be cool, calm, and collected. Most of the time they were in front of us calling in targets, often when they were very close to the target themselves. Talcot started from the right, fired a battery volley, and shifted left until he covered the whole hill. We could actually hear the Krauts scream and moan, so we knew our artillery shells were doing their work. The Germans also dropped a few rounds our way. That hastened our digging even more.

We found a small ditch on the forward slope that we used for an OP. With me were Charlie Raymond, Lieutenant Bergdal, Sergeant Reinecke, and a new lieutenant who had recently joined Company F. We had just completed stringing our communications wire from guns to the OP when the Kraut artillery became more intense—and more accurate.

After you've been subjected to incoming artillery for a while, you learn to judge approximately where it will land. We heard a battery volley coming and knew it would be close. We all hit the bottom of our ditch. That was the last thing I remember because (as I later learned), four rounds of 105 fell right on top of us. Those who were not directly hit with shrapnel were temporarily knocked out by the concussion and powder gas, including me. I don't know how long I was out.

The first thing I remember was hearing someone gurgle. It was sort of like listening to someone gargle mouthwash, but slowly and softly. I rolled over and shook my head to clear it, and as I did spotted Charlie Raymond. I had seen a lot of wounds, but his was the nastiest I had ever seen. Charlie's left jaw was split from his ear to his mouth about an inch wide. Part of his tongue and jawbone were gone, as were many of his teeth. He had also been hit in the back. I remember saying, "God be with you, boy."

A medic was nearby, so I called over for help. The medic said we had to get him out. He bandaged Charlie up the best he could. He stood on his own power and I helped him back to the battalion CP, about a hundred yards to our rear. There was a light rain and it was cold. Charlie was trying to speak, but I could not understand him. I grabbed a medic and made him redress Charlie and give him some more morphine. I also made him promise to get Charlie out. I pulled a sniper jacket off a Kraut POW and wrapped Charlie with it. It was raining hard now. The Krauts were still firing at us. Every time an artillery shell came in, someone was hit.

The same barrage that had gotten Charlie got everyone else in the hole but me. The new lieutenant was unconscious. When I came to and heard Charlie, I didn't see Sergeant Reinecke. I later learned that he was hit in the back and shoulder and made his own way to the rear. Lieutenant Bergdal, who was hit in the shoulder and neck, was getting faint from loss of blood. Even so, he kept insisting that he find Captain Talcot and plaster the Kraut bastards. I later saw him in the battalion CP hole, leaning against a rock with his eyes closed, his face white, and his wounds bandaged as he relayed fire orders from Captain Talcot, who was a little farther forward.

After I had taken Charlie to the rear I began to shake. Was I going into some sort of shock? I was not sure. My CO, Capt. Jim Farrell, grabbed me and said, "Lieutenant! Charlie's gone. The 81s are your babies now, Andy. Snap out of it!" I looked him the eye and nodded, letting him know I understood, and made my way to the mortar gun positions to check on things. The men were still digging in. I told them about Charlie and they said, "We'll get even with those bastards." I got Sgt. John Koors, one of my mortar squad leaders, to come to the OP with me. We started digging our OP a little deeper, too. Another lieutenant from Company F had been sent up to replace the one who had been hit.

Lieutenant Lou Cox wasn't getting along too well. He was on the right flank with his machine gun platoon. A shell had landed in the hole alongside two of his men. Private First Class Meyers was blown to pieces, and Private First Class Shrock had both his legs torn off. Shrock lay there by his gun, whimpering and quivering. There was absolutely nothing we could do for him. Captain Farrell took off his raincoat and placed it over Shrock's quivering body. The machine gunner died a few minutes later.

We dug with our entrenching tools and our hands until it got dark. When you're close to the enemy you have to stop digging when it gets dark, because digging makes a lot of noise. The night was cold, wet, and miserable. Occasionally, the Krauts fired their damn artillery. We rolled hand grenades over the side just in case the Krauts tried to come in.

Each time the artillery came in someone would cry out, "I'm hit! I'm hit! Medic! Oh God, help me! "In daylight we were a perfect target for the Kraut's artillery observers on the hill to our front. We had a little cover, but no camouflage whatsoever. We were too concentrated and too close together.

An artillery barrage is the most frightening and terrifying experience any man can go through. There is absolutely nothing you can do but find cover, hunker down in your foxhole, and pray to God. Barrages lasted anywhere from a few seconds to several minutes. One particular barrage I remember clearly. I was in my foxhole when it began and I hugged the ground until it ended. I carefully raised my head and looked around. There was another foxhole not ten yards away. A shell had landed directly inside, obliterating both men completely. Their body parts were blown all over the place. It was a sickening sight. Tree bursts are also very dangerous, because the shells tear apart limbs and the splinters turn into missiles; sometimes they cause more damage than an artillery shell.

When you first look up and see you are alive but your buddy in the next foxhole is wounded or killed, you thank God for letting you live through another one. But after a while, you a tremendous guilt feeling takes over and a big question lingers: "Why am I allowed to live but my buddy is not?" You carry that feeling the rest of your life. You constantly think of your buddies and sometimes, especially when you experience a certain sound or a certain sensation, you can see your buddies just as they were fifty years ago.

* * *

When daylight came it finally stopped raining. Sergeant Koors made me a cup of coffee by heating water over a burning K-ration box. About the middle of the morning, we could see Krauts moving around in the little town of Nomeny, to our left about eight hundred yards away. I threw a few mortars in there. Every time we fired the 81s, it seemed to bring in more Kraut artillery.

Captain Farrell soon came up to me and said, "Andy, don't shoot those 81s any more. Give the boys a rest. Every time you fire the 81s, it brings more artillery in on us."

During the afternoon the Krauts threw everything they had at us. Snipers also hit our men. Every time a shell came in, it cut our telephone lines from the OP to the guns. It was dangerous to try to repair it, because each time someone moved, the movement attracted more artillery. This was especially true if the Kraut observer saw someone walking or crawling (as was mostly the case) with a reel of wire.

It was on one of those occasions when I was trying to straighten out the tangled mess of phone wires when I thought I'd shaken hands with my maker. I was about halfway between the OP and the gun positions when I heard it coming. I didn't have much time. I dove for a ditch. The artillery and I landed at the same time, me in the ditch and the artillery where I had been. Sergeant Joe Pawlak yelled, "Lieutenant, are you all right?" I was, but I decided I'd sit for a spell. Staff Sergeant Alex Mulheron, platoon sergeant of the 1st Machine Gun Platoon, who had seen most of his men either killed, wounded, or captured, yelled out, "For God's sake, Lieutenant, don't mess with that damned wire anymore!"

Lieutenant Saul "Kad" Kadison, who has just joined the Company H mortar platoon, was calm and collected for a man under artillery for the first time. He had everything under control. Private Rozniarek and a couple of other men had been hit. A platoon of Company F riflemen that was behind the 81s had really been hit hard. Word came down that we were pulling off the hill that night. It didn't make any difference to us where; any where was better than The Volcano.

It was then I learned Major Warmbrod, Doc Furnish (our battalion surgeon), Lieutenant McDonell, and Lt. Jess Barton had been hit shortly after Charlie had been struck. Ray Wadsinski had been killed the day before; Lt. Doug Cox was given command of Company G.

That afternoon, elements of the 1st Battalion moved into the woods in front of us. They encountered nothing. When darkness came, we were moving into the Bois de la Rumont, east of Millery and south of Morey, when the Krauts let go with a barrage on The Volcano. The blast of the shells made us shudder. Company F and Company E went up near the top of the hill. What was left of Company G stayed near the base of the hill with the CP and the 81s.

We settled down for the night, hoping everything would be quiet so we could get some rest. Since Charlie had been hit, I inherited his runner, Junior. We crawled under a bush, spread one raincoat beneath us and another on top of us. It was a very quiet night, and I slept well.

* * *

Rations and fresh water greeted us when we woke the next morning. I got a can of spaghetti, the first of the new type C-ration. There was no telling when we'd get rations again, so I took my time enjoying mine.

About 9:00 a.m. I went out with Lieutenant Cox and Company G to occupy the left flank of Hill 412. I was looking for a place to set up the 81s. Doug sent two scouts ahead to reconnoiter the route. They came back and said they knew the way. Junior and Whitwell were with me. The deeper we got into the woods the thicker the foliage got. The scouts lost the way so Cox left to find his own way. We went back to the base of the hill again. We hit the ground when someone spotted

Krauts in a hedgerow about fifty yards to the left of our wooded hill. Cox decided to try to talk them into surrendering. He took an interpreter with him and crawled to a vantage point. The interpreter yelled for a few minutes before he was answered with a burst of burp gun fire. We hugged the ground a little closer.

That pissed off Cox, who decided to go in after the Krauts. He took one squad of riflemen to sneak around from the right, and left one of his new sergeants to use two squads as a base of fire. It was a very tough situation. Most of the men were replacements that had just come in the night before and didn't even know their squad leader's name—if they had a squad leader at all. They just lay there, doing nothing except praying to stay alive.

A couple of the men moved to the edge of the woods to shoot at the Krauts they could see behind the hedgerow. I had a grease gun that I had carried for a few days but had never fired. I crawled up beside a rifleman. Every now and then he cut loose. I'd say, "Did you get him?" "Yes, sir," he replied.

It was an excellent view but a very dangerous position. I saw three Krauts run out of the hedgerow. The two on the outside were carrying the one in the middle. They were about a hundred yards away. I cut loose with my grease gun. It was nice to see them fall, but I lost faith in grease guns on the spot. I expected the damn thing to shoot fast. Instead, it fired slow and sounded like an old man trying to cough. The damned sight was so wide and covered so much territory, I could probably see an entire battalion through it.

Things really began to heat up now. While we were trying to sneak around the Krauts, the Krauts had successfully sneaked around us! One of them with a burp gun opened on us from behind and another from our right flank. They were throwing rifle grenades at us, too, from the top of the hill. They were getting too close for comfort.

A wounded Kraut lay on the ground about thirty yards to our left front, behind the base of the hill and the hedgerow. A German medic came out of the hedgerow. In addition to a red cross on his helmet, he had a white apron with a red cross on it tied around his body. Our boys let him get to his wounded. Instead of treating him, the bastard reached in his aid bag, drew out a grenade, and hurled it at us! Two of our men were hit; one of them was a medic. The rifleman next to me drilled the Kraut medic several times, making sure he didn't treat any more wounded.

We started walking toward the top of the hill. Lieutenant Cox's new plan was to form his rifle company in a line of skirmishers and move through the woods. I sent the two wounded men back and told them to tell Colonel Murray that we had run into a little difficulty and would like someone to come up on our left rear, because now fire from coming from there, too, in addition to the fire from our right front. It's no fun when the foliage is so thick you can't see thirty yards in front of you, but can hear bullets cracking twigs over your head when you're lying with your face pressed into the ground.

Cox was having one hell of a time. He was yelling orders and getting no cooperation in return. He had two new lieutenants who didn't know one man from another, and the replacements were not about to do much in this situation. He yelled at the officers to form their men as skirmishers and move forward. As soon as Cox left, one lieutenant asked me, "Does he want us to dig in?" Imagine someone digging into woods so thick you can't see the end of the rifle. Did the guy think we were going to have a picnic lunch, too? Didn't they teach anything in OCS?

We moved a few feet forward when the burp guns opened up on us again. We hit the ground. I was sweating. What the hell were we going to do?

"Hello, Company G. Where are you?" The voice was behind us.

Cox hissed for us to be quiet and was reluctant to answer because he thought it might be a Kraut. They were known to use such tricks.

"Send a runner up to us," the lieutenant finally answered.

"You send a runner back here," answered the voice behind us.

"What Officer Candidate Class were you in?" yelled back Cox.

"Class 311. And what area were you in at Ft. Benning?" said the voice.

"Harmony Church area," said Doug.

This was enough to satisfy Cox, so he sent a man back to guide them up. We all breathed a sigh of relief when it was learned the element on our tail was not a bunch of Krauts but a rifle platoon from Company F. The men were badly needed reinforcements. On the way up they had killed a few Krauts, including a kid about fourteen or fifteen years old who had been firing the burp gun in our rear.

Colonel Murray was on his way up when, for the second time in two weeks, Company G was almost completely annihilated. Lieutenant Doug Brown had cleared the woods and was reorganizing his company. They had not dug in because they knew they would be moving out soon. The men were fairly concentrated. The Krauts threw in about fifteen or twenty rounds. You can't hear mortar shells coming. All you hear is a split-second swish. Most of the rounds landed among the troops. Many were tree bursts. A piece of shrapnel hit Brown in the head.

I cannot think of anything that tears at your insides more than hearing a wounded man cry out in pain for help when there is nothing you can do for him. We had very little aid to give the wounded. We had long ago exhausted our bandage supplies, and the possibilities of getting more were slim to none. A rifle company at full strength carries a complement of about 193 men, including six officers. After this battle, fourteen men were all that was left of Company G. The colonel attached the survivors to Company F.

General Summers, the assistant division commander, was there to see Colonel Murray. When the colonel received the news of Company G's annihilation, he almost begged the general to relieve us, but it was not in the general's power to do so. We were to continue the attack. As he left, the general said to Murray, "Good luck, boy."

In the early part of the afternoon, Company F, positioned near the top of the hill, also sustained quite a few casualties from artillery and mortar fire. The German artillery was simply relentless. We pulled out late in the afternoon to continue the attack to the east. I think we were to take some other damn hill. The woods were thick and we had a lonely track to guide on. Snipers kept picking at us. Everyone was tired, hungry, and thirsty. We had a half-canteen cup of water issued to each of us that morning; most of us had already consumed that. Darkness came and Colonel Murray decided to hold up for the night. We set up a perimeter defense. It rained a little, but we rested.

* * *

We moved out early the next morning, September 21, in a column of companies winding along a slippery muddy road. We were still in the thick woods. I gave my men a cigarette ration that had been brought up the night before. I was with the command group and my 81s were on the tail of the column. Our new objective was the high ground west of Moivron and Villers-les-Moivron.

Normally, a heavy weapons company has one mortar platoon consisting of three mortar sections. Each mortar section is commanded by a lieutenant and consists of two squads, each with its own 81mm mortar, making six mortars in a heavy weapons company. I had skeleton crews with four mortars left.

When the head of our column took machine gun fire from the left front, the colonel asked me to fire the mortars. We couldn't find any smoke for mask clearance, so he decided instead to fire a little artillery. Captain Talcot set up his radio and sent back a fire mission to his battalion. He added a P.S. to his order: be particularly careful because he had to adjust by sound and he was only a hundred yards or so from the bursts.

After a while, we moved on. The mud was thick and everyone was covered with it. We picked up two Krauts, an old sergeant and a young kid. The sergeant said he had a mortar section, but the rest of the crew had deserted him. He had destroyed his mortars.

The woods were thinner now and we were nearing a highway close to Bois de la Rumont. As we moved single file down the path, a sniper opened up with a burp gun on our left flank and hit the kid in front of me. "I'm hit, I'm hit!" he cried out. "Please help me!" He was lucky, because the slug had struck him in the leg. We dragged him to cover and the medic dressed his wound.

We hit the highway and turned right for a few hundred yards, then turned left into thick, wooded underbrush. We moved slowly for a while and then stopped, so I ate the last of my K-rations. We heard firing behind us. Word came up the column that part of Company F and the 81s, at the tail, had lost contact and been cut off. Captain Jerry Sheehan, the battalion S-3, had taken command of Company F when all of that company's officers had become casualties. He and I went back to get them with about six riflemen. I borrowed a couple of grenades from someone. We backtracked several hundred yards.

The reports were that a Kraut machine gunner had sneaked into an abandoned car on the edge of the highway, where we had turned left. We worked our way back and sneaked up on the car. I was scared as hell. Instead of finding a Kraut, we found our men. They were as glad to see us as we were to see them. They had been in a little fire fight which they had won. A couple of dead Germans littered the ground to prove it. We got the column straightened out and moved on.

In the late afternoon we held up in the big woods. The 3d Battalion was catching hell on our right flank. Colonel Murray set up a perimeter defense. The woods were so thick that it was impossible to fire the

81s, so we filled in as riflemen. We stayed in those thick woods without food and only a little water for three days and three nights.

* * *

The Krauts had all approaches to the woods covered and apparently had us surrounded. Every road was blocked and they had the support of 150mm guns and 120mm mortars. We had had a hard fight to get into the woods, and when we finally did get in we were totally exhausted. We had no food or water to revive our strength. The ground was very hard and rocky, and we didn't have strength enough to dig ourselves adequate foxholes. The men ate what synthetic lemon juice and sugar cubes they had. Every time Tom Jennings, the battalion S-4 (supply), or anyone else tried to bring rations in to us, they were either ambushed or couldn't get near us.

On the second day in the woods, Lt. Henry Walker, one of Company F's rifle platoon leaders, took a combat patrol and tried to get to the edge of the woods and take a look. Some Krauts tried to ambush him, but he drove them off. He found a kid from the 318th who had been hit pretty bad in the arm and had been lying in the woods for two days. He wanted water, but we had none to give him.

Several times the Krauts captured rations intended for us. Finally, on the third day, we heard tanks rumbling through the woods. At first we didn't know whose they were. It turned out it was our tanks breaking through to bring us chow. There was almost enough for each man to have a half canteen cup of water and a K-ration. The K-rations were a little short, so Kad and I split one. Boy, that tasted good! When the medics and our jeeps came in later, we raided the jeeps for cookies and chocolate. Disappointed in my grease gun, I took the opportunity to trade it for a carbine. At this time, friendly troops also came up on our flanks and relieved the pressure somewhat. We got orders to move out late that afternoon to the east and seize Hill 418.

We were all lined up and well concentrated on a wooded trail, waiting to move out, when it happened. I was sitting in a jeep with Junior when the mortar shells plastered us. Sometimes you can hear a split-second swish, and sometimes you can't hear anything at all. We heard nothing. About thirty or forty rounds poured onto our position in two or three waves. Most of them were tree bursts, which inflicted heavy casualties on us. The Krauts fired at us from Hill 401, south of Bratte.

Several of the casualties were shock cases, men whose nervous system was shattered by concussion. They weren't shaking, they were vibrating. Their buddies carried them out. We spread out and waited for orders to move out. We lay there until darkness, under an intermittent mortar barrage.

There were so many casualties from this attack that it was necessary for us to reorganize before we attacked, so word passed down to move back to our original position. The night was pitch black with no moon or stars. We had to hold hands and follow the phone line back as far as the group of foxholes that composed the battalion CP. From there we went to our own holes.

* * *

Kad and I slept under a jeep. A lot of artillery and mortar fire came in that night, and our battalion suffered more casualties. We resumed the attack early the next morning. It was drizzling rain and cold. We suffered several casualties just trying to get to the edge of the woods. One of Lou Cox's boys took a bullet in the head and died before we could get him out. One of Company H's machine gun platoon leaders cracked up and had to be taken back to battalion aid. He had seen half of the men he taught how to fight killed before his eyes. A man can only take so much death before he just shuts down. No one thought any less of him.

We pushed out of the woods, down across an open field, across a road, through a vineyard, and up over a bare hill. It was a wonderful feeling to be out in the open again. I think a lot of us were getting claustrophobic from being in those woods for so long. We pushed on to another partially wooded hill, Hill 418, the high ground southwest of Villers-les-Moivron against only minor opposition.

While we were waiting for the rest of the battalion to come up, Henry Walker and I shared his K-rations. He showed me that K-ration crackers with a piece of cheese and some sugar sprinkled on it tasted good, even if soaked by rain.

We set in a few outposts and were shooting the breeze in the rain when Capt. Jim Mullins, the CO of Company E, came up with a POW, a young kid in a Luftwaffe uniform who had been transferred to the infantry. He had a dispatch case on him. Lieutenant Moye, Henry Walker, and I dove into his bag. Moye came out with a beautiful compass, Henry with a handy little stove, and I came out with a bar of soap. Now what in the hell would I do with a bar of soap? We had barely enough water to drink, much less take a bath. Besides, it was cold!

We dug in on the forward slope of Hill 418, overlooking the town of Villers-les-Moivron. Ahead was rolling open terrain with scattered towns and woods. The 3d Battalion dug in on our right, but later moved to another position.

Captain Talcot and I found an excellent OP that overlooked the whole valley to our front. Occasionally the rain stopped and we could see for miles out into the valley. I found myself wondering how such a beautiful country could be so torn up with war.

Villers-les-Moivron was a small town with about a dozen houses. A railroad track ran through the town, and there was a cemetery just west of the tracks. We had been told that this was the last of the high ground, and that from now on we would be fighting in open country. It was a good feeling.

Colonel Murray was relieved as our battalion CO and Maj. Jim Hayes, the regimental S-2, was made our new battalion CO. It seems that Regiment had been dissatisfied with the way Colonel Murray had been running his battalion. I wondered how they came to that conclusion. I had never seen any of them while the fighting was going on. Colonel Don Cameron, our regimental CO, was also relieved. Over his vigorous protest to attack an objective with his depleted regiment, he had the guts to tell the commanding general, "What in the hell do you want me to take it with? My bare hands?" Lieutenant Colonel Henry Fisher, the regiment executive officer, became the 317th Infantry Regiment's CO.

Major Hayes gave me permission to send Private Stanley back to the kitchen. Stanley was a good soldier, but he was too old to be on the front line and just didn't have the strength that was necessary to fight. He was the oldest man in the company. He had no business in a line outfit in the first place. I thought of the millions of men back home dodging the draft boards.

Captain Talcot and I spent most of our time looking through our glasses, but we couldn't see anything worthy of shooting. We didn't mind, because our hill was relatively quiet and we didn't particularly want the Krauts to start slinging artillery at us.

On the second afternoon, September 23, about 3:00 p.m., while Captain Talcot and I were looking out over the valley, we saw something very strange. Two columns of infantry marched out of the east and cut across our right front. There was not a vehicle of any sort and the column was long—as far as the eye could see. We didn't know whether the men were Americans or Germans.

We reported this back through channels—and waited. Nearly two hours passed. It now about 5:00 p.m. and the column was still moving. It was still about three miles to our right front, and by that time we learned the whole damn thing was composed of German infantry, strung out for about five miles. Talcot received word not to worry about them because elements of the 6th Armored Division were moving on our right, preparing a little surprise for the marching Krauts.

They were moving over open exposed ground. There was not a single vehicle in the column—not even a damn jeep! It was rather odd. At about 5:30 p.m., the guys from 6th Armored sprung their trap. Tanks rushed from hidden positions and opened up with their machine guns. The Krauts hit the ground and the machine guns chattered.

A few minutes later artillery opened up on them with time fire. Later, I learned that a whole corps artillery group had let them have it. The Krauts didn't have time to dig in. It was a beautiful sight to see. Captain Talcot was itching to fire his artillery, but was told the Krauts were out of our sector. All through the night, we could hear the slow TAT-TAT-TAT of our machine guns and see the flash of our time fire.

Opportunities like that don't come along often in war.

Chapter 5

VILLERS-LES-MOIVRON

September 25, 1944–September 27, 1944

The next night, September 25, we were informed that we would attack the following morning. I went to see Lt. Robert Moye, who was now commanding Company E after Capt. Jim Mullins took over as battalion executive officer. He would lead the attack and was in the process of getting his company oriented.

The night was cold and rainy. Water filled up my slit trench. I just couldn't get any sleep. It wasn't the weather, either. I kept thinking about tomorrow—another day, another battle, more death.

We moved out at 3:00 a.m. so we would be at the objective by daylight. This time we had another hill to take. In order to take that hill, we first had to secure the little town of Villers-les-Moivron. It was reported that there were a couple of squads of Krauts dug in there. My mortars were to follow Company F, now commanded by Capt. Ira Miller, formerly the Headquarters Company CO.

I took the platoon to the edge of the woods where Company E was dug in, and we waited there for Captain Miller, who arrived shortly thereafter. It was pitch black. Major Jim Hayes came storming and stumbling through the dark looking for Miller.

"Miller, why haven't you got your company on the move?" barked the major. "Get off your butt and start moving."

"Major, I can't move until I get my company lined up," answered Miller.

"What do you mean, can't? There's no such word as can't in the American Army, and I don't want to hear that word again!"

Kad whispered to me, "The major's got a lot to learn, hasn't he? He ought not to snap at the Captain like that when the Captain's men are around!"

We finally got straightened out and moved down off the hill toward Villers-les-Moivron. It was a little village of perhaps a dozen houses, but it would prove to be the venue of one of the bloodiest battles ever for my battalion. It was still drizzling rain at daylight, and the ground was very muddy. We were late getting started. We had taken a round-about way so we could push through Moivron from the south and southeast. We went through the little town of Leyr, about three miles south of Moivron, where elements of the 6th Armored Division were positioned.

I talked to a Captain there who told me that some of his tanks were going to give us a little support. We cut across country and moved in on Moivron from the southwest. We didn't know what we were going to run into, so we fixed bayonets. The ground was so muddy I could hardly take a step without slipping. We were attacking in a column of companies across open, sloppy fields.

When we were about five hundred yards from town our tanks and TDs opened up with their main guns. Our artillery opened up, too. Shells were bursting in the air, some falling short over the heads of those in front of the column. We still hadn't seen a Kraut and had not drawn any fire, but why take chances? The Krauts almost always let you get on top of them before they did anything, and then they really cut loose.

Company G peeled off to the right and Company F on the right came in from the southeast. Company G took some prisoners as it closed in on the railroad station on the edge of town. Parts of Company F had crossed the railroad tracks and still not fired a shot.

About 11:00 a.m., a Kraut came out into the orchard across the railroad tracks with a white flag. Major Hayes, who stood on the railroad tracks, told the men to hold their fire. He yelled in German for the Kraut to come out. The Kraut just stood there. Quite a number of Company F's men moved into the orchard to close in on the town.

Without warning, the Krauts started cutting loose on Company F with machine guns, burp guns, and rifles. The son of a bitch with the white flag ran for cover. A few minutes later, artillery and mortars opened on us. Company F, with Bill Butz's machine gun platoon, was caught in the open orchard. Company G started taking automatic fire from the vicinity of the railroad station as well as artillery and mortar rounds. A lot of the fire seemed to be coming from the cemetery on the west side of the tracks, along a road running east and west on the south side of town.

Kad set up the 81s behind a head-high stone wall. An unpaved narrow road paralleled our position. It had a shallow impression rather than ditches along the sides. That's where the men were. Junior and I crawled up as close as we could along the railroad embankment and adjusted the 81s on the cemetery. We only fired a few rounds before one of the 81s was knocked out by an artillery round. The men had to set up in an open field and were catching fire from small arms as well as artillery.

The Krauts seemed especially interesting in hitting the railroad track. Junior and I went back to a railroad culvert that was just to the right of the east-west road to try to get a SCR536 radio. Our phone wire had been shot out. Captain Talcot was there, calm as ever, trying to set up his radio. A Kraut machine gunner was shooting along the east side of the track, so we had to get in waist-deep water into the culvert to avoid his rounds.

Several of the wounded were lying around, waiting on the litter bearers. Captain Jim Farrell screamed, grabbed his crotch, and rolled to the ground. At first he thought his balls had been shot away, but the bullet had zipped between his legs, leaving a nice hole in his raincoat and his testicles firmly in place.

"God damn it!" I yelled at my CO. "Get your ass under cover! We're short enough on officers and noncoms without you getting killed!" I could not believe the words coming out of my mouth! It was the only time I ever spoke like that to a superior.

Everybody was catching hell. The artillery increased everywhere and we got lots of tree bursts. The men in the orchard really had it tough. Every time someone tried to bring a wounded buddy back across the track he got it himself Lew Hing, Bill Butz's medic, did a wonderful job getting his boys back. He was the only medic who repeatedly went into the orchard and came back with wounded. He was as brave as they came.

I dropped back about fifty yards to where the guns were positioned. Several of the men there had been hit. I would not ask my men to expose themselves by standing up in the open to fire the mortars. I told them to spread out in the ditch along the road until the fire lifted a little. We could move back a piece and set up in a draw. But instead of lifting, the artillery fire increased. The Krauts were trying to zero in on the road where we lay. A lot of wounded were moving down the road toward the aid station, which was set up in a farm house to our rear. That day I saw more men moving (and being moved) toward the aid station than I saw moving forward.

Every infantryman knows he is going to get hit. It's just a matter of time. Few talk about it much, but everyone just knows that, sooner or later, their turn will come. They just pray to God that when their time does come, they won't get hit in the guts or in the face. Anywhere but in the guts or in the face.

Several artillery shells landed on top of us as we hugged close to the ground. Sergeant Martin Roach got hit in the back and legs, and was screaming in agony. Sergeant Volk tried to get up, but he couldn't; both his legs were broken. I was knocked out for a little while from the concussion of a near-miss. When I regained my senses, Private Freeman was yelling. He was one of Bill Butz's boys. He had a hole all the way through his side, and he was hurting bad. I cut his shirt off, but saw I couldn't help him, and had someone carry him to the aid station. Sergeant Ralph Freeman, my platoon sergeant, was dazed from a concussion. I slapped him a few times and he finally came to. That one little barrage took out nine of my men, so I told Kad to get the hell out of there and pull back into the draw behind us.

Company F couldn't move, so the major decided to send Company E through with tanks from the 6th Armored Division. Five Shermans came up the road with riflemen hunched and trotting alongside them. Lieutenant Henry Walker's rifle platoon was leading, and as usual he was up front with the first tank.

I grinned and yelled, "What the hell's the matter? You getting scared and have to have tanks with you?"

He smiled back and shouted, "Hell no! But I do know that my life's not worth two cents!" That was the last time I saw Hank alive. He was killed a few minutes later.

Hank Walker and Ray Wadsinski had two sweet girls waiting for them back in the States. The girls later wrote us and simply couldn't believe that Hank and Ray had been killed. They wanted to know all about it—how they were killed, and how and where they were buried.

After the tanks got across the railroad tracks, they were to cut right along the road, roll through the orchard, and get into the town. As they approached the track, Kraut artillery fire increased. When the tanks reached the orchard, the artillery and small arms became heavier and more concentrated. The Krauts were directing their artillery against the Shermans. The shrapnel from the bursts didn't hurt the men inside the tanks, but the infantrymen around the tanks caught it. That's how Hank was killed, from one of the shrapnel bursts.

Company G was getting the hell beat out of it up near the railroad station on the north side of town. We had been seeing Kraut reinforcements coming in from the north all along. The tanks stopped; they would not go into town. Lieutenant Robert Moye chewed them out. They said they were going to back up so they could give supporting fire. Instead they pulled out completely, that is, with the exception of two that were stuck in the mud. Without the tanks we didn't have enough men left to take the town, so about 2:00 p.m. we got orders to pull back to the high ground south of the town and set up a defensive line.

Bill Butz and Sgt. Alex Mulheron had caught hell, too. Bill's runner got a slug right between the eyes as he started across the track. Bill had two machine guns left. Sergeant Mulheron, who was now commanding the 2d Platoon, had three. I had three mortars. Despite all the Kraut artillery, Doc Price, our battalion surgeon, and his medics stayed to care for the wounded long after we pulled out.

It was still drizzling rain, as it had been for several days, and the ground was muddy and slippery. We pulled back in a hurry and in great disorder. It took several hours to get everything lined up. Our new position was two miles uphill over a muddy, winding ditch that was supposed to be a road. I put the 81s in with Company G.

We had no more started digging in than the Krauts started throwing artillery shells our way. Company G had a few casualties, which hastened our digging. Kad got the men lined up while Junior and I set out to see what was cooking.

We stopped and ate a belly full of grapes from the plentiful orchards. Boy did they taste good. We found Capt. Jim Farrell, who told us to dig in and that he was going to a meeting and would give us the dope when he got back. Kad had the mortars under control and was digging in. I finally got to relieve myself, something I had wanted to do all day.

Kad and I only had one shovel between us, so we took turns digging. About dark we got word to pull out and join the rest of the battalion down at the railroad station in the little town. When we got there, we found that we were to return the old positions on Hill 418 that we had left fifteen hours earlier.

We lined up along the road in columns, waiting on orders to move out. It was again black as pitch. Everyone was tired and tense. We heard someone at the far end of the column whistling. Word was quietly passed back to knock it off. It didn't stop and came closer to us. When the whistler reached our point in the column he said, "What's the matter? There isn't a German within a mile of here." The whistler turned out to be Major Jim Hayes, our battalion commander.

Everyone was so dog tired we stumbled more than walked. It took all of the strength we could muster to climb back up that hill. We took frequent breaks. There was a bright moon and everything was misty and looked so peaceful. I thought of how the moon must look over Kingsley Lake and the peacefulness I always experienced out there. I hoped our recently killed buddies had also found peace.

We got back to our holes about 3:00 a.m. They were a welcome sight, and our cooks brought us dry blankets. I told the men to bed down and get some sleep, and that we would only post two guards tonight.

We always slept in all our clothes, but Kad and I decided to pull off our boots that night. As we started to bed down we heard shots and saw firing in the distance. It was the Krauts burning the two Sherman tanks that had been left down in the town. I slept in late the next morning.

The next day, September 27, was perfectly clear. It had finally stopped raining. We spent our time reorganizing and resupplying. The supply sergeant brought up a few dry clothes for the men. The town of Moivron was quiet except for the tanks that were still burning. We could see the bodies of our dead buddies lying around in the town. It hurt just to look at them. A little after noon about ten of our planes flew over and bombed and strafed Moivron. I think that took care of whatever Germans were left in the town.

Late that afternoon our cooks brought us hot food and mail from home. The chow tasted good. It was the first time we had hot food prepared by the kitchen since our hedgerow fighting days in Normandy about two months earlier. I also had in the mail an absentee ballot for the coming fall election. I put an X by the name of the candidate of my choice and sent it back with one of the cooks to be mailed. I wondered if the rain at home kept people away from the polls.

Chapter 6

SIVRY, FRANCE

September 28, 1944–October 5, 1944

The next day, September 28, we moved several miles to the south to dig in and occupy a hill that had already been taken. It was a nice warm day, but we had to do a lot of climbing. My feet were swollen and hurt because they had been wet for so long.

We were put in regimental reserve for a couple of days of much needed rest on Hill 418, southwest of Villers-les-Moivron in the Bois de la Rumont. We spent our time cleaning our equipment, getting resupplied, and training. A number of replacements joined us, so we spent some of our time teaching them the art of warfare the books don't cover. Company G again had suffered heavy casualties, so it was given ninety replacements. Lieutenant Henry "Bud" Leonard and Lt. Henry Ackermann joined Company H around September 29. Captain Farrell gave Leonard to me and Ackermann took over the 2d machine gun platoon.

On September 30, Company G, Ackermann's machine gun platoon, and Kad's section of 81mm mortars were moved up about a mile away to take over the forward slope of the big hill we occupied from elements of the 1st Battalion. The hill overlooked the town of Sivry, France. We were again having spells of sunshine mixed with drizzling rain.

On the night of October 1, the rest of us moved up with Company G. As we walked through the woods in a single column, we had to step over a body of a dead Kraut. A sharp limb had gone all the way through his body and pinned him to the ground. I guess it was one of those freak accidents caused by artillery bursting in the trees.

Company G had been reinforced with heavy weapons and was ready to lead the attack on Sivry the following morning and Company F was to occupy Company G's old positions. It was a fairly clear night and it didn't take long to get the rest of our guns in with Kad's.

Kad and I went to Lieutenant Ellsworth's hole to get the plan of attack. Ellsworth was having quite a time because he had had Company G only a few days. To top that off, he had just received ninety green replacements. The plan was nothing more than a sneak attack— no preparatory fire at all. The Germans occupied the hills to the north, and we had to attack from the south. Ellsworth had to move his troops through a mine field in front of our position before he could go into his attack formations. It was a difficult attack to plan.

Sivry was smack in the middle of a big valley about one mile from our hill. In between was perfectly open terrain, all of which was under observation by the Germans. Behind the town, almost straight up in appearance, were two huge mountains: Mt. Toulon and Mt. St. Jean. This terrain consisted of a broad plain, studded with little villages and several small forests.

Ellsworth wanted to leave at 3:00 a.m., so he could be at the edge of town by daylight. Kad and I each would have an SCR536 radio and Kad would call me every hour on the hour. The terrain was almost perfect for radio communications. Ellsworth jumped off on schedule. After he cleared the mine field, one rifle platoon would go into town from the west and the other platoons, with their heavy weapons, from the south. At dawn we heard small arms fire. Even though it was a clear day, we couldn't see any movement through our glasses.

Our battalion was out of radio contact with Company G (we learned later that Company G's radio had been shot up), so Major Hayes sent a carrying party into town with another radio and some ammunition. Later in the morning the guy who took the carrying party down came back up. Bud Leonard and I were at the OP. We asked him if he got the radio in okay and how Company G was getting along. He said, "Sure, I got the radio in. Company G's just fine; they're just cleaning the place out now." We believed him. We could hear small arms fire but couldn't see any movement in the town.

I had been trying to contact Kad all morning over the radio, but every time I tried, the Krauts would cut in on our frequency. Finally, about 11:00 a.m., I heard "How 3-2 to How 3-1; How 3-2 to How 3-1. Praise the Lord."

It took a few minutes for that message to soak through my dull brain. I finally realized that Kad was trying to tell me that he was either low on ammunition, or out of it altogether, and that the full message would have been "Praise the Lord and pass the ammunition," a common phrase used by infantrymen. I called back to Sergeant Freeman to send me six volunteers with one cloverleaf each of HE light to go with me into Sivry.

The new guy, Bud Leonard, wanted to take them down or at least go with me but I wouldn't let him. In a few minutes the six men came up. Private Clyde McCauley was leading them. They all said they were tired of sitting in the woods and wanted to see what this little town looked like.

By this time the Krauts were throwing a lot of artillery on the open spaces around the town as well as on the town itself, so I instructed the men to stay at least fifty yards apart and to follow the man in front of them. I tried to find out the best way to get into town, but nobody knew anything. About halfway down was a streambed leading into town. I decided this was the best way in. At least it provided a little cover. Total concealment was out of the question.

We followed the tape through the mine field that Ellsworth's men had staked out and headed for the stream. We met stragglers coming back up the hill. Some were without helmets or rifles. They were wild-eyed and crazed with fear. I asked one guy why the hell he was running out on his buddies. He said, "Lieutenant, they can shoot me tomorrow morning, but I will never go back into that hell town." I let him pass. He was of no use to anyone like that.

The artillery was coming in heavy and close now, but we had to keep moving. It would have been suicide to stop when the barrages were that close. As we got closer to town and started following the streambed, we came across several of our men who had been killed trying to get into town. I still couldn't see anyone even as we approached closer. I didn't know if the Krauts had the end of the town we were trying to get into or not. I figured we would know for sure when someone opened fire on it. Just a few seconds later, when we were about a hundred yards from town, a sniper opened on me with a burp gun. The bullets hissed through the air all around me as I dove for the ditch. Obviously we were going into town the wrong way. While I was lying in the ditch trying to locate the sniper and figure out the best way to get into town, a soldier came piling in on top of me.

After he got his breath he told me the Krauts had this end of town and that Lieutenant Ellsworth had seen us coming. He had sent the soldier out to guide us in. Meanwhile, I had located Pvt. John Piko, one of Bill Butz's boys, and some more of our men who were supposed to have already gotten into town with machine gun ammunition. Piko told me that the leader of the first carrying party had put his radio on the outskirts of town and had left him and his men stranded. I told Piko to keep spread out and fall in on the tail of the column.

The guide said the only way we could get in was to swing around and come in from the south. This meant going over open, rolling terrain under direct observation of the enemy. The only way to do that was to keep spread out and keep moving. We did this, and no one was hurt. The guide told me that the rifle platoon that was supposed to go in from the west had been pinned down since dawn and hadn't moved an inch. That's where the stragglers had come from. The last hundred yards had to be run over an open field, and we didn't waste any time covering it. I didn't know I could move that fast.

We went into the back end of a courtyard in which Kad had placed one of his mortars. It was easy to tell at a glance that things had been rough for quite some time. I got the men to cover as soon as they came struggling in. It was no easy job, carrying that heavy load of ammunition.

I counted heads. Everybody was there. That is, all the men carrying mortar ammunition and the machine gunners carrying ammunition for their buddies. The guys who had been carrying the other stuff on the first trip were nowhere to be found. I told Private McCauley to take his six men back as soon as they had rested up. The fight was still going on in the town and there was no need for them to stay around and get hurt. I went to see Kad. There was a lot of street fighting going on, building to building, and it was one hell of a job getting to him.

Heavy mortar fire–120mm–was falling on the part of the town that we had captured. The Kraut machine gunners and snipers were also picking at us from their positions on Mt. Toulon and Mt. St. Jean. We ran like hell across the open and sneaked through over the rubble. I found Kad sitting on the inside steps of what had been a house. He was calmly smoking a cigarette and looked up and said simply, "Hello." He was tired as hell and his eyes were bloodshot.

"Kad, move over and give me a cigarette."

"What the hell took you so long to get here?" he asked.

"Hell, fella, why don't you use your radio every now and then, and tell a guy how to get into a place like this? I called you for an hour trying to get you to tell me which route to take to get into this place. You never answered, so I took off anyway and almost got my ass shot off trying to crawl in on the Krauts from the rear. If you had answered my call and told me which way to come in I'd have been here an hour ago and my britches would still be dry!"

He laughed a slow, tired laugh. "I heard your call, but so did the Krauts." They had been jamming our frequency for two days. Kad continued: "If I had told you which way to come in they would have heard me and would have waylaid you." That was, of course, true. But the fact that the Krauts had been listening to our radio conversations for two days never entered my thick skull.

Kad quickly brought me up to date. Ellsworth and Company G only had half the town. It was still a slow process of taking one rubble of a house, and then another. The Krauts were stubborn as hell. Company G had made it to the edge of the town before it was discovered. The lead scout had seen a Kraut calmly walking down the street and clipped him. That started the fireworks. Krauts popped up from all the windows in the town and started cutting loose with everything they had. It had taken Company G quite some time to inch along to where they were when I arrived.

Because of its high casualty rates during previous fighting, Company G was pretty much depleted and had no 60mm mortars and only one light machine gun. As a result, Kad and his boys had to use their 81mm mortars as 60mms and bazookas.

To shoot an 81mm mortar, you use a firing table that indicates how to adjust the sights to fire the mortar at given ranges. This firing table doesn't have any data for firing at ranges under three hundred yards. When a mortar shell bursts, it covers an area of about fifty yards with fragments. Kad had been firing at 125 yards! And when you think that an 81mm mortar packs the wallop of a 105 howitzer, that's quite a feat. Things like that aren't covered in the field manuals or at Fort Benning. Sergeant Hubbard's mortar had been firing quite a bit, but he had no data to put on the sights, so he had fired by using turns on the elevation knob. When the number two gunner dropped the shell into the tube he had to put his hand on the tube to make sure the shell wouldn't go straight up and come back down on top of them. To top it all off, Kad and Sergeant Quinn, who had been doing the observing, were in the top of a house on one side of the street, firing at a house directly across the street, just a few feet from the bursts.

The Krauts increased their mortar fire. Parts of the house we were in started coming down on top of us, so we retired to the cellar. In a few minutes it quieted down a little, so we went to the OP. Kad had his ammunition now and he wanted to use it. There was a Kraut Panzerfaust man about seventy-five yards down the street, and every time one of our boys tried to get in a few shots from some window, the Kraut would cut loose at him with his Panzerfaust. Brother, when Panzerfaust shells are around it's no time to play peeping-tom! Every now and then a Kraut popped up in a window to take a potshot down the street. We put our heads together and crafted a plan: our boys would sling it at the Krauts and keep their heads down while Kad did his adjusting. After he had adjusted on his target he would cut loose with a barrage that was usually sufficient to kill the enemy, or at least make him think twice about staying put.

The trouble with shooting a mortar in a town is that you rarely see the bursts and have to adjust by sound, which in itself is very deceiving. Kad was having a hard time. He couldn't sense his rounds, and every round was precious because he only had so much ammunition.

We signaled our boys to slow down their shooting. In a little while, the Krauts started to poke their heads up. Kad let go with a round. When the first round landed, we saw a Kraut look sharply over his right shoulder. We knew the round was too far and needed to be brought in a bit. Using this process, Kad eventually eliminated the Panzerfaust man.

We went back to the guns to see how the men were getting along and see if Private McCauley had left with his men. It was worse trying to get back to my mortars than it had been to get to Kad in the first place. "I'm going to see how Lieutenant Ellsworth is doing! I'll be back in a little while!" I yelled to him over the noise of the shooting.

I found Ellsworth in the rubble of a house. He was mad as a wet hen. He was running low on ammunition. He badly needed BAR clips, hand grenades, bazooka rounds, rifle grenades, and grenade launchers. All of this was what the earlier carrying party was supposed to have brought in, but none of it ever got to him. His radio had been smashed along with its operator, and the only contact he had with the battalion was intermittent phone conversation over a line the Krauts frequently knocked out. If Battalion expected him to hold what he had *and* try to take the rest of the town, he had to have that stuff, and he had to have it now.

I told him that I was going back up on the hill as soon as my men rested a little and that I'd see Major Hayes for him. He gave me a written message to give the major, and a tongue lashing to deliver as well. The men's canteens were getting low, and as yet they had found no water in the town. When you're under the tension of heavy fighting it's very hard to refrain from drinking your canteen dry and, you're always hungry.

The Krauts were raising pure hell now, and it was risky to move around. Kad and I went back to the OP. When we got there all that was left was the end of the telephone wire. The Krauts had blasted the OP with Panzerfaust fire, and the phone had been blown to pieces. Kad decided to risk his ammunition and put in a lot of shooting before dark in the hope it would inflict some damage on the Krauts and keep them quiet for the night.

We got together with Ellsworth and decided to raise hell with the mortars while the riflemen closed in. Ellsworth's ammunition was running low and it was his last chance to take the entire town before dark. We started laying it on heavy where it seemed most of the Krauts were positioned. The Krauts had machine gun emplacements on top of Mt. Toulon behind the town. We could see them, so we raised hell with them, too.

Suddenly, the Krauts stopped shooting. We could hear them hollering to one another around the town and on the outskirts of the town. They were yelling, "Kamerad! Kamerad!" From past experience we knew it might be a trick, and that maybe they wanted us to come out in the open so they could ambush us. Every American outfit has someone who can speak German (or any other language that needed to be spoken). Through his interpreter, Ellsworth told the Krauts to lay down their arms and come out with a white flag and their hands over their heads.

After what seemed an eternity, the first Kraut came out with his hands over his head, carrying a white flag. There were about thirty Krauts altogether, and every one of them was wounded. They were the only ones still alive. We talked to a German lieutenant who was in command. He said all of his men, including him, were wounded, and that he had no choice but to give up.

Darkness was closing in and I wanted to get back on the hill while there was still light. It would be a tough job trying to find my way through the mine field at night. I started back with the machine gunners who had brought the ammunition down for their buddies. I told Ellsworth that I'd give the true picture to the major, and I told Kad that I'd see him tomorrow. There were two wounded boys of ours who could walk, so I took them with me. I told the men to be sure and stay spread out, because it was suicide to close up, and that if the Krauts started shooting at us to keep moving. Although the Krauts within the town had surrendered, the wooded slopes of Mt. Toulon and Mt. St. Jean were still infested with them.

It wasn't going to be an easy job getting out. We had open ground to go over that offered no cover, and we had to run quite a piece to keep the snipers behind the town from picking us off. It was a two-mile trip uphill over open terrain in full view of enemy troops we could see on Mt. Toulon. To top that off, we also had to pick our way through a mine field.

We got along okay until we were about halfway up the hill, when the Krauts started throwing that damn artillery at us. It was heavy stuff—150mm—and it shook the earth when it hit. I hadn't looked back for quite some time. When I looked around, I discovered the men had closed up. They were so tired they hadn't realized what they were doing. Their heads were down and they were putting one foot in front of the other only by super-human strength. It was too late now. If a man stopped to get some interval between himself and the man in front, it would be suicide. So we had to keep moving the way we were, with the Krauts shooting like hell. My legs were numb; that fast pace uphill was rough going. I kept thinking, "one well placed shell and we all will get it."

When we were halfway through the mine field, Pvt. Charles Trunak yelled behind me that he had been hit in the leg and couldn't walk anymore. I yelled for him to lay there until the rest of the column had gotten into the woods and then I'd get him out. We were only a few hundred yards from the woods of our hill now. After the column entered the trees, the medics helped me get Trunak back to safety.

I gave my message to Major Hayes. McCauley had one man in his column hit, too. He got him out okay. It was dark now. I got a blanket, dropped down in my hole, and prayed.

* * *

The next morning the weather was clear. Although Ellsworth had the whole town of Sivry, I knew it was suicide for anyone to stay there. We were now fighting German officer cadets who had been reinforced with SS troops, and they were tough nuts to crack. They were out of a big officer cadet school at Metz. The country around here had been their training ground, and they knew every nook and cranny of it. It would have been like invading Krauts trying to take a combination of Fort Benning and Fort Sill defended by American boys who had been trained there.

My 81mm mortars belonged up on this hill, where they could get observation all around the town and all the ammunition they needed. They didn't belong down in the town of Sivry, where they were being used like hand grenades. Through our glasses we could see the Krauts swarming all over Mt. Toulon and Mt. St. Jean, and knew they were looking right down the necks of our guys in Sivry.

About 10:00 a.m. a little guy about half my size came barging up the hill alone. Where the hell is the major?" he asked. I asked him how Kad and the boys were. This guy was mad as hell. His name was Crone, and he had a little mustache showing over his beard.

Lieutenant Ellsworth had sent Crone up to talk with the major. Ellsworth still hadn't received any of the supplies he needed so badly. I told him I'd go to the major with him, because I was going to get my boys out of that death trap. The major wasn't in. He had gone to Regiment, so we talked with Big Jim Mullins, now the 2d Battalion executive officer.

Captain Jim and I were old buddies, but he couldn't do anything until the major came back. While we were at the CP, the S-3 had the balls to report to Regiment that everything was okay in Sivry when he had just heard a minute before from Crone that the ammunition was almost gone. They had to have a radio, and there was no water.

"Captain, this is no place for 81s! If you give me permission, I will take the 60s from Company F—those boys can't use them in their present position—and personally see that water, rations, ammunition, and a radio get to Company G. All I want back is for you to let me bring my 81s up here, where they belong."

"Lieutenant, I can't give you permission to do that. You will have to wait until the major gets back. The division commander ordered your 81s into the town."

"Jesus, what the hell does he know about 81mm mortars?" I was really ticked off.

Captain Jim was sympathetic to my plight. "I promise I will talk to the major as soon as he gets back. I will call you immediately."

Crone and I went back to the edge of the woods where the rest of the battalion was dug in, and waited. About noon, the major called me up and told me he was sending the logistics officer to me with rations and ammunition, and that I was to take the 60s down and bring my boys back. Bill Butz was with me, so we went to work rounding up the Company G stragglers who, for one reason or another, had come back to the hill.

I got them all together and told them my plan. Most of them looked at me like I was crazy. They were scared to death. The bulk were replacements who had come up only a couple of days before. They hadn't been broken in gradually to infantry fighting; instead, they had been thrown into the toughest fight we had yet.

I told them that we had to go down over terrain for two thousand yards that was exposed to the enemy. No matter what happened, they had to get the things through because their buddies needed the ammunition and rations they would be carrying. The men in town had no blankets. I wanted to take them some, but they needed ammunition and rations worse.

Crone suggested we go back exactly the way he had come up—a straight line from our hill to the town. He would lead the way, and I'd feed the men to him. He was just a little guy, but he had guts. He wasn't about to leave his buddies alone down there. The first ten men carried K-rations, the next few carried BAR clips of ammunition and grenades, and the next group carried bazookas, bazooka ammunition, cigarettes, and chocolate. Chocolate helped a lot even if it is as hard as a rock. The last man carried one precious radio.

I looked through my glasses and watched as Crone entered the town even before I started out. I brought up the rear. On my way down I saw some of our boys lying around who would never fight again.

The Krauts were shelling the town, so we had to be very careful. I saw Ellsworth first. He was sure glad to see us and the ammunition and radio, but especially the rations. I told him that I brought him some 60mm mortars and that I was going to take my boys back with me. He gave me a guide to take me to Kad.

I had visions of my boys with no water, no rations, and no blankets on the brink of death. God, they must be about gone from hunger, thirst, and fatigue. When I entered Kad's house—his cellar—I smelled something like Mulligan Stew and heard a pig squeal. The men had found the one water spigot in town that worked. They had also found a bin of potatoes and some dried vegetables. And, they had found a wine cellar! They were preparing a feast and I had arrived just in time to help them enjoy it.

Private First Class Terribilini, the best gunner we had, came walking in wearing a white, if not somewhat dirty, apron and a white chef's cap stuck on top of his helmet. He was the chief cook. The men even had a table set with a cloth and dishes.

The meal was good—if you liked to dine while the plaster is falling in your plate and the house is shaking from shells falling on it. Occasionally, a big piece of plaster fell and clanked off my helmet. I barely paid attention as I scooped out the stew into my mouth as fast as I could!

Our artillery observer with Ellsworth was blasting away at the machine gun and snipers that we could see dug in on the side of the hill that looked right down our necks. Every time he would let go with a barrage the Krauts did too, and that made it risky to fool around on the streets. It was especially rough with the snipers and machine gunners. The artillery observer was really enjoying himself. Every time a barrage would land he slapped his leg and said, "Hitler, count your children." He also noted, "You know this is the first time I've ever had to look up to observe artillery."

I went to see how Lieutenant Ackermann and his boys were getting along. I found him and one of his gunners lying on a bed in a dark room of a house. They were both worn out, as was everybody else. Ackermann had a piece of shrapnel in his shoulder, but he said it wasn't too bad and that he could manage okay. One of his guns was placed in the back door of his house and the crew tried to keep the Kraut machine gunners and snipers quiet. Kad had a little ammunition left, so we decided to throw it at the Krauts before we left. It would be dark before long, so we had to rush things up a bit.

He stayed at the guns while I strung a phone wire to the house on the outskirts of town. Cover was out of the question. I had to crawl behind some rubble on the second story of a rubble house. The Krauts were raising hell with their 120mm mortars now. It was ticklish business moving around.

I got to my OP okay and started adjusting on a machine gun emplacement a couple of hundred yards up the side of the hill. I had only fired a couple of rounds when the next thing I knew, Kad was slapping me! I focused on his face. It felt like my left leg wasn't there. I hurt from my stomach to my toes. I had no idea how long I'd been unconscious.

A few of the Kraut 120s had landed on the house I was using as an OP. Part of the house structure had collapsed on me and knocked me out. When Kad couldn't get me on the phone, he came out after me. A beam had my leg pinned down, so he had to dig me out from under it. I tried to stand, but my leg was so weak and sore it would not support me. Kad rubbed it briskly for a couple minutes to get the circulation going and bound it tightly with a bandage. I was finally able to hobble. No bones seemed to be broken, but my leg was bleeding a little.

Ellsworth, meanwhile, had interrogated a couple of prisoners who told us the Krauts were going to attack the following morning at 3:00 a.m. with a battalion of officer cadets. They also said they had heavy weapons replacements and about thirty heavy machine guns. We believed them, because the Krauts pounded the hell out of the town with mortars and artillery. There was only one way that we could get out of town and that was the same way Crone and I had come in. The Krauts had the other three sides of the town blocked off.

Kad got all the men together and I told them that we had to make our way to the west edge of town and move out single file. We also had to keep several hundred yards apart because the artillery and mortar fire was heavy all up and down the valley.

Several of my men were wounded, including Cpl. Sidney Folmsbee, but luck and the Lord were with them. All of them could walk, even though it hurt like hell. The pain in my throbbing leg was severe, but I knew the way back and was the only one there who knew the way through the mine field. I had to make it no matter what.

We got to the edge of town and I tried to show the men the route we would take. It was two miles uphill over rolling ground, and it was quickly getting dark. I knew we had to clear the mine field before nightfall or someone would trip a wire and blow himself to bits.

"Heh, Lieutenant," asked one of the men. "We don't have to lug this ammunition we have left back up the hill, do we?" I thought about it for a few seconds and shook my head. "Dump it in a well in town."

Sergeant John Quinn had to help me walk. I would lead the way out and Kad would feed the men to me at intervals. As we were standing there getting ready to move out, the Krauts started using us as target practice. Brother, let me tell you being on the receiving end of target fire is not any fun.

The wounded were to be sprinkled in between the other men so that if one of them couldn't make it, someone else could carry his equipment and help the wounded man. I wanted to hang onto the guns if at all possible because replacements were hard to get. Remember, they were having strikes back home.

The artillery pestered us all the way up. The men were dog tired from carrying their heavy equipment, but stopping meant death. They knew that, and that helped everyone keep moving.

When Quinn and I were about halfway through the mine field, we heard some rounds coining in that were going to land too close for comfort, so we dove for a gully. As fate would have it, I landed on my leg and for a minute or two, I lost my senses from the excruciating pain. When we got to the edge of the woods we both sank down and didn't say a word for quite some time. We didn't have the strength.

The men straggled in and dropped down from sheer exhaustion. It was getting dark fast. I told Sergeant Hubbard to pull the column down the path that ran parallel to Company F's lines for a few hundred yards and hold it up. Darkness closed in, but Kad and a few others had not yet come up.

I sent word up and down Company F's lines for the men to be on the lookout for my men and not to fire. I was afraid they might hit some trip wires in the mine field. My leg felt like it was about to fall off, it hurt so badly. But I took the men I had down to where the company was holed up, and in a few minutes Kad came in with the rest of the men. He had gotten lost in the darkness, but managed to come through the mine field without touching a trip wire.

The wounded men were in a lot of pain from their hard grind. One of them had been hit in the stomach and he was really hurting. The wound didn't look that bad, but I know his insides were probably torn up. We still had about two hundred yards to go over muddy clay to get to the rest of the platoon.

Sergeant Zane Turner, one of Bill Butz's machine gunners, had a phone from his gun back to my platoon. I called Sergeant Freeman to get three jeeps ready to take the wounded to the medics. Koors and Quinn helped me through the mud because my leg was almost useless. My boys were glad to be together again. Shaultz, the guy who asked me earlier if he could dump his ammunition, had filled his bag with bottles of wine, so we had a little nip.

I called up the major and gave him a report on the situation, told him about the wounded that couldn't walk, and that I couldn't bring them out with me. Ellsworth had run out of medical supplies, including morphine, and his wounded were hurting bad. The major told me that he would get the wounded out that night. Later, Major Carey, the regimental surgeon, and Captain Price, our battalion surgeon, drove an ambulance down and brought out the wounded. Tom Jennings, the battalion S-4, carried rations down.

It started to rain, so Kad, Bud Leonard, and I decided to sleep on the ground. About midnight, one of our guards told us the artillery shells were coming in really close, and that maybe we should crawl into a hole. I tried to get up, but my leg wouldn't stand it, so I got Doc Tillman to give me another shot of morphine. Within a few minutes I drifted off to sleep. Did I mention how wonderful that morphine was?

* * *

The next morning, October 4, at 3:20 a.m., the Krauts attacked Sivry with what we estimated was a full battalion of infantry. At about 8:00 or 9:00 a.m., communications with Ellsworth and Company G were cut off. A few stragglers from Company G got out. They were wrecks of men. With hollow eyes and hollow voices they pieced together their story.

The Krauts had launched a sneak attack. They attacked with burp guns, grenades, and bayonets. They outnumbered our boys about forty to one. When it had gotten to the point where it was a matter of every man for himself, Ellsworth told his guys to get out the best way they could. Ellsworth, apparently, was still holding out and needed help badly. His CP was in a church in the middle of town, completely surrounded by Germans. The major decided to take down Company E himself and try to get into town.

Company E moved forward, circled around the mine field in a dense fog, and succeeded in reaching the houses on the edge of town. That's as far as they got. The Krauts stopped them cold with heavy small arms fire. Every street in the small town was covered by Kraut machine guns. Major Hayes and his boys were on open ground and the Krauts had the advantage of buildings. Our artillery smoked the hill behind the town and raised hell with high explosives, but it didn't do much good.

My leg was really swollen now; I couldn't walk on it at all. Late in the day at the aid station I ran into the major. He had a high temperature that later turned into pneumonia. He didn't want to leave, but he had no strength left. He told me what happened in Sivry.

Company E had also recently received lots of new replacements. Initially, two rifle platoons made it to the edge of town. It wasn't until the middle of the afternoon that the other two rifle platoons reached the rest of the company. When they got on the outskirts and the Krauts turned their guns on them, the men dropped face down into the ground and wouldn't move. The old timers were picked off trying to show the new kids how it was done. When the situation became hopeless, we were ordered to withdraw. This was about 6:30 p.m. on October 4.

* * *

I'll never know why we were ordered to take that damn town. What possible benefit could we have derived from taking Sivry, without also taking the strategic and commanding Mt. Toulon and Mt. St. Jean? I guess when you're looking at maps from a comfortable position several safe miles to the rear, things look entirely different.

There were a few medals given out for the little action around Sivry. About 380 men had taken part in the attack, but only 191 escaped from Sivry, half of them wounded. Kad broke up a counterattack while he and his men were trying to get in, and he received the Silver Star. A sergeant from Company G, Jimmy Adkins (no relation), got the Distinguished Service Cross. Only forty men were left in Company G. These men probably owed their escape to a rearguard action fought by Sergeant Adkins. He was wounded, but made his way back through the village after covering his buddies. Lieutenant Ellsworth refused to surrender until all of his men were gone. For my piece of the action in Sivry, I was awarded the Bronze Star.

About 3:30 p.m. on October 4, Monahan, Ackermann, Ellsworth, and a few others were captured by a German force of about four hundred men. As Monahan was being taken back up Mt. Toulon he stopped, turned around, and waved to us. We could see him through the glasses. There were now only two of the original thirty-seven line officers left in my battalion. The others had been killed or wounded.

After the Krauts took Sivry, they set up a public address system on Mt. Toulon and called for us to surrender. The guy on the PA spoke perfect English and called us by our code name, "Headache." He said one of our other regiments (Hayseed) had been annihilated. "Lay down your arms, form in a column of twos, bring your mess gear and your best girl's picture, and chow will be waiting for you." We answered with artillery.

Some of my boys took me to the aid station. The medics also brought in a couple of men who had shot themselves. One kid had put his left hand over the muzzle of his M-1 and pulled the trigger with his right hand. Boy, those bones were splattered. The other kid hadn't been as smart. He had put an M-1 slug through his knee, and it was a mangled mess. I couldn't see how the medics could do anything but amputate his leg. Of course, both of them were "accidental," but it does seem as if they could have chosen a more fleshy part of the body.

Before I went to the aid station, I had a feeling the doc wouldn't let me stay with my men, so I called them together and told them that I would be gone for a few days and for them to take care of themselves until I got back. I realized then how close we had become during the past couple of months. Usually I could get my men together and talk to them for hours on end, but this time I got all choked up and could only sputter a little. The men who came out of Sivry with me said, "Thanks, Lieutenant."

A few days later, on October 8, two of our regiments supported by XII Corps Artillery and a battalion of .50-caliber machine gun squads, stormed Sivry, Mt. Toulon, and Mt. St. Jean. My mortars fired 985 rounds in fifteen minutes on Mt. Toulon and were credited with killing between five hundred and six hundred Krauts.

Chapter 7
MEDICAL EVACUATION AND RECOVERY

October 5, 1944–November 21, 1944

When a man was wounded on the front lines, he was carried toward the forward aid station by whatever means possible. Sometimes there were litters available, but most of the time the wounded were carried or dragged by one or two men to get them out of the line of fire. After he was moved back, litter bearers from the forward aid station came up to evacuate him. They hauled the man to their jeep, loaded him up (ambulance jeeps usually carried up to four litters), and drove like mad to the battalion aid station, which was usually a mile or so to the rear.

Doc Bobb, our medic, and Doc Furnish, our battalion surgeon, put me into an ambulance after they examined me at the battalion aid station. I was to be evacuated to the rear for further evaluation and recovery. My first stop was to the collecting company, and from there I was transferred to the clearing company. I finally ended up in the 39th Evacuation Hospital located near Nancy, France, around October 6. Boy was I feeling good because of the morphine! I was floating through the clouds with absolutely no pain and no fear. I was completely relaxed, without a care in the world. Did I mention how wonderful morphine was?

I looked at my field jacket. The medics through the various aid stations had each tagged me as to their diagnoses. The stretcher bearers set me down in a small office in the hospital. A hatchet-faced woman with tight lips and wearing a nurse's uniform came over and looked at my tags. She was an old maid, and a second look at her old me why. I tried to talk to her, but all I got in reply was a "Shhhhhh!"

After she read my tags, she said in a sharp voice, "What's the matter with you?" I replied, "I'm in labor and expect to give birth to twins any minute." She turned red around the gills and briskly walked away.

They moved me to a cot, but in a few minutes the same hatchet-faced woman came up and rammed a thermometer down my throat. I tried to talk again. I got a "Shhhhhh!" After she removed the thermometer, she asked in that same shrill voice, "Have you had a bowel movement today?"

"No, have you?"

She turned red again. "Lieutenant, we will have none of your brashness around *this* hospital."

I must have dozed off. Someone was holding my hand. I opened my eyes and saw a big smile and a pair of deep blue eyes looking at me. I said, "Hold my other hand. It hurts, too." The pretty nurse said, "I'm not holding your hand; I'm taking your pulse." She started to put me through the procedures that all new patients go through.

I must have been quite a sight to behold. I hadn't shaved in several weeks and hadn't brushed my teeth in quite a while. When I looked at my teeth in a mirror, they were black! The nurse said I must check my valuables, so I emptied all my pockets. I put everything in a pile beside me: my wallet, K-rations, cigarettes, toilet paper, gum, can opener, a leather thong I used to tie up my raincoat, a can of powdered coffee, some dirty oily rags I had been using as handkerchiefs, and a pair of binoculars I still had around my neck.

In my left-hand fatigue jacket pocket I had a .45 Colt pistol that I always carried in case my carbine failed. I had even forgotten about that. In addition, I had a few little souvenirs I had taken from some prisoners we had captured: a piece of silk from a parachute and some emblems and patches ripped off Kraut uniforms.

After the pocket inventory came the process of undressing me. That was rather embarrassing because the last time I had a bath of any nature was out of a helmet thirty-nine days earlier, and except for my socks, had not changed clothes. I hadn't had a hot bath since I left the States.

Naturally I couldn't smell myself, but I know the nurse could detect a distinctive barnyard aroma about me. Nevertheless, she was an understanding American gal and didn't make any comments. I was wearing a field jacket, fatigue shirt, fatigue pants, OD (Olive Drab) pants, two OD shirts, two wool undershirts, wool drawers, cotton shorts, and a cotton undershirt. All of them, particularly my underclothes, were black as the night and almost stiff enough to stand up by themselves. My cotton shorts still had a hole in them where a piece of shrapnel had come through them several weeks earlier. There was still dried blood on them.

The nurse helped me down to the last mentioned item and then the ward boy took over. My body was black with dirt. I was on the way to the most wonderful experience I had in quite some time—a hot bath! The ward boy wanted to bathe me in bed, but I said, "Hell, no. You just help me to the shower room and I'll take over from there."

While we were arguing about the bath, the doctor came in to examine me. He asked me what was wrong. I told him nothing except that I couldn't walk. That didn't seem to set so well with him, so I decided that from then on, I'd be a little more discreet.

I learned later that a doctor's time in an evacuation hospital was precious. They worked all day and all night on men who were brought in from the front to try and save them while they still had a chance to live. The doctors and nurses were an incredibly dedicated group. His pulling and twisting on my leg didn't help any, but I let him have his way. He said he'd X-ray my leg later.

After the doctor left, I bribed the ward boy into carrying me to the showers. My leg hurt like hell, but that shower felt mighty good. I couldn't sleep that night, even with the sleeping pills the nurse gave me. I asked her for some more, but she refused.

The next morning the doc came back to take a look at me. He had X-rays with him. I forgot to be discreet again and told him to fix my leg up and let me get the hell out of the joint. My leg was still swollen and I couldn't bend it. The doc said he couldn't do anything for me here. They didn't have the necessary facilities, so they were sending me to a general hospital in Paris, where they have modern equipment. He showed me some funny things on the X-rays, things I didn't understand. He said I had chipped my knee cap and torn the ligaments and the cartilage. I asked him how long before I would be able to walk again. He replied that depended partially on me, meaning that I must take it easy for a while.

The doctor and I talked a little. "I see that the Third Army is on the move again."

"What do you mean, Doc?" I asked.

"Oh, we can always tell. Whenever we have a lull here in the hospital, we know things are comparatively quiet. But just as soon as the casualties start pouring in we know that the Third Army is on the move again. Yesterday a lot of wounded starting coming in."

That night I noticed a black patient walking up and down in front of my cot. After a while he came up and said, "Pardon me, suh, ain't you Mr. Adkins' boy?"

That surprised the hell out of me. "Yeah, why?"

He let out a big grin. "Why, I used to rake your daddy's yard when you was a little shaver."

"Sit down here. I want to talk to you," I said. His name was Allen Leggett and his mother still lived in Starke, Florida. We talked about everybody we knew in Starke, and I promised him that I'd write Dad and tell him to go and see his mother. It was indeed a small world.

Next to me was a soldier who had been hit in the stomach. The doctors had rubber tubing running all through him. He looked like a laboratory experiment. I guess I wasn't in such bad shape after all.

One day while I was in the 39th, I heard a ward boy bitching like hell. When I asked him why, he replied that his clean laundry had been late in getting to him this week. I tell you, the nerve of these people. Late laundry?

I stayed in the 39th Evacuation Hospital from October 6 to October 9. From there, I went to an air evacuation point and stayed overnight. There was no plane available, so one night they loaded us on a hospital train and sent us to Paris. It took all night to get there. Since sleep was impossible (and had been for several nights), I became acquainted with Capt. Norman Ogilire, a tank commander who had one eye all bandaged up. He wore glasses and one day, while his head was poking out the turret of his tank, a machine gun bullet seared his temple and broke his glasses. A piece of the lens hit him in the eye.

We pulled into the Paris station early in the morning. Groups of Frenchmen stood around staring, their tongues clucking in their cheeks. Captain Ogilire couldn't see and I couldn't walk, so we combined my eyes and his legs to get us off the train.

The 108th General Hospital in Paris was really a modern affair. I was put in a wing on the top floor with several other officers. There I lay on a bed with clean, crisp sheets and the first mattress and sheets I had slept on since I left the States. In the same ward with me was Capt. Johnny Wooten, an old acquaintance. He was with the 12th Army Group and had a badly infected ear. We had a big time teasing Johnny. We told him the reason he was in the hospital was because both of his thumbs were sore from doing nothing but pushing pins in maps. In the next bed was a Lieutenant Jones from the 1st Infantry Division, who had been hit pretty good in the butt. His hole was much larger than mine had been. (Yes, we did compare butt wounds.)

They told me the same thing here as they had in Nancy: they couldn't do anything for me. I would have to go back farther, to another hospital where they had better facilities. The doctor in Paris told me that they only kept patients there that they could cure and return to the front line in fifteen days.

The wing I was in had huge windows that offered a great view of Paris. From my bed I could see the Eiffel Tower, the Arc de Triomphe, and the section of Paris known as Montmarte. We heard tales of the famous night spots and of the pretty mademoiselles in the Montmarte district, but the nearest we could get to them was through secondhand reports. I had heard of the wonders of Paris all of my life, but it was impossible for me to get out of bed.

One of the duties wounded officers had was to censor mail. We censored the mail of the enlisted men who worked at the hospital and from their letters I could read of the wonders of the city they were relating to their loved ones at home. One letter was a peach. It was written by a medic stationed at our hospital. It read something like this:

My Darling,

I miss you so and if I ever needed your faith in me it was yesterday. We launched our attack yesterday morning at daybreak. Darling, it was awful. We had gone only a little way when the Germans saw us coming. They let us get almost on top of them before they started shooting. All at once dozens of machine guns and rifles started opening up on us. I clung to the ground. My best friend (I can't give his name) lying next to me was hit in the head. I did all I could for him, but he died in my arms.

A machine gun right in front of us kept us from moving. That gun had to be annihilated before we could advance. The captain shouted, 'Men, we can't move and we will all be killed unless that machine gun is knocked out. I want a volunteer to go forward and quiet it. Who will go?'

My beloved, I felt a strange impulse come over me. My best friend had died in my arms. My blood began to boil when I thought of those Germans killing my best friend. He had saved my life, for the bullet that took his life could just as well been meant for me. In that instant I thought of you and knew that if I wanted to see you again, my love, and if my comrades wanted to see their loved ones that machine gun had to be silenced.

No one answered the captain. What were they, cowards? I knew that if our company was to be saved I had to silence that machine gun. The Germans were shooting artillery at us now. I crawled toward the captain. How I ever crawled through that intense artillery and am still alive, I'll never know. I finally reached the captain and told him that I would go. He gave me his two grenades to go with the two I had, and I started working my way toward the machine gun.

Darling, I can't describe to you what horror I went through trying to get to the machine gun. Every inch I crawled was a nightmare. The German riflemen saw me coming, and every one of them tried to shoot me. One bullet did scratch my leg, but it was only a flesh wound, so don't worry about it.

Finally, after what seemed an eternity I reached a position from which I could throw my grenades. I threw three. The machine gun was silent. When the rest of the Germans saw that the machine gun was out of action they threw down their rifles and got up and ran. I shot three as they were running. When the Germans started running, the rest of my company came up and finished them off.

When things quieted down I realized that I was a little scared, but not very much. Guess it was because I was thinking of you. The captain shook my hand and mumbled something about the Congressional Medal of Honor, but of course it's not official yet. Those things take quite a while, you know, all this army red tape. Don't say anything about what I am writing you, but I just wanted you to know.

* * *

I stayed at the 108th from October 10 to October 14. In the early afternoon of the 14th, they put me in an ambulance and carried me to an airstrip on the outskirts of Paris. In a few minutes I was aboard a C-47 on my way to England. From there I was taken by ambulance to a hospital for a one-night stand. When they rolled me into the reception room, I saw Cpl. Sidney Folmsbee from my company. In addition to being hit a couple of times, he was having trouble with his back, so they had sent him to England to have it looked after.

The next morning they loaded us on a hospital train and started us rolling to another hospital. Late in the afternoon, after a train ride and an ambulance ride, I arrived at the 216th General Hospital. When I got to the reception room I asked them if I had to go to any more hospitals. They said no, this was my last stop.

While they rolled us into our respective wards, the Red Cross gave us cigarettes and a smile. After I had been in my bed a little while, the doc came in to take a look. After checking me out, studying my case history and X-rays, and after I recited the history of my life, all he said was, "We'll see."

For the last two weeks I had done nothing but ask questions of the doctors, and the answers I'd received in return would not have filled the back of a postage stamp. It didn't do any good to tell or ask them anything, because they weren't going to tell me anyway.

A few minutes later I looked up and who should I see come hobbling in on crutches but Phil Bible, an old OCS buddy. He had a machine gun bullet through his ankle. After the excitement died down, he told me that J. L. "Murph" Murphy, a Citadel classmate of mine, was in the same ward, but at the moment was taking a sightseeing tour of the grounds in his wheelchair.

In a few minutes Murph came rolling in. He had been the I&R Platoon leader of the 318th Infantry of my division and had been hit on September 13 when we were all trying to repulse the Kraut counterattack near St. Geneviève. He had been hit pretty badly. Two fingers and the thumb of his hand were useless and he had a gash in his leg about two feet long. I learned from him what happened to the 318th that night, and it was really a nightmare.

The ward I was in was quite an affair, full of men with every type of wound imaginable. There were two lieutenants across from me whose legs were in casts and had those pulley systems tied to the ceiling. One of them, Harry Sales, had a bullet through his leg. He had been knocked off a halftrack, and when he came to and looked down at his leg, he saw the bone sticking out and covered with mud.

In another bed was Bill Tucker from Atlantic, Iowa. He was a P-47 pilot. His plane had caught fire and he bailed out. When he jumped, part of the plane's tail caught his leg and tore the hell out of it. He had a nice plaster cast. After we got to feeling better and could move around a little, Bill, Harry, and I would pull our beds together and play bridge.

Most of the guys were infantrymen, so we kidded Bill Tucker who was with the Air Corps. Whenever Bill would start to say something, someone would yell, "Bombs away," and someone else from the other end of the ward would reply, "Give him another Oak Leaf Cluster to add to his Air Medal!" We kidded the Air Corps about the numerous medals they awarded. They received about as many air medals as the Infantry received Purple Hearts. It was all in fun. Bill knew it and laughed with us.

Lieutenant Bill Walsh, of the 313th Field Artillery Battalion from Chicago, and Murph palled around together. He had a bullet enter the top of his shoulder and stop just above his heart. He was quite a sight, all bent over and his left arm practically useless. Joe McAnnula from New York City took a bullet that went through his hip. He hobbled around with a cane.

Lieutenant Butler from the 318th Infantry, who had a wife and two kids back in the States, had enough metal in him to build a couple of machine guns. His back and legs were so scarred from shrapnel wounds that he could have easily have been converted into a wash board. Still, this guy wanted to go back and do some more fighting. Even though he had to limp around on two crutches, every time the doc came to look him over, he'd say, "Doc, when are you guys going to let me out of this joint? I want to get back to my outfit. All I need is a little exercise and I'll be all right."

Lieutenant Butler had had a machine gun platoon when the 318th was trying to storm the castle atop Pont-a-Mousson. He had had a little argument there with the divisional artillery commander. Butler and his guns had been momentarily stopped by grazing fire and couldn't get up the hill. The general came over to Butler and said, "Lieutenant, get those machine guns up that hill." To which Butler replied, "Sir, I can't put bayonets on these things, you know. What do you want me to do, pick them up and shoot them from the hip like Clark Gable?" That ended the argument, because before the general could reply, a little artillery came in on top of them. The next thing Butler knew some Frenchmen were hauling his mangled body down the side of the hill in an ox cart.

When we were all well enough to get out of the bed to go to the latrine, they moved us to another ward. There we all acquired nicknames. The blond kid from Alabama with shrapnel in his eye was called "Blinky." The tall brunette from Texas, the one with the plaster cast around his chest, and extending around his right arm so that his arm stuck straight up in the air, was "Flagpole." Tompkins had a big cut across his chest and when they sewed it up he, of necessity, had to hunch his shoulders. He was "Scrooge." I was "Limpy."

* * *

While I was lying in the hospital bed one night, it finally struck me that I was going to be there for some time, recovering and getting my strength back. I didn't have much to do, so I started thinking about the events over the last few months, ever since we arrived at Normandy. The next day I started my journal, listing everywhere, everything, and everyone I could think of. It became quite a piece, my journal. That's how I am able to remember so many details, otherwise long forgotten. I decided also, then and there, that I would continue to keep my journal up to date when I got back to my company.

The hospital encouraged us to take passes once we were able to get around. I went into Salisbury several times. It's a beautiful old English City. I also went into London a couple of times with Harry Sales. Harry used to be stationed in London and knew his way around. We did everything that could be done in London on several three-day passes, including seeing the sights.

After touring Bond Street on one of our visits, Harry and I started walking back to our hotel. On the way back this guy walks up to us and says: "Say, Gents, I know a quiet little spot where you can get a drink if you want one." Harry laughed and said, "Okay, lead us to it."

"Harry, what's going on?" I asked. On the way he explained to me that all the bars in London were closed for several hours during the afternoon, and there were several black-market places better known as "five o'clock clubs," where a person could get a drink. They were quiet little places usually upstairs, and when we got there we would see a small bar and several girls sitting around. After a while the girls would give us the eye and we, of course, would ask them over to our table for a drink. Usually they would tell us that they were waiting for someone, but with a little persuasion they would come over and say something like this: "I really am waiting for someone and I shouldn't do this, but he's late and perhaps this will teach him a lesson."

To our surprise, the gal would turn out to be quite a drinker, and every time we would ask her if she wanted another drink, she would say yes. Of course, we were served a little diluted whiskey and (unbeknownst to many men) she got colored water, which we paid for the same as we paid for our diluted whiskey.

After Harry oriented me, I asked why we were going if he knew the set up. "Just for the experience, son, just for the experience. It will be a nice yarn to tell your children." The man led us up a few flights of stairs. Sure enough, there it was: three rooms with a bar, soft music, lounges and tables, and several gals "waiting for someone."

The first time I went to London I went to the officers' sales store to get a set of greens (I'd come to the hospital in a pair of G.I. pajamas). I ran into my old friend from Starke, John Torode. Boy, was it good to see him! He had to leave London right away, so we didn't have long to spend with each other.

When Harry and I returned from London, I thought I was tired. After the lights were out I still could not go to sleep. I tried to relax and think through our trip to London, but still no sleep. I tried smoking cigarettes, but that didn't help, either. The voice in my mind would not leave me alone.

"What's the matter with you, Adkins? Why can't you sleep? You know why you can't sleep? You are thinking about something. You have a problem on your mind and are afraid to face it. You are going back to France soon, and you don't want to go. You like it here, don't you? It is nice lying around in clean warm beds with no worry and no care and no responsibility and having someone to wait on you.

"You were anxious to get back to your men when you were in the hospital in France, weren't you? You were a hero then, and felt out of place in the rear. But you have changed your mind since you got back to England, haven't you? You like it here, you've had it so good, you'd be a fool to go back.

"Hell, you are a pretty smart fellow. It wouldn't be hard to convince these doctors that your leg couldn't stand combat duty. You've done your share, buddy; let somebody else live in that hell for a while.

"Have you really done your share? Did Bob Strutz do his share? He got his head blown off, remember? And how about Ray Wadsinski and Hank Walker. Did they do their share? What would they say if they could read your mind now? Hell, you're no hero. They were the heroes. But, then, you're no coward either, and if you live through this war you will have to live with yourself."

The doc came around the next morning to look at my leg. He said, "How is the leg, Adkins?"

"It's okay Doc. I'm ready to get back to my outfit."

Chapter 8
BACK TO THE FRONT

November 21, 1944–December 14, 1944

I left the 216th General Hospital on November 21 and transferred to the 10th Replacement Pool. Our train had a four-hour stopover at Bristol, so I took some time to do a little sightseeing. I stayed at the 10th Replacement Pool until November 23 and then went to another branch of the 10th at Phesy Farms, on the outskirts of Birmingham.

Birmingham was only a ten-minute bus ride away from Phesy Farms. It was truly a soldier's paradise. There were very few American troops stationed there, but girls flooded the place. Another buddy of mine named James was with me. It was our last fling before we started back to France.

At Phesy Farms, we were able to fully resupply our equipment, supplies, and ODs. We also got all our back pay and a twenty-four-hour pass. We went to the British Red Cross Club and were assigned to a room. After cleaning up, James and I went downstairs to eat. We found a quiet table in the corner. In a few minutes, a quaint, pretty voice with a distinct British accent asked, "What would you like?" I looked up and saw the most beautiful sight I'd seen in months.

The young lady took our order and left. When she brought our food, I asked her in a roundabout soft sort of way, "How about a date tonight?" She told me that she was a volunteer worker in the club and was not supposed to talk to the men there. But . . . she was getting off from work in a few minutes and if I cared to meet her in front, she would think about it.

I gobbled down my food. Here name was Jean, and she gave me her address and directions on how to get to her place. At 7:00 p.m., I started out with ulterior motives. When I reached her home, she introduced me to her mother, father, and aunt, all of whom lived with her. On a table in the corner I noticed sandwiches and cakes. She had changed clothes and looked like a million bucks.

Their house was very comfortable and made me homesick. Her father turned to me and said, "Our daughter is a volunteer worker in the club, you know. We like for her to invite some homesick American soldiers to visit with us in our home. We haven't very much, but we like to share what little we have with you American boys who aren't able to be in your own homes." That put a lump in my throat, especially given the way I had been thinking about his daughter.

Then, as if talking to himself, he said in a quiet voice, "We lost our two boys at Dunkerque." Now I felt like a first-class heel. Here was this nice English family that wanted to share what little they had with a total stranger, and I wanted to take their daughter out to some park or hotel room. I looked at Jean apologetically. How could I have ever thought of such a thing? Had this man's war turned me into a barbarian?" "Forgive me," I thought, "Forgive me."

Our casual company at Phesy Farms was quite an affair. All of the men in it had been wounded and knew they were going back to France to be either killed or wounded again. As a result they didn't particularly give a damn about anything. They all knew what war was about and weren't in too much of a hurry to get back. Time passed quickly, as it always does, and on November 28 we started loading on our ship at Southampton to take us to Le Havre, France.

We arrived at Le Havre on November 29. The heart of the city around the harbor had been completely wiped out. Not even the walls of buildings were standing. They claim ten thousand civilians were killed when the city was bombed. I guess that's why the remaining Frenchmen weren't too friendly. We walked about five miles uphill to a tent city and stayed there overnight.

On November 30 they loaded us on the small French "forty and eight" cars. Printed in French on each of these cars were the words, "This car will hold 40 men or 8 horses." So *this* was the "40 and 8s" I'd always heard about! I looked inside my car and saw a five-gallon can of water, a box of C-rations, and a roll of toilet paper. Forty of us with full gear crammed into that little square-wheeled icebox. What a contrast to those nice comfortable hospital beds.

During our second night on the train, we stopped longer than usual. I looked out the door and saw we were in a big freight yard. A Frenchman walked by. I asked him where we were. "Paree," he said. All I could see was freight yards, miles and miles of freight yards. The men got out to stretch, relieve themselves, and, as always, look around.

One of the men found a huge wooden cask on a flat car on our train. He punched a hole in it with his bayonet. A liquid streamed out. He tasted it while most of the men crossed their fingers. It was wine! The word spread quickly. One of the men came up to me and said, "Lieutenant, I know we aren't supposed to drink, but it's awful cold in that square-wheeled icebox, so why don't you give me your canteen while you take a little walk up the other way?" Every container imaginable was filled with wine—canteens, canteen cups, empty C-rations cans, even helmets! The remainder of our ride wasn't as cold as the first part.

Finally we reached the 9th Replacement Pool at Fontainebleu on December 2 and stayed there until the sixth. We traveled farther and arrived at the 17th Replacement Pool at Neufchateau the next day and stayed until December 11. Before going back to the Company, I stopped off at the division reinforcement company. They didn't call new troops "replacements" anymore; now they were "reinforcements." Lieutenant Doug Brown was in charge of the company. He had been hit when we first tried to cross the Moselle. He wanted to rejoin his company, but the medics wouldn't let him. I rejoined Company H on December 14.

The division was in army reserve at St. Avoid, France, and scheduled for two weeks of rest, training, and reorganization. We had a new battalion commander, Lt. Col. Bill Boydstun. I went by to see him. He was a big, broad-shouldered man with a flat nose he had earned as a collegiate boxer. He shook my hand like he meant it and said, "Adkins, I've heard a lot about you and we're mighty glad to have you back."

* * *

It was a strange mix of emotions to be back with the company. There were many familiar faces. We had grown close over the months of fighting. But many of my friends were missing—killed, wounded, or captured. On one hand, I was glad to be back with my buddies. On the other, I knew sooner or later we'd be fighting the Germans and once again be in the middle of blood, guts, and death.

I was also glad to be back with Bill Butz. Same old Bill, only he had acquired a handlebar mustache. "How's the new battalion CO?" Bill said, "He's a swell guy; you'll like him."

The men hadn't been too impressed with Major Hayes. Sure, he was a West Pointer—and that was a good thing—but the men remembered too well that in the two attacks at Moivron and Sivry when he was our Battalion CO, we had gotten the hell beat out of us. The way both of those attacks had been ordered was not only useless, but foolish. That left a bad taste in the men's mouths. Then too, Major Hayes sported the Silver Star for "personally leading his troops during an attack on Sivry." Okay, so the guy did kill a few Krauts and ran around shouting, "Follow me!" Still, he never got into the town of Sivry. The men couldn't quite understand that.

Kad was still the same. In addition to crossing the Seine and fighting their way through the Maginot Line while I was gone, the boys had a little fun in a town called Farberswaller. Kad told me about it.

Kad's 81mm mortar platoon was too far behind, so Colonel Boydstun sent word for Kad to move them into Farberswaller. The colonel told him that the town had been cleared and for him to just take his men on in and bed them down for the night. Kad woke up the platoon and the men sleepily dragged themselves into the small town. There were no American troops there, so Kad shrugged his shoulders and thought to himself, "Well, if the colonel says the town has been cleared, I guess it is okay."

He found a big house with outside steps leading to the second floor and stuck the platoon inside. The sleepy men filed into a large room on the second floor to get organized. Kad heard some tanks rumbling in the distance and thought they were Shermans arriving to provide a little moral support.

A few minutes later, Sgt. Joe Pawlak said, "Lieutenant, they don't sound like our tanks to me." He grabbed his helmet and went out to investigate. Pawlak walked down the hall to the front door and looked outside. To his stunned amazement, a German Tiger Royal tank was sitting in front of the house! He hurried back to the big room in which the platoon was still assembled and told Kad. He quickly closed the door leading to the hall and whispered, "Men, out the back window, and be quiet about it."

Private Ray, one of the ammo bearers, was the first to the window. As he started out the window he saw a squad of German infantry fanning out in the back of the house. There was nothing to do but stay inside, be quiet, and pray. Ray was a great collector. In addition to having several German pistols on his belt, he had on a German sweater and a pair of German socks. It wouldn't do to be captured with any German equipment on him. He got the sweater off okay, but he couldn't get the socks off because his bootlace was broken.

Sergeant Albert Melcolm had his radio, so Kad told him to call the colonel. They heard hobnail boots coming up the stone steps leading into the house. Melcolm was trying frantically to call the colonel on the radio and be quiet at the same time. "How Three to White Six, How Three to White Six, come in."

The hobnails clicked their way down the hall. Pawlak reached in his boot, pulled out his trench knife, and stepped to one side of the door. The boots stopped in front of the door. Kad told me he could hear his heart beat, but try as he might it kept pounding. He couldn't understand why the Krauts didn't hear his heart.

The men waited. Silence. The boots started down the front steps and Melcolm finally reached the colonel on the radio. "For God's sake, come get us!" Finally the colonel arrived astride a Sherman tank. "I gotta get my boys," he said. The colonel had several tanks and a handful of riflemen with him.

The Krauts must have not been looking for a fight that day. They pulled out when the colonel and his crew reached the edge of town. Kad was mad as a wet hen. "Colonel, sir, the next damn time you tell me that a town is clear and you want me to move into it, I'm going to tell you to go straight to hell."

Colonel Boydstun laughed. "I'll try to do better next time."

Chapter 9
THE BATTLE OF THE BULGE

December 15, 1944–January 16, 1945

I had only been back a couple days when Field Marshal Karl Gerd
von Rundstedt, the German commander in the West, launched his
big counteroffensive known today as the Battle of the Bulge. The
weather was bad—snow, freezing cold, and fog. Under this cover, the
Germans moved up three field armies and surprised the Allies and
overran part of the front, heading for Antwerp to cut off our supply
port and supply lines. German infantry and tanks attacked along a
ninety-mile front in an effort to split Allied armies on the Western
Front. This caused a "bulge" in our lines, and the battle to flatten
out this bulge by troops for the next month was to become known as
the Battle of the Bulge.

One of Rundstedt's spearheads was headed for Luxembourg City,
with the objective of taking the place and the famous radio station
known as Radio Luxembourg. The 80th Infantry Division was given
the mission of holding Luxembourg City at all costs. I believe Patton
said, "Hold to the last man."

It had started snowing and was getting colder every day. On the
night of December 19 we were loaded on trucks and within twenty-four
hours had traveled 150 miles. We rode in open vehicles. It was freezing
cold and there was no way to keep warm. We had a few blankets and

huddled close together to try to keep warm. There were no rest stops and no delays of any kind. When we had to relieve ourselves, we did so off the back end of the truck while hanging on for dear life.

It seemed as if we were in an endless stream of army vehicles. The 305th Engineers went first, checking the roads and bridges for mines. Division Military Police (MPs) acted as road guides to keep the convoy as closed up as possible so no one would get lost. Next came the trucks carrying the three infantry regiments (317th, 318th, and 319th), followed by the 702d Tank Battalion, the 633rd Anti Aircraft Artillery Automatic Weapons Battalion, and the field artillery battalions (313th, 314th, 315th, and 905th). Last in the convoy were the service companies, headquarters units, and the division HQ.[1]

It was a good night with a full moon and good visibility. General Patton ordered us there as quickly as possible, so our convoy used full beams instead of just "cat eyes." Headlights of the various vehicles had a covering over them (the "cat's eye") so that when driving at night, the lights pointed down at the road just in front of the vehicle. This made it more difficult for planes or infantry to spot us.

We dug in near Junglinster, Luxembourg, just north of Luxembourg City, about eight miles from the front line. There we found remnants of every outfit imaginable—a dozen from a rifle company, a few quartermaster trucks with their drivers, kitchen personnel, wiremen, artillerymen—all of them who had been separated from their outfits when the Germans launched their attack.

The next day, December 21, we moved twelve miles to Steinsel, Luxembourg, and into Division Reserve. We moved out at 10:00 a.m. and got to Steinsel about five that evening, just as it was getting quite dark. We needed billets for our men, so Kad and I walked to a house and knocked on the door. A scared little man stuck his head out. "We're Americans and need shelter for our men," Kad told him.

The man asked, "You are Americans?"

"Yes."

The man smiled and said, "Come in! We have been expecting you and have some rooms ready."

The man had a wife and two young sons. I hung up my dirty, torn field jacket and lay down on the floor for the night. The next morning when I reached for my jacket I noticed the tears had been mended and the dirt scrubbed away. I thanked the family for their hospitality and their kindness and wished them well.

The next day, December 22, we marched nine miles to Beringen. The German spearhead had penetrated quite a distance past our front, and we were given the mission of hammering at the shoulder of the spearhead with the intention of cutting off a pocket. It had snowed overnight, and in a way, the fresh snow turned the dreary landscape into a beautiful picture-postcard scene.

* * *

At 3:15 p.m. on December 23, we started a cross-country attack on Bourschied, 2nd Battalion leading, followed by the 1st and 3rd Battalions. There was a foot of snow on the ground. It was still snowing and very cold. We had to cross open rolling terrain, and the ground was frozen and slippery. The conditions for fighting a war were absolutely horrendous.

We attacked with two companies abreast, G and F. It was rough going all afternoon. We had a lot of new men who had not learned the little tricks of warfare. A lot of them still carried their full field packs in addition to their heavy loads of machine guns, tripods, and pieces of mortar. The result was that many fell out or tried to fall out.

The 1st Battalion was attacking on our left. There was a bright moon that night that silhouetted us beautifully against the snow. We met no opposition until about 9:00 p.m. Then word came up from the tail of the column that a Kraut patrol estimated at fifty men was sneaking up on us. That was a combat patrol, most likely with automatic weapons that could cause us a lot of trouble.

Kad and I called Lieutenant Colonel Boydstun, our battalion commander, on our radio. He told us to stop and spread out. Some of our men were on the tail of the column, so Kad and I went back. Luck was with us. The Germans were caught between us and 1st Battalion, so they decided that the best thing would be to get the hell out of there. The boys killed five Germans and captured two more. I snagged a German Walther P-38 pistol from a dead Kraut.

The terrain was very rugged, with a series of valleys and ravines running generally northwest by southeast that had to be crossed. It was necessary to cross the skyline to attack, and the Germans defended each reverse slope with machine gun fire. Up ahead of us was a deep wooded gully. The colonel decided to send Company F around its right flank and Company G through it. About five hundred yards on our side of the gully was a little knoll. We had hoped to catch the Krauts off guard, but when we were almost to the gully, a Kraut machine gunner opened up on us from the left flank. He fired in bursts of belts. Everybody hit the ground and quickly spread out.

Kad and I had been walking together. About fifty yards to our right flank was a wooded draw. We decided to crawl over there and keep a lookout. While we were in the process of lighting a cigarette beneath our overcoats, another Kraut opened up from across the draw. We postponed our smoke. The Germans seemed to be everywhere.

Company G was getting ready to go into the wooded draw. The colonel wanted some mortar fire on the draw to clear out any Krauts who might be hiding there. I had Sergeant Quinn set up a couple of guns behind the little knoll so the muzzle blast wouldn't be seen. That's one disadvantage of shooting an 81mm mortar at night: the blast from the muzzle shoots into the air about thirty feet, making it nearly impossible to mask from curious enemy eyes. I crawled up on the knoll and adjusted by turns.

We had a platoon of medium tanks with us. The colonel decided to send five of them into the woods with Company G. The mortars were to follow Company G in. The draw turned out to be much deeper than first anticipated. Captain Frank Caputo, who was now commanding Company G, got most of his company and three of the tanks into the draw before the Krauts opened up on him.

Kad and I were on our way down the steep, slippery banks when the Krauts let loose. Brother, they threw everything in the book at us! Direct-fire weapons opened up on the tanks. That was death, because the tanks were stopped cold. They had no room to maneuver. The slope of the gully was too steep for them to get back up on and the thick, scrubby trees kept them from moving ahead. They were pinned down like ducks in a shooting gallery. It was a ambush from beginning to end, and putting tanks in that situation was lunacy.

Frank Caputo's boys were closely packed together, catching hell, too. When the situation became hopeless, we pulled back behind the little knoll. The two tanks that went down with Frank were knocked out, but some of the crewmen managed to get out.

We formed a perimeter defense around the little knoll. The cold was unbearable. We were in the open and had nothing to break the fierce wind that was blowing. We helped the wounded the best we could and saw to it that they were taken back to the aid station.

Sleep was impossible because of the cold. I lay down beside a tank with Lt. Bill Mounts and Kad. Mounts had come overseas as Company H's executive officer. He had been wounded in northern France and rejoined the company while I took my turn in the hospital. It was about 3:00 a.m, and it was still too cold to sleep. After a while I tried to get up, but found that my coat was frozen to the ground, so I had to wake Kad to help me rip me loose.

When daylight came on Christmas Eve Day, the cold was unbearable beyond description. It was at this point I had an interesting conversation with Sergeant Quinn, who stomped over to me mad as hell.

"Lieutenant, you want to see two yellow son of a bitches?"

"What are you talking about Sergeant?"

"Well, Sergeant J— and Sergeant K— are lying in their holes with frozen legs."

I was not sure what he meant. "Why do you call them yellow sobs?"

"The yellow bastards deliberately stayed in their holes without moving so their legs would freeze."

"How do you know?"

"Koors and I tried to get them to stand up and stomp around last night, but they wouldn't. You know, Lieutenant, as well as I do that no man can remain still for any length of time in this weather without freezing."

"Where are they now, Sarge?"

Quinn replied, "They are still in their holes and the bastards can stay there as far as I'm concerned."

"Go pull them out and we'll get them to the medics."

Quinn shot me a confused look. "Lieutenant! I have always done what you asked me to do in the past, but I will rot in hell before I help those yellow bastards!" It was hard to disagree with him.

We had no communications with Regiment. We were just outside the town of Welscheid. Our wires were out and none of our radios worked. We knew the Krauts would often cut the wire and wait for someone to come out to fix it, and then either take him prisoner or ambush him. We had no natural cover, so we kept digging in. This helped us keep warm while we were waiting on orders from regiment. We saw a broken old farm house to our left rear, well out in the open. Around it were five tank destroyers, and inside the building were the crews and part of our headquarters company. Some of our troops were partially dug in between us and the building.

The best foxholes are the ones where you dig a shelf on the sides and deep enough so that if it rains, you won't have to sit in the water. The holes were usually rectangular, and under the best condition about four or five feet deep, two or three feet wide and six feet long. Most of the time, however, the foxholes we dug were just holes in the ground, because we were so tired we could barely move our arms, and the ground was so damn hard it was like concrete until you dug below twelve inches. Many times I needed to go to the bathroom, but just couldn't because Germans were in the area and would sling mortars at us if we ventured out. When that happened, I usually used an empty K-ration box or even my helmet as a temporary toilet, and then threw the waste over the side. It was crude, but I lived to write about it.

About mid-morning, the Krauts opened up on the parked tank destroyers with an antitank gun. It was a pitiful, hopeless sight. The Krauts not only pounded the TDs, they also shot up the house where the troops were staying. We sat and watched, unable to do anything.

The crews ran for their TDs and tried to back them up the slope to some cover. While they were in the process of doing so, a Kraut tank on the ridge about five hundred yards to our right flank opened up on them, too. The TDs and the farm house were caught in the cross fire of two Kraut direct-fire guns. It was well planned and deadly.

Two of the TDs were knocked out as they tried to back over the slope to safety. Some of the crewmen got out, but others didn't. The helpless TDs rolled down the slope in flames. Later, one of the TDs managed to get to cover, poke its gun over the crest of a hill and knock out the Kraut tank on the right. The farm house was really taking a beating. Some of the men got away, but many others died on the spot. Captain Jim Mullins, the battalion executive officer, was hit there.

After a little while a Kraut automatic rifleman opened up on the boys who were desperately trying to dig in between us and the farm house. It was suicide for them to move. Some of them tried to come back to where we were behind the little knoll, but only a few of them reached us. Several were killed, caught in the wrong place at the wrong time. Two of them were our artillery liaison captain, and a guy named "Froggy," who had come overseas with Company G. The reason for his nickname was because of his deep voice. I remember one day we were sitting on the deck of our ship off the coast of Utah Beach. Company G was having a bull session and Froggy was called upon to make a speech. After shooting the bull for a little while he became serious. He told his buddies that some of them would not see their home again, and for those who did get home, not to forget their buddies who lay dead on enemy soil. That was a very sobering speech. I will never forget it or him.

Once the Krauts were done with the TDs and the farm house, they threw mortars at us. That was rough, because we were close together in the open and had little cover. Why didn't Regiment get off their butts and tell us something besides "Hold what you've got!"

We couldn't see who was shooting at us, but we threw lead into the woods to try to keep the Krauts quiet while our boys out in the open worked their way back behind the knoll. Our rations had run out the day before and we were getting hungry. It was cold and the wind kept blowing snow all over the place, making it hard to see.

I gently suggested to the colonel that we pull back a little piece so we could spread out. He said, "Nothing doing. I'm staying here until Regiment tells me what they want next." Later that afternoon, we finally received orders to pull back about half a mile and dig in on the forward slope of a small hill.

Max Kelly, who was now commanding Company F, was out ahead of us, and Bill Butz was with them. They were cut off. The colonel sent Lt. Michael Damkowitch, Jr., from Company G, out to them several times to tell Max he could sneak back or fight his way back. About five that evening, Max decided to sneak back. I was glad to see Bill. We found out later from S-2 that there was an estimated five hundred enemy troops on three sides of us. I sure am glad I didn't know that at the time.

* * *

We moved out when darkness set in. The moon was very bright and it was very cold. We had frozen C-rations and frozen blankets waiting for us. Kad and I got the mortars placed and then tried to figure out some way of heating our frozen rations. There was a burning farm house nearby, so we thawed our rations there and decided to try and get some sleep.

We found 1st Sergeant Bloodworth and Lt. Bill Mounts huddled in a chicken coop. It was the only thing left standing on the farm. They had a little fire going, and some skinny chickens were roosting.

Between the smell, the smoke, and the cramped conditions, it was almost impossible to breathe, so Kad and I moved outside.

It was Christmas Day. At first light, we got orders to saddle up and move back. We were to dig in on the high ground about a mile north of Niederfeulen. We were in regimental reserve while 1st and 3d battalions attacked Kehmen. What a way to start Christmas. The head of our column moved slowly and, as a result, the men began to bunch up. The Krauts noticed this opportunity and opened on us with artillery as we moved up the side of a hill. They were firing what we called "screaming meemies"—large-caliber rounds fired in clusters. We heard the rockets coming, but there was little we could do other than spread out and run like hell. There was no cover around.

The German Nebelwerfer was equipped with six tubes for the rockets. Due to its design, the rocket made a screaming sound as it flew through the air. They used high explosives, but were not very accurate. They did, however, scare the crap out of us. Hence the name "screaming meemies."

Several men were hit. Some of the men hit the ground and wanted to stay there. That would have been suicide, but it was tough to get them up and keep them moving. When we got over the top of the hill and out of sight, the Krauts stopped shooting at us.

We were to set up the 81s behind Company G. A small patch of woods was near our proposed position. We had to search and clear that area first. We found two dead frozen Krauts who had been killed during the first part of the breakthrough. About two hundred yards from the guns was a huge house.

It was Christmas Day. Kad and I were determined to get our men warm. We went to investigate the house and found that an antiaircraft outfit had been there before the breakthrough and, from the equipment and supplies left behind, it was easy to see that they had moved out in a hurry.

We left a skeleton crew with the mortars and moved the rest of the men into the house. The company and battalion CPs were in Niederfeulen, so I went to see Bill Mounts to find out what was cooking. Junior, my runner, went with me. The Krauts were shelling the town and it was difficult to get around, but we finally found Bill. He was sitting in the cellar of a house eating withered apples.

When you're within range of German artillery, you want to be in the cellar. In many cases, the first and second floors had been blown away, but even if they weren't, they were inviting targets for German artillery. Anyone other than an infantryman walking into one of those cellars would immediately consider it uninhabitable. It smelled bad—the air was a mixture of sweat, brick dust, soot, cigarette smoke, urine and crap. It would not be breathable by a normal human being. But, every infantryman who was lucky enough to find one of those cellars thought it the most desirable place on earth. They were secure from all but a direct artillery hit. Most important, they were dry and out of the direct weather. The exhausted soldier could push some straw into a corner, lie down, and plunge into a deep sleep, completely relaxed.[2]

As we walked up, Bill Mounts said, "Sit down and rest your weary bones. Have an apple." My feet were swollen and hurt like hell, but so did everybody else's so I couldn't complain. Bill had talked with the colonel and said that nothing was brewing, and that we were to sit tight and wait for orders. He also told me the kitchen was going to bring us up a real Christmas dinner with all the trimmings.

On our way back to our platoon, Junior and I saw the bodies of our men who had been killed the day before. They had been retrieved from the battlefield and were laid out in neat rows in the snow. Some of them were covered with blankets; others were not. Those left uncovered looked to the sky with fixed dead eyes that seemed to ask, "Is this my Christmas present?"

When I got back, Kad had the men and the mortars all straightened out and had set up a roadblock about five hundred yards down the road that ran by our house. The men were tired and gloomy, their spirits were low, and their feet hurt. When I told them about the Christmas dinner with all the trimmings, they brightened up a bit.

About 1:00 p.m., one of our cooks brought us our Christmas dinner. We had turkey and cranberry sauce with all the trimmings—and all you could eat, too. I thought about the 1st and 3rd battalions. They had moved out to attack Kehmen at daylight. I hoped they might get some relief and warm food this Christmas Day.

* * *

We stayed in the house until December 28. During that time we were shelled quite a bit. Many of the men had trench foot and were evacuated to a hospital. Kraut patrols tried to come through our lines and our patrols tried to go through the Kraut lines. The Germans had a trick of sending unarmed men on patrols, so that if they got caught they could say they were trying to surrender.

We tried to dig in the mortars, but that was impossible. The first foot or so of earth was frozen, and below that was water. The engineers helped us with our holes. We'd shoot a couple of rifle rounds into the frozen ground, then use explosives to get down into the earth. From there we would dig deeper with our shovels and entrenching tools.

We got a lot of Christmas packages from home and decided we would pool all the chow together and have ourselves a feast. As a result of eating so much rich food and candy, I got a bad case of the GIs. It's really rough to have to go to the can every few minutes when it's snowing and freezing cold.

* * *

On the night of the December 28–29, we moved about four miles northeast of Niederfeulen to relieve the 3d Battalion in a defensive position just west of Kehmen. We stayed there until January 10. Those thirteen days and thirteen nights were the most miserable days of my life. I had never been as cold before or since. It constantly snowed and the days were dreary. There was no warmth to be found anywhere.

The Ardennes is not a distinctly defined region, but more a series of rolling hills and thick patches of fir trees. The typical village in the Ardennes had a number of stone houses and narrow streets, all centered about a large road intersection, with the largest villages numbering between 2,500 and 4,000 people. The winter weather is often raw and cold, with heavy rainfall, deep snows, and biting winds. The days are short with early morning fog and mist that last well into the morning.[3]

Our position resembled that of a shallow volcano. Two rifle companies were dug in on the perimeter. The 81s were behind them in a sloping draw, and the battalion CP, the company CP, and the reserve company were in some woods about a mile and a half to our rear.

Almost every night, the Krauts tried to send a combat patrol around our position and come up the draw from the rear of my mortar platoon. As a result, I had to keep an outpost down the draw about four hundred yards out. They almost got through one night, so I borrowed a .50-caliber machine gun and set it up to cover the draw. That would make them think twice before they tried to sneak up on our rear again.

To our front, about a mile down in the valley was the little town of Kinston, which the Krauts held. We tried to burn it down with white phosphorous from my mortars, but that didn't seem to pack enough wallop, so the colonel called in a platoon of 4.2-inch chemical mortars. Those babies really packed a wallop; the shells weigh about thirty-five pounds each.

To our right about a mile away was another little town on the side of a hill. It also had Krauts in it. Every now and then we threw some rounds in to keep the Krauts worried. To our front, a couple of hundred yards out were two stationary Tiger Royal tanks. They didn't have a hole in them. They had simply run out of gasoline. When Rundstedt started his counterattack, he had counted on capturing large quantities of American oil and gasoline. He figured wrong.

We had been receiving sniper fire for a while, but we couldn't tell where it was coming from. After a few days we found that the German would sneak into one of the abandoned tanks just before daylight. He would wait until one of our men got out of his hole for one thing or another, and then pick him off. He killed or wounded several men in this manner. We had some tank destroyers sitting on that hill with us. After we realized where the bastard was, they opened on the tank and blew the hell out of it. That sniper didn't bother us again.

It was dangerous business, trying to observe from our OP. We had established it with the outpost to our front. But with our olive drabs against a backdrop of white snow, we stood out like sore thumbs. Every time we poked our heads over the top of the frozen hole, the Krauts threw artillery at us. Every time we tried to move from the OP to the guns, or vice versa, the Krauts shot at us.

Outposts were normally anywhere from ten to fifty meters in front of the line of our foxholes. Enemy outposts were sometimes within fifty yards or so of ours. No one liked being in an outpost, but everyone took their turn.

We had heard rumors that command was going to send us some new-fangled shoe packs that were supposed to keep our feet really warm. They were one-piece rubberized boots worn over several pairs of socks. But where were they? Why didn't we have them? We needed them now, not next summer!

The artillery and the mortars of the Krauts were becoming more effective. The ground and snow were frozen, and when a shell hit, it exploded as soon as it hit the frozen mass and wouldn't penetrate even a little before it went off. Almost all of the metal shrapnel flew around instead of digging a hole in the ground. Everything was frozen—our guns, our water, our food, and our feet. At the slightest provocation, the snow came tumbling down in masses into my hole with me. We always slept in all of our clothes. We were given dry socks every day, and we always wore two pairs of socks and rubber overshoes over our combat boots; even with all that, it was impossible to keep our feet warm. We learned to dry our wet socks by tying them together and hanging them around our necks. That way, wet socks would dry and be warm from body heat, and we could change them out the next day. I also put socks over my gloves, but my hands remained cold.

About five feet in front of our OP was a dead Kraut laying on his back. He had been killed earlier in the battle. Because of the intense cold, his body was frozen in a rigid position. By some freak of nature, his right arm was extended up into the air. In locating targets, we would use his arm as a base point from which to measure angles. Occasionally, the snow would fall so heavily it would completely cover the dead Kraut and his arm. When this happened, we had to crawl out and brush the snow away from our base point. It was crude, but effective.

Sleep remained elusive. The best way to describe it is that we dropped off into a trance for a few minutes at a time. At least that is the way it was with me. Bill Butz enjoyed a good artillery barrage. When the shells came in heavy, he just curled up in his hole and went to sleep. He said the jarring of the earth rocked him to sleep.

We were fed two meals a day, one before dawn and the other after dark. The first two or three days we could get out of our holes and eat, but the Krauts picked that up and thereafter put down a barrage at chow time.

Sergeant John Quinn came by, and I asked him for a drink of water. "For Christ's sake, Lieutenant," he said laughingly. "Don't you ever have any water? It took me thirty minutes to thaw my canteen out yesterday and just as soon as I did, you drank it all!" I smiled and said, "Sergeant, if you don't give me a drink, I'll have you court-martialed."

John rubbed his chin a minute and then, as if talking to himself, said, "A court-martial . . . court-martial. Let's see, if I'm court-martialed, I'll have to go back to the rear, won't I? And back in the rear they have warm buildings, don't they? And in the warm buildings they have warm water and warm beds, don't they? And they will have to feed me, won't they? And they will probably feed me what they eat, because it will be too hard for them to find any of this frozen shit we've been eating, won't it?" He laughed. "Okay. It's a deal, Lieutenant! I won't give you any of my water, and you send me back to be court-martialed. When I'm in that nice warm bed awaiting my trial, I'll be thinking about all you poor guys freezing your balls off up here. And, I'll think of all the wives and sweethearts at home who will call you "numb nuts" when and if you get home, because you got your balls frozen sitting out on this damn godforsaken hill for so long." I threw a flaky snowball at John, but he ducked out of the way.

John's bitching about the food (and everything else) was on target. The cooks tried to keep our food warm, but when the marmite cans were opened and set in the snow, the chow soon became cold.

Frank Caputo had his CP right above me about thirty yards. His was a dugout that could accommodate about six men. When things were pretty lax, I went up and shot the bull with him and his crew.

A day or night didn't pass that we weren't shelled. Because of the constant artillery fire, someone was either killed or wounded every day.

One of the rifle companies was relieved about every other night. The men went back about a mile into the woods, got up, and moved around a little. Not so much with the machine gun platoons, though. There was no one to relieve them and the men had to stay in their holes day and night. There they were stuck in foxholes with limited, if any, physical activity—ideal conditions for getting trench foot or frostbite. When you're on the front line, somebody is always watching, and usually it's the enemy. It's a necessity of life to stay in your hole whenever you can.

The mortar crews were a bit more fortunate. We were in a little gully shielded from direct observation by the Krauts. Occasionally, when there was a lull in the firing, the men could get out of their holes and build small, smokeless fires and try to restore some of the warmth to their bodies. The water in our canteens stayed frozen.

One morning, after I thawed the water out in my canteen, I poured it into my canteen cup. I set it to one side away from the fire while I opened a K-ration to get the coffee out of it. When I finally got the coffee out, I reached for the canteen cup of water only to find that it had frozen again, so I had to start the process all over. It was mighty cold in the Ardennes that winter.

Any movement at all on our part would bring down artillery fire on us. After a couple of days it became a problem to feed chow because every time we tried to form a chow line of any description, the Krauts started shooting at us. Every night the Krauts brought up an assault gun near our position and threw in a few rounds. Frank Caputo had several of his CP group killed or wounded one night from this fire. We had to bury our mortar ammunition to keep the Krauts from hitting it.

Every night, Kraut patrols worked around our area. They managed to get through our lines and raise a little hell before they were taken care of. It was a miserable existence—a cold hell on earth. We had to stay all day in two-man foxholes without getting out. Someone had to be awake in the hole at all times, so one man would try to sleep for an hour while his buddy kept watch, and then they'd switch out throughout the night. If they both went to sleep, a Kraut could easily kill them without a sound, and that was not uncommon. To make sure both men in a two-man hole would not sleep at the same time, they were allowed only one blanket between them. That way, only one man could gain any semblance of warmth. The other had to stay awake or freeze to death.

It is impossible to fully convey what we experienced in the Ardennes. The word "miserable" does not describe those thirteen days. The men would say, "For God's sake, let us attack. We'd rather attack and die trying to take something than stay here and freeze to death." Even some of our weapons froze on us. We pissed on them to get them working again. It was a temporary, yet effective solution. But, it played hell with the weapons.

Sergeant Wilbur Peck came up to tell me that Lindblom, one of the ammo bearers, was having trouble with his legs. They couldn't take this cold. Lindblom hadn't told him about it; he was that kind of a man. Even though he was nearing forty and had a couple of kids back home, he wouldn't tell anybody his legs were killing him. I called him over and asked him about it. He looked surprised that I knew about it and said they were all right. But I could tell by the way he walked up to me and by the expression on his face that they were bothering him. I sent him back to the kitchen to get warm.

Most of the nights were bright and the snow reflected everything. All the patrols, both ours and the Krauts', wore white uniforms and capes to make it difficult to seem them. To make matters worse, heavy fog was common, and reduced visibility to almost zero.

It's hard to describe how this cold affected our senses. We called it a "deafening silence." It was so quiet we could actually hear our hearts beat at a normal pace. After a long period of stillness and quietness, our senses became so acute every sound was amplified to every German soldier within a mile and every bush became a potential Kraut trying to sneak up on us. After a while, you come close to losing your mind.

One night about 11:00 p.m., a runner brought me six or eight replacements. I crawled out of my hole to greet and orient them. They were young kids in their teens and had left the States only a few short weeks ago. I always hated to see kids taken right out of the States and put into a hell hole like this. At the time the men came up, there was a Kraut patrol reportedly working down in the draw about two hundred yards to our rear.

"Lieutenant, how far are we from the front?" asked one of the new kids.

"Private, all you have to do is turn around and walk about three hundred yards that way," I said, pointing directly to the rear, "and you will be at the front. Or that way, or that way, or that way," I continued, pointing in almost every direction. His eyes widened in shock, but he got the point.

It was awfully cold and a little schnapps would do us all good, so I asked the platoon transportation NCO to try to scare us up a couple of bottles. He brought some and I dealt it out to the men. It warmed our insides and helped a little. We also snagged a couple of bottles of cognac and champagne. We placed the champagne in the snow and in a little while it was ice cold.

Bud Leonard was a man of true ingenuity. He had rigged up a stove using 81mm ammo canisters and his foxhole became a haven for everyone. He also found different things to cook and eat. His palace in the ground quickly became known as the Leonard Foxhole Furnace.

Almost every night we heard a plane flying low overhead. We knew from the sound of its engine that it was German, and probably a reconnaissance plane. It became known as "Bed Check Charlie II." We had had a similar plane with us in Northern France.

Sergeant Koors, Kad, and I received a few boxes of goodies from home during this time. As usual, I ate too much and I got a good case of the GI's. Relieving yourself in that climate under those conditions was quite an ordeal, and one I wouldn't wish on anybody. For two days I had to take a crap about once every hour. Answering nature's call during an artillery shelling was bad enough, but I had to rake away snow, dig a hole in the frozen ground, take off my overcoat, field jacket, and coveralls, and let down two pairs of OD trousers, a pair of long handles, and a pair of cotton shorts. By then, my hands were so cold I hardly had enough strength to button all that stuff up again.

We got a lot of ammunition. Just for the hell of it, every night we'd plaster the daylights out of the little town to our front just to keep the Krauts on their toes. If the Krauts were just like us, harassing fire bothered the hell out of them even if no one got hurt.

The afternoon of New Year's Eve we stocked up heavily on white phosphorous and high explosive shells. At the stroke of midnight on New Year's Eve, we let go with about two hundred rounds. At the same time, our artillery laid down one hell of a barrage—just to give the Krauts a New Year's greeting. They had planned a similar one for us and did the same thing at the same time, but theirs wasn't as good as ours.

Nothing much different happened during the next ten days. We were cold, and the Krauts were cold. We'd send a barrage, and they'd send a barrage. We sent out a patrol, they sent out a patrol. The days were long, and the nights were longer.

The colonel gave me the mission of running a patrol between my position and his CP. It was a hard grind for the men because the road was just like ice with heavy snow banks. On our last night there, McCauley and Junior were running the patrol. They both slipped and fell hard. Junior broke his ankle, and McCauley badly sprained his leg.

* * *

The 1st Battalion moved up to relieve us at 1:00 a.m. on January 10. We didn't know exactly where we were going, but anything was better than sitting on that windswept iceberg. Kad moved out ahead of us on the advance party. My platoon was the last to be relieved, and those long hours waiting were the most miserable I had experienced in a long time. There was absolutely no way to keep warm. When we were finally relieved, we had to walk three or four miles over the frozen snow-drifted roads with all our heavy equipment just to meet the trucks. They carried us to Heidersheid, where we arrived at about 2:00 a.m. Sergeant McQuain met us there and told us we had billets down the road a piece. Kad was waiting at the billeting area. He had found a couple of stoves and built some nice warm fires, but because we were several hours late, he had run out of wood. Nevertheless, the inside of the house was warm and it cut off the piercing winds.

We stayed in Heidersheid, in regimental reserve, until January 16. While we were there the kitchen fed us three hot meals a day and the supply sergeant brought us clean dry clothes. I hadn't had a bath in several weeks and decided come hell or high water I was going to bathe. I gathered up every can I could lay my hands on and heated water on the stove in preparation of a delightful bath out of my helmet. It's not the same as a hot bath or shower, but the joy of a warm bath—especially after being so cold for so long—was sheer heaven. The clean clothes felt good, too.

The chaplain came and held services for us here, which most of the men appreciated.

We lost a few more men from trenchfoot. I rounded up all the stationery I could lay my hands on so the men could write their mothers a letter. I told them they could write all they wanted, but I was going to check the roster to see that they all wrote home. After the men turned in their letters, I found that one of my old men from California hadn't written a word. I knew that his mother was still living, so I called him in. "Bo Bo, why didn't you write your mother?"

"My mother can't read, sir."

"Write it anyway," I ordered. "Your mother will find a friend to read the letter to her."

I needed a new runner. I called Pvt. Clyde "Mac" McCauley in. He was a long, lanky guy with stooped shoulders and a cigarette always dangling from his lips. He was twenty and had a wife and baby back home.

"Yessir?"

"Mac, how about being my runner?"

"I thought I already was," he replied. "Every time you want to go some place you never can find Junior, so you call me."

I chuckled. "I mean my *official* runner. I might even make you a corporal."

That got his attention and he nodded in agreement. "I can use the extra money, Lieutenant." As he was leaving, he turned around and asked, "If I'm your runner, which of you guys do I gotta sleep with when we are in the open, you or Lieutenant Kadison?" Kad was in the room and heard the question. Now Mac had his attention, too. "Which one of us do you want to sleep with?"

"No offense against Lieutenant Kadison, but he snores too much and too loud." Mac grinned and ducked out the door as Kad threw a can at him.

They brought us some scotch, gin, cognac, and champagne while we were in Heidersheid. The same day we got the liquor, Kad and I learned that we had been promoted to 1st lieutenants. That called for a celebration. Kad went outside and returned with a bucket of snow. He placed the champagne in the bucket and twisted it slowly.

"Ain't you a fancy dude now?" I said.

"You southern hicks don't know what living is," he replied. "This is the way we enjoy living in Brooklyn."

"You mean they drink something in Brooklyn besides beer?" I chuckled.

"Every night we go out, always a different gal. Blonde one night, redhead the next night, and brunettes in between. And we drink champagne, too. Every night."

"Kad, when this war is over and I come to see you, will you take me out with a blonde or redhead and give me champagne?"

"Sure, buddy, but you have to wear shoes in Brooklyn."

I really liked Kad. He and I had become good buddies and shared a lot of the same values. He cared for his men as much as I did for mine. His men respected him and would do anything he asked. They knew he wouldn't ask them to do anything he wouldn't do himself.

We decided to call in Lts. Mike Damkowitch, Bill Butz, and Bill Mounts to help us celebrate. I called Mac. He came in, the ever-present cigarette hanging from his lips. "Yessir, did you want something?"

Kad answered. "Private McCauley, our respects to Lieutenant Mike and tell him that 1st Lieutenant Adkins and 1st Lieutenant Kadison request the honor of his presence to help us celebrate this auspicious occasion."

Mac shot Kad with a queer look. "This what kind of an occasion?"

"This auspicious occasion."

"Now ain't you guys getting fancy. This ain't no war between the states."

"Private McCauley, you will have respect for your superior officers or I will have you shot at sunrise."

Mac drew deeply on his cigarette and exhaled the smoke. "Where do you get that superior stuff? The only thing you guys are superior in is when we are running for cover."

We all laughed and Mac went for Mike Damkowitch.

I had found a pair of skis in the house next door and decided that I wanted to learn how to use them. (I had never seen snow in my life until this campaign.) I put them on and started down a steep hill. I lasted about ten feet before I started my somersault. Kad almost laughed his fool head off. I decided to abandon the art of skiing and take up something more rugged, like poker or shooting craps.

Like so many men, Kad's legs and thighs were infected and he was having a tough time walking. During the attack on Sivry several months ago, he had to lie in a muddy ditch for several hours. The following days were rainy and he had not been dry for many weeks. As a result, his legs and thighs had become infected. He went to see Doc Bobb, who sent him back to the hospital where they could fix him up in a few days. He didn't want to go because he knew that we would be moving up in a couple of days and he would be needed, but Doc made him go. Kad was lucky, because his trip to the hospital allowed him to miss the hardest ordeal this battalion had ever been through.

Chapter *10*
THE RELENTLESS, BITTER COLD WINTER

January 16, 1945–February 5, 1945

At 7:00 p.m. on January 16, we moved out to relieve the 3rd Battalion in position about three miles north of Heidersheid on the forward slope of a mountain looking across a valley at the Krauts, who were dug in on the forward slope of a mountain across the valley. The company and battalion CPs were in the little town of Tadler on the banks of the Sure River, off to our left front down in the valley. To our immediate front were two little towns at the base of the mountain; both were held by the enemy. I tried to dig in behind a little ridge near the front edge of the mountain, but every time we moved, the Krauts opened up on us. I got permission from Lt. Colonel Boydstun to move back about half a mile, which was the only place around suitable to set up the mortars.

I went back to the 3rd Battalion to get the map overlays they had used. I finally found Company H's mortar platoon sergeant in a room, trying to get warm. In the corner was a blonde lieutenant. "Sergeant, who's your buddy over there?" I asked.

He looked at me and answered, "Lieutenant, he's no buddy of mine! He's a yellow son of a bitch if I ever saw one. He's been trying to get back to the hospital ever since he's been with us. Claims he's got frozen feet. He first went to the battalion medics bellyaching about his feet. They saw nothing wrong with them and they told him to get the hell out of their aid station and quit trying to goldbrick. That didn't suit him, so he sneaked off from the platoon and went to the collecting company. He pulled the wool over their eyes long enough for him to talk them into believing he had something wrong with his feet. Now he's waiting for an ambulance to take him to the hospital."

I decided the sergeant had this under control. I had enough to worry about my men, let alone some coward. I didn't care if he was an officer.

Movement in Tadler and on the front edge of the mountain was strictly verboten. Any movement at all on our part prompted the Germans to open fire on us. They had a lot of machine guns and burp guns, and they could see our every move. They picked at us all day and, in turn, we picked at them all day. It was about the same affair we had had a couple of weeks earlier.

There were a lot of dead spaces in our defensive line, so we had to do a lot of night firing to keep the Kraut patrols out. Our foxholes were very good. The engineers had blasted them out for us, and we cut logs to make dugouts. My dugout was about ten feet long, six feet wide, and four feet deep. I could burn candles in there at night (when I could find them) and read *Stars and Stripes* to see how hard the war workers were having it back home, how rough it was for them to go weeks without butter, and having to work overtime. As cold as I was, my blood boiled every time I read something like that.

We were having a lot of snow storms now. Sometimes you couldn't see more than a few feet. Snow banks formed everywhere. One night, about 3:00 a.m., I had to get up and take a leak. But when I tried to slide the shelter half back from the entrance to my hole, it was frozen and buried under a bank of snow. Even though Sergeant Koors, Sergeant Melcolm, Private McCauley, and a few others were with me, they were sleeping like logs and I didn't have the heart to wake them. I had telephone communication to all the guns as well as to everybody else in the battalion, but I couldn't get a peep anywhere and I just *had* to get out and take a leak. Finally when I was about to bust, one of the guards heard me and came to my relief.

The kitchen brought us two hot meals a day. That is, they stayed hot until the marmite cans were opened, and then the food and the coffee turned cold within seconds. It still beat the hell out of frozen K-rations.

One of the seemingly endless rows of tents at Camp LaGuna, Arizona, where Lieutenant Adkins and his men prepared for war. *A. Z. Adkins, Jr. Collection*

Lieutenant Bill Butz (r) and the author (l) at Camp Laguna, Arizona, early 1944. *A. Z. Adkins, Jr. Collection*

Lieutenants Charlie Raymond, Bill Mounts, and George McDonnell, Camp Laguna, Arizona, early 1944. *A. Z. Adkins, Jr. Collection*

Training on the 81mm mortar. *A. Z. Adkins, Jr. Collection*

SERGEANT RALPH FREEMAN (L) AND THE AUTHOR (R) IN LATE AUGUST 1944, AFTER THEIR BAPTISM OF FIRE AT ARGENTAN, FRANCE. *A. Z. ADKINS, JR. COLLECTION*

A BRIDGE SPANNING THE MOSELLE RIVER IS KNOCKED OUT IN SEPTEMBER 1944. *U.S. ARMY*

An aerial shot of the Moselle River taken in September 1944, showing where the 2d Battalion, 317th Inf. was pinned down by MG fire. *U.S. Army*

Ferrying tanks on the Moselle River, September 1944. *U.S. Army, 80th Division Signal Company*

80TH DIVISION ARTILLERY SHELLING THE MOSELLE RIVER CROSSING IN
SEPTEMBER 1944.
U.S. ARMY, 80TH DIVISION SIGNAL COMPANY

81MM MORTARS FIRING FROM A FARM LANE IN FRANCE, AUTUMN
1944. *U.S. ARMY, SIGNAL CORPS*

THE VAUNTED SIGFRIED LINE, PIERCED DURING THE AUTUMN OF 1944.
NOTE THE "DRAGON'S TEETH" CONCRETE TANK OBSTRUCTIONS.
U.S. ARMY

CROSSING THE SIEGFRIED LINE.
U.S. ARMY

(ABOVE) SGT. JOHN KOORS STANDS IN THE FROZEN VILLAGE OF HEIDERSCHEID, LUXEMBOURG, DURING THE BATTLE OF THE BULGE, JANUARY 1945. (BELOW) KAD AND THE AUTHOR IN THE SAME VILLAGE, *A. Z. ADKINS, JR. COLLECTION*

FROM LEFT TO RIGHT: LT. SAUL "KAD" KADISON, LT. HENRY "BUD"
LEONARD, CAPT. JIM FARRELL, AUTHOR LT. ANDY ADKINS, AND
LT. BILL MOUNTS, ST. AVOLD, FRANCE, DECEMBER
1944. *A. Z. ADKINS, JR. COLLECTION*

MEMBERS OF THE 80TH DIVISION ADVANCE ACROSS FROZEN GROUND
DURING THE BATTLE OF THE BULGE, DECEMBER 1944.
U.S. ARMY, 80TH DIVISION SIGNAL COMPANY

St. Vith, Houffalize Road, Belgium. January 1945.
U.S. Army, 80th Division Signal Company

Lieutenant Emmett Taylor joined Company H in March 1945.
A. Z. Adkins, Jr. Collection

LIEUTENANT EDWIN HELLER. HE WAS ASSIGNED THE MORTAR PLATOON
DURING THE WAR'S FINAL WEEKS. *A. Z. ADKINS, JR. COLLECTION*

A SNIPER AND A POLE HAVE A DISCUSSION IN NUREMBURG, APRIL
1945. *A. Z. ADKINS, JR. COLLECTION*

(ABOVE) LIEUTENANTS ANDY ADKINS AND BILL BUTZ IN
MOLSCHELBAN, GERMANY, APRIL 9, 1945. *A. Z. ADKINS,
JR. COLLECTION* (BELOW) SLICK BANNERMEN, ONE OF THE
AUTHOR'S BUDDIES. *COLLECTION OF ALICE F. GULLEDGE*

THE OVENS AT BUCHENWALD CONCENTRATION CAMP, APRIL 1945.
MANY DIFFERENT AMERICAN UNITS, INCLUDING THE AUTHOR'S OUTFIT,
DISCOVERED FIRSTHAND THE HORRORS OF NAZI GERMANY WHEN THEY
CAME UPON BUCHENWALD. *U.S. ARMY*

THE DEAD OF BUCHENWALD CONCENTRATION CAMP, APRIL 1945.
U.S. ARMY

Surrendered Germans in Nuremberg, April 1945. *A. Z. Adkins, Jr. Collection*

A German soldier and his family walk past the author's jeep in April 1945.
A. Z. Adkins, Jr. Collection

THE DAY MY JEEP BROUGHT BACK 850 POWS. AUSTRIA, MAY 1945.
A. Z. ADKINS, JR. COLLECTION

DACHAU. SLINGSHOT POSES WITH A MAN NAMED ONLY "DALRIMPLE,"
JULY 1945. *A. Z. ADKINS, JR. COLLECTION*

80TH DIVISION MORTAR FIRE AT NEUSTADT, GERMANY, APRIL 1945. *NA*

AUSTRIA, MAY 7, 1945, 1400 HOURS: SLINGSHOT AND THE AUTHOR
READ GENERAL EISENHOWER'S PEACE PROCLAMATION, *A. Z. ADKINS,
JR. COLLECTION*

Doc Bobb, who played a central role in saving many of the men of Company H.
A. Z. Adkins, Jr. Collection

It was also a problem to keep up the phone wires from the guns to the OP. Sergeant Melcolm had his SCR300 radio. When we tried to use it, the Krauts would cut in. Not every time, of course, but occasionally they would figure out what channel we were on. They played scales on an organ for hours on end, which almost drove Melcolm crazy because he had to stay with his ear glued to the receiver.

* * *

About 9:00 p.m. on the night of January 20, Lt. Bill Mounts sent for me. I knew what he wanted; he was going to give an attack order. When I got there, Butz and Hartnett, both machine gun platoon leaders in Company H, were already there. Mounts was grinning like a bride. He gave us a shot of gin before he got down to business. Bill was always happy and smiling when he called his platoon leaders in to give them an attack mission. He knew what an attack order meant and his jovial mood helped. We were going to clear out the town of Bourschied the following morning, and were going to move out at 3:00 a.m.

We had already seen part of the terrain we would have to cross over during the attack. It was the roughest yet: rugged hills covered with trees and piled with snow banks. We were to go parallel to the line held by the Krauts, up steep hills, and down steeper valleys. We knew it would not be a surprise attack. We also knew the Krauts would likely spot us from the mountain they held to our left flank. Their mountain was higher than ours, and now we would have to go into valleys where they had excellent observation. Needless to say, I was not overly thrilled with this plan.

We were part of a larger attacking force. The 1st Battalion and the other regiments in our division were ordered to support us along with tanks and TDs. We were given the hardest mission. The route we were to take was strictly cross-country where tanks could not operate. Because of the nature of the terrain, we knew that artillery would be of little or no use to us. Our orders were to provide flank protection to the other attacking unit, and attack at the same time.

Mike Damkowitch's Company G was slated to lead, followed by Max Kelly's Company F. One rifle platoon from Company E would go in and take the little town down in the valley at the foot of the mountain on the Kraut's side. I sent Sergeant Quinn down with Lieutenant

Meyers's rifle platoon from Company E to act as mortar observer. I only had enough men to man four guns. Sergeant Pawlak's mortar section would stay in position near the front of the mountain for Quinn's use. The other mortar section would follow Company G.

I thought it was better to leave the mortars in position; I could observe from the attacking companies and when we had gotten out far enough, then I could move the guns forward. I wanted to do that because I knew it would be almost impossible for my own men to carry that heavy equipment over such terrain. The colonel overruled my suggestion. None of us liked the attack plan, but there was little we could do about it. Before I went back to the platoon, I stopped by to see Mike Damkowitch to make arrangements for the following morning. He had some aerial photographs of Bourschied and the ground we would have to cover. He showed them to me and asked, "Andy, there's my baby, whatta ya think?" Mike and I had been buddies a long time, and I told him what I thought. He didn't like the idea, either, but there wasn't much we could do about it. I told him I'd be there with him in the morning.

When I got back to the platoon, I found three new replacements had just arrived. I hated to see them. They were young kids just in from the States, and in only a few hours they would be part of a pretty rough attack. They were loaded down with equipment and clothing. I oriented them a little and Sergeant Koors helped them get rid of stuff they wouldn't need.

I got the sergeants together and gave them the dope. I kept Sergeant McQuain and Sergeant Dodson a little longer. Their mortar squads were going with me in the morning, and I wanted to pep them up a little. Dodson had just been promoted to staff sergeant, and I told McQuain he had been recommended for the Bronze Star for a neat piece of work he had done back in Moivron.

We had to get up before 3:00 a.m. on Sunday morning, January 21, in order to be at the LD in time. The 81mm mortar platoon from 3rd Battalion moved in to relieve us and give us support if we needed it. The rest of the 3rd Battalion relieved our battalion.

Daylight brought a snowstorm with it. We were to attack in a column of companies, which was the only way to attack over such terrain. Mac, my runner, and I went up with Lieutenant Damkowitch. Sergeant Koors had the mortars behind Company G.

We had only moved a short distance when things started getting worse. I am not exaggerating when I say that the slope of the hills we were trying to cross was just a little less than vertical. It was covered with trees and there were several feet of snow on the ground. After a few people had walked on the snow and packed it down, it was as slick as glass. One could only take a few steps without slipping. The only way to move halfway decently was to pull yourself up by grasping trees and roots. It was an exhausting, freezing, nightmare that was about to get much worse.

We had only gone a little way when Lieutenant Meyers's rifle platoon ran into a Kraut patrol over to the left, down deeper in the valley. The Krauts had spotted us before we even got a good start. He got rid of them with a little help from the rest of the company.

The Germans were clever bastards. Every few yards we moved, someone would step on a trip wire the Krauts had buried in the snow. There was no way to avoid those wires; they were invisible buried in the snow. Some were attached to antipersonnel mines that blew a man's foot and leg off if it didn't kill him outright. Most of them, however, were attached to flares, and every time one of them was set off, the Krauts knew exactly where we were. These flares sent a chill up and down our spines. Some burst above the tree tops, like a roman candle sending yellow, green, or red fire scattering in all directions. Within seconds the Krauts would lay down a concentration of fire that had already been zeroed in on that spot. It would either be mortars, artillery, or screaming meemies. Every time this happened, someone got hurt or killed. It wasn't long before we ran short of litter bearers. They had all been used up carrying the wounded back and there were none to take their place. The possibility was slim to none that they or other litter bearers would get back to us before quite a few hours.

According to the map, the town of Bourschied was only three miles from our LD, but the way we had to go was approximately ten miles, and we could move at only a snail's pace. When we were about two miles out we came to the steepest hill yet. It was almost vertical and slicker than glass. Mac and I almost broke our necks sliding down its side. We had to climb hand-over-hand to get to the top of the hill on the other side. There was a little ledge near the top where Mac and I stopped to wait on our boys. We knew that it would take more than physical strength for them to climb up there.

While we were waiting the Krauts laid down one of the worst barrages I've ever been in. It was apparent that they could see the men
coming slowly down the opposite hill and climbing slowly up the one
we were on. The artillery came first, then the damn screaming
meemies. The valley echoed and re-echoed the bursts. The barrage was
a continuous shell burst that lasted for about ten minutes. It was deafening. The shock of the bursts was frightening, and the ground literally
danced and knocked us off balance. But the worst—the absolute
worst—was to find out how many men fell beneath that barrage.

Private John Piko came up and told me that some of my men had
been hit and two had been killed. He didn't know who they were. A
little later, Sergeant John Koors came up with the mortar platoon and
also reported several men had been hit. At first they thought Dodson
had been killed. A piece of shrapnel went through the top of his helmet, but he was still breathing. Some of his buddies dropped their
ammunition and carried him back. My men never left their wounded.

The column was halted, so Mac and I went up to join the command group. On the way up we ran across some of Bill Butz's machine
gunners who had been killed. They lay beside their guns where they
had fallen, their blood frozen in the snow. One man had been blinded
and there was blood streaming down his face. He was crying, "I can't
see, I can't see. Don't leave me. Please don't leave me. Somebody help
me, please!" We comforted him the best we could and left a man to
stay with him until the medics could get there.

We came to a long ditch and found Lieutenant Hartnett there with
his machine gun platoon. Part of Company G was a little to the left of
him. Frank Caputo came up. He was white and blood was dripping
from his arms and legs where he had been hit. He told me that the
entire command group had been hit. We had no communication with
Regiment; all our radios were broken and our telephone line had been
shot out. He was going back to get in touch with Regiment. It wasn't
safe for him to go back alone, and I didn't think he could make it. I
told Corporal Hildebrandt to go with him. He told me later that Frank
almost walked them to death.

Bill Mounts had two holes in his ankle where shrapnel had gone
completely through. It was broken and he was suffering with a great
deal of pain, but he had guts. Lieutenant Colonel Boydstun was hit all
over and was turning blue. The colonel was a big man, an ex-collegiate
boxer. He called for Lieutenants Damkowitch and Kelly and told them

that Kelly was in charge, and that he wanted them to continue the attack.

The cry of a wounded, helpless soldier is the most heart-tearing experience in the world. To hear his wounded soldiers cry around him tore the heart out of the colonel, just as his terrible wounds were tearing the life out of him. Lieutenant Colonel William Boydstun died a few minutes later, January 22, 1945.

Communications were utterly disrupted early in the attack. Sergeant Albert Melcolm, my radioman, took it upon himself to reestablish communications. Without hesitating, he advanced through heavy hostile fire to an exposed hilltop, from which he relayed vital field messages on his SCR536 radio from forward to rear elements. For eleven hours straight he was subjected to German barrages.

One of the first things Max Kelly did upon assuming command was to order a perimeter defense. He contacted Capt. Jerry Sheehan, the battalion executive officer, through Sergeant Melcolm. Jerry said to hold up, that he was coming to us. Mac and I went back to help set up the defense. We didn't mention the colonel's death because it wouldn't help the men at all if we did.

Jerry Sheehan arrived a little before dark. As he came up, he asked, "How's it going, Andy?"

I replied, "Pretty rough, Jerry. What are you going to do?"

He replied, "Probably get court-martialed for disobeying a direct order."

I didn't get it then, but I later learned that Jerry had been ordered to continue the attack. Nevertheless, after he saw the situation, he decided to pull us back and stop the assault. A little while later, Regiment approved of our withdrawal, mainly because the 3rd Battalion had taken Bourschied without any casualties.

Jerry told us that we would move back at darkness the same way we had come in. We had no litter bearers and very few medics, but we would not leave our wounded to freeze to death.

Lieutenant Lemans, a swell guy who was very dedicated to his men, was given charge to get the wounded out. We made makeshift litters by putting two poles through the arms of a buttoned up overcoat. Each company was to furnish a certain number of men to carry the litters.

All of the BAR-men from Company G were ordered to guard the litter bearers and the wounded going back. I told my men that Bill Mounts had been wounded; every man volunteered to get him out, which made me very proud. I picked Sergeant McQuain and a few other big guys. It was foolish for me to tell them to be sure the sergeant got out. "Lieutenant," they each replied in unison, "we'll freeze to death before we'll let him stay out here."

I told the men to bury their ammunition in their holes. I pulled Sergeant Koors aside and told him that if the going got too rough to let the men dump their guns. I knew that it would take superhuman effort to get back without having to carry fifty pounds of mortar equipment.

After we got started, Mac and I went on ahead to see if we could get some jeeps to come up to a spot near our LD to carry the men the remaining mile. We had received orders to return to our old positions.

The night was fairly bright, so we followed the telephone wire back. Along the way, I ran into Lt. Virgil McAlpin, our battalion S-2. He was sitting in the snow with a Kraut he had picked up. Captain Ira Miller of Company E had been badly hit when he took the rest of his company down to help Lieutenant Meyers. The Kraut had helped drag Captain Miller a couple of hundred yards to safety. Meyers had lost a number of men. The Krauts right above him on the high mountain had been dropping 120mm mortars on him. Captain Miller died while they were trying to get him out.

The last mile was the hardest. The hills were covered with ice and my leg was killing me. I had to stop every few yards. Mac helped me on in. There was no way to get jeeps to us, so Mac and I waited with Mike Damkowitch until our platoon caught up. Mike had a little schnapps and a big slug of that helped a lot. Sergeant Benifield, the mess sergeant, arrived with chow the same time Sergeant Koors got to us with the platoon. The men were almost gone, but they still had their guns. I was mighty proud of those boys, and I told them so. Benifield helped them carry their guns back to our old position. The chow was cold, but we were hungry and it tasted so good.

Lieutenant Lemans got in about eight o'clock the following morning with those wounded who were still alive. About nine had died of exposure on the way back. Sergeant McQuain and his boys got all of Company H's wounded in. The courage and superhuman strength exhibited by the men who brought in the wounded could never be paralleled.

We took it easy for a while as we waited for orders. My leg hurt and was stiff. It was hard just trying to get comfortable. I got in touch with Bill Butz, who took over Company H after Bill Mounts was evacuated.

We couldn't account for all of the men in the company, so I went back to the battalion aid station to see if they had any record of our men. The collecting company was set up near our battalion aid station, and both of them had more wounded than they could handle.

One of Bill Butz's machine gunners lay on the operating table. The right side of his face, including his right eye, was missing; shrapnel had ripped it away. The rest of his body was lacerated. I don't know if he made it out alive. From the looks of his wounds, I don't think so.

I accounted for most of the men. They were putting Bill Mounts in an ambulance. He was smiling and so grateful they had brought him out. I brought him his toilet kit, some cigarettes, and three letters from his girl, Carolyn. I teased him and pretended that I wasn't going to give him the letters. He almost climbed out of the ambulance to crown me!

It's hard to describe the bonds that form between men during war. We're all destined to Fate—whether we live or whether we die. Behind the lines we can laugh and take it easy. But up on the front lines we depend on our buddies and our buddies depend on us. In the heat of battle, some men rise and perform far beyond what you think they can do. It doesn't matter who stands out or who doesn't, as long as we all stick together as a team. But those men who fight the front lines together form a strong, never-ending bond, a relationship of respect, admiration, and loyalty that stays with you throughout your life. I believe it stays with us in the afterlife, too.

* * *

At 4:15 in the afternoon of January 22, we marched to Heidersheid and climbed aboard trucks for Wiltz, Luxembourg, at 7:30 p.m. It was cold and the roads were very slick. Some places on the road were only suitable for one-way traffic. It was about twelve miles from Heidersheid to Wiltz, which was a ghost town. From what was left standing of the buildings and homes, one could tell that it had been a very beautiful and modern city. The homes had many modern features I had not seen in the States.

Kad was back from the hospital there, waiting for us. I put my mortar platoon in what was left of a once-beautiful mansion. It had no lights and no windows, but at least it helped cut off the sharp winds and snow.

Jerry Sheehan was now our battalion CO. He called us together early in the morning of January 23. Captain Charles Jones was his executive officer and Capt. Tom Mattlock his S-3. He told us that our XII Corps had lost contact with the enemy and it was believed they were pulling back to the Siegfried Line. Our regimental combat team's mission was to go out and make contact with the Krauts. That's army-speak for "Find the enemy."

It was quite a plan. We were ordered to push out in a column of battalions. The 1st Battalion would lead the way, followed by the 313th Field Artillery Battalion. We moved out at 5:30 that afternoon. Our 2d Battalion moved to just outside the little town of Weidingen, on the outskirts of Wiltz, where we halted in a column for quite some time.

We bedded down in Weidingen. It too was demolished, but we found enough walls and roofs to keep out the driving wind and snow. We told the men to get as much sleep as possible, because we were going to move out at midnight. Right on schedule we moved out cross-country to attack the town of Lellingen, which according to the map was four miles away. We were on the right flank of the 1st Battalion. Max Kelly's Company F was in the lead, and I was directed to take a section of mortars from Company H with him. Kad took the other mortar section with Company G, which was behind Company F.

It was a bright night, but the cold was horrible. We headed cross-country over steep hills covered with trees and snow. As usual, after only a few men had walked on the snow, it became packed slick as glass. Private Francis Rajnicek, one of my gunners, was having a hard time. He had to wear thick glasses, which became iced over. A couple of times his battalion commander had to help him over the very rough spots. Snipers forced us to stop about 3:00 a.m. There was no way to keep warm when we stopped. We were cold all over, but our feet hurt the most. No matter how much stomping or kicking we did, they were still cold.

When daylight came, we pulled out our smokes, which always seemed to help. We started to move out. I saw a man sitting in the snow with his shoes off and his feet wrapped in a blanket. When I told him to get up and start moving, he said he couldn't because his feet were frozen. I told him if he stayed there he would freeze to death, but he didn't seem to care. He finally put on his boots and his buddies helped him along until his legs had a little feeling in them.

We pulled up on the right flank of the 1st Battalion about mid-morning. The Krauts opened up on us, but the firing died down pretty quickly. Lellingen was to our right front. We went to the edge of the woods to take a look at it. It was a peaceful looking little town, sitting right out in the middle of a small valley with a frozen creek and a railroad embankment along the edge of it. Although it looked very quiet and peaceful, we knew better.

Everybody was dog tired and as miserable from the cold and the rugged terrain as human beings could be. Max Kelly's men in Company F were more tired than the rest, for they had been beating their way through the snow all morning. Jerry Sheehan decided to send Mike Damkowitch's Company G through him. Mike was to go around the right flank of the town and Max straight in. I set up the guns. Mac and I went up to the edge of the woods and sat a while with Lieutenant McAlpin, our battalion S-2. Mike got around the flank of the town and was getting ready to go in when the Krauts opened up on him. He was caught in the open. There was no other way to get into town, and he couldn't move until Max came in with Company F and relieved some of the pressure.

When Max started out he ran into some Kraut tanks and armored cars. A number of his men were hurt and he couldn't move without help. The only communication we had within the battalion was by SCR300 radio, and Mike's batteries were getting weak. There was no way to get fresh batteries to him.

Jerry Sheehan called Regiment and asked for tanks. Regiment told him there were no Kraut tanks in our area. About that time the Kraut tanks threw in a few rounds. Regiment still wouldn't believe there were tanks in our area! I often wondered why those so-called staff members never came up to see for themselves when the going was a little rough.

On the morning of January 26, Bill Butz called me right before daylight over the radio and told me to move into Lellingen right away. As we were entering the town about daylight, some Kraut artillery started falling around us. We hurried into town and got the men under cover. Doc Morris, my medic, came up and said he thought Pvt. Jay Miller had been killed. He was behind Jay on the tail of the column. I asked Sergeant Koors to go back and take a look. I didn't think I could stand it.

Jay had been with the platoon since it was activated and had just returned from the hospital a few days earlier. Sergeant Koors came back in a few minutes and said that Jay had been hit in the head and his legs had been blown off. He and Jay had been together longer than I had been with them. I had no right to ask Koors to go back. It hurt him deeply.

We went into a house and tried to get warm. We got a girl and her mother to make us some coffee. Bill Butz came in and told me that we were moving out cross-country on the 1st Battalion's right flank, and that we were to drive for the division objective by clearing the woods and taking the little town of Fennberg.

I looked at the terrain we would have to cover. Our first obstacle was a huge, steep mountain. It, too, was as slick as glass and the men would have to muster superhuman strength to get to the top. But that was only the beginning of our obstacle course. I wondered how long men could be driven like this. Would we ever get relief?

As we started up the hill, the Krauts dropped a little artillery, not on top of us but near enough to make us nervous. It was rugged going up that damn hill. Every few slippery steps we had to stop to get our breath. My men were carrying fifty pounds of bulky mortar equipment in addition to their own personal stuff.

About halfway up, Sergeant Koors told me that Corporal Rozniarek was hurting badly. Leo Rozniarek was about five and a half feet tall and thirty-four-years-old. He was an old-timer with the company and had been hit back in September. He was carrying a bipod for his mortar crew. His back was hurting him, but he was the type of man who wouldn't tell me about it. He thought too much about his buddies to let them do his work. I stopped and waited until he came up. He said his back was giving him a little trouble, but he could make it okay. I knew better, so I sent him to down the aid station. I thought of those poor 4-Fs back home who had busted ear drums, high blood pressure, and suffered from ingrown toenails. How rough they must have it working eight hours a day and not making enough money to buy a Cadillac. And here was Leo Rozniarek, a little man thirty-four-years-old whom I had made a corporal a month ago. He was making $66.00 a month and had forgotten how it felt to be warm because he had been cold for so long.

Company G was leading the way. Lieutenant Damkowitch had to change his scouts every few minutes. It was bitterly cold with a hard wind blowing and fine snow falling. Visibility was very poor. Plodding through heavy unbroken snow and trying to keep from freezing was very difficult. A man's legs would last only a short while in that deep snow.

Late that afternoon Mike ran into small arms and automatic weapons. It was still snowing and the wind was still cold. We only had maps to go by, and the Krauts knew this terrain by heart. Mike had to use a compass, and it was rough. The Krauts were shooting at short range and it took the shells only a very short time to reach us. We didn't have much time to dive for cover, what little there was of it.

The men were miserable, their strength was gone, and their morale was at its lowest ebb. Their bodies were racked with pain from the cold. If a man had any water at all in his canteen, it was frozen solid and there was no way to thaw it out. Our hands had no strength left in them and it took two of them quite some time to open one K-ration in an inside pocket next to their body. In that way, the meat would thaw out enough to chew it. We ate handfuls of snow to quench our thirst, but the snow, as always, tasted flat and did not help much.

Kad and I crawled into a hole under a blanket to wait out the night. I pulled out my flashlight and my Bible and read the 91st Psalm. Dad had told me that if I read it, I would come home. I prayed continually in combat. I believe that is why I'm alive today. But this particular night I prayed a little differently. I asked God to protect us throughout the night, because we didn't have the strength to protect ourselves. No Krauts got through our lines that night.

January 27 was very similar to the day before. Driving through the snow, we only ran into occasional small arms and artillery fire. We stopped here and there to contact the flanking units and Regiment. The only thing to do was stomp your feet to try and warm them up.

During one of these breaks Kad and I decided to cheer each other up. "Kad, how'd you like to be by a nice warm fire in a huge fireplace with big logs, dressed in a pair of slacks and moccasins, with a good-looking blonde with you who had eyes only for you and a big juicy quart of Scotch sitting on the table beside you?" His eyes lit up just thinking about it. "And," I added, "every time your gal kissed you, you'd reach over a take a little nip of Scotch. How does that sound?"

Kad was sitting in the snow. He was a dark-completed man and hadn't shaved in a couple of weeks. He looked like one of Bill Mauldin's characters and that was his nickname now—"Mauldin." He let out a big grin and nodded his head in a vigorous yes. I mimicked kissing a blonde and taking a nip of Scotch.

I did this until the Scotch was gone and each time he would nod his head in a vigorous "yes!" Then we would discuss juicy steaks, smothered in onions with mountains of french-fried potatoes. He would argue the merits of a down comforter and I would argue my grandmother's homemade quilts.

Kad's home was in Brooklyn, so I sang, "I'm going to hang my hat on a tree that grows in Brooklyn," and dedicate it to him. Then I tried to rake up an argument about how I was going to lie on the sunny beaches of Florida and watch the girls go by in their bathing suits after this man's war was over. But he wouldn't argue with me. Instead, he consented to come and live with me in warm Florida. After a little while we returned to reality, split our last frozen K-ration, and dove for cover when the artillery came too close.

After moving slowly all day we came to a point where we could see our objective, the town of Fennberg. It was nothing more than a few houses and barns at the top of a gradually sloping hill. To get to it we would have to go uphill for a 1,000 yards across open terrain. There wasn't one single piece of cover between us and the top of the hill. The objective had to be taken that night. The 5th Infantry Division was on our right and it would relieve us after we took our objective.

Jerry Sheehan asked for tank support. It was denied with the excuse that we "didn't need tanks." A little while earlier, we had seen two tanks with another one of our battalions try to get into that little town, and they had been knocked out by Kraut tanks. The refusal pissed off Sheehan, who then asked for a fifteen-minute artillery preparation before his men went in. He was denied artillery with the excuse that his troops "were too close to the objective and our artillery fire would fall on them." I wondered why some people didn't come up and look for themselves instead of looking at a damn map! This wasn't the first time I cursed divisional HQ, and it certainly wouldn't be the last. A map had a lot of information, sure, but it couldn't be oriented with the terrain because the terrain was nothing but a white sheet of snow and very few terrain features shown on a map could be found on the ground.

We were cold and our strength was gone, but we had an objective to take. We also knew that if we could take the objective, we would get some relief, and that helped us muster up the needed strength. We were to move out at seven that night. Company G was to work straight ahead until it came to the flank of the town and then it was to turn right. Captain Ropers' Company E was to bear a little to the right and protect Company G's flank. A driving snow set in and visibility was poor.

The 81s were the only artillery we had. Kad and I set the mortars up. It was almost impossible to adjust them because of the snow. Company G had to attack 800 yards uphill through several feet of snow with no cover whatsoever. It was a Kraut machine gunner's dream. All he had to do was to lay his gun along the top of the snow; he could not miss if he tried. Every time the boys started out they got caught in grazing crossfire and mortar fire. Lieutenant Hartnett's medic, one of the old boys, was killed trying to get to a wounded man. Lieutenant Lemans was hit in the leg, and Sergeant Bars was hit in the face.

Despite the terrible conditions, our machine gunners and mortars held the Krauts quiet long enough for our boys to get on the objective. We were finally relieved at dawn.

* * *

It was a pitiful sight, seeing the men coming back. Their feet were so swollen and sore that there wasn't a man who didn't limp.

We were moving back to Lellingen. We had to stop every few minutes for the men to rest. A lot of men had to be carried in. We tried to lift their spirits by telling them the cooks had hot chow waiting for us. That helped a little. Our cooks did have warm rooms and hot pancakes waiting. That chow was mighty good.

The 101st Airborne Division was moving into our area. We left Lellingen at 11:30 a.m., January 28, and moved 38 miles to Crutchen, Luxembourg. When we arrived there late in the afternoon there were no billets waiting for us, so Kad and I tried our French on the Luxembourgers. They were very nice to us. They considered it an honor to have American soldiers stay in their homes. Crutchen was just a little farm town, and most of the houses were one-quarter house and three-quarters barn—but they were warm!

Kad and I and our crew stayed in a house with a man, his wife, sister-in-law, and two small daughters. We slept on the floor in the living room and kitchen. They were very nice to us. Every night they came for a little visit. Kad was pretty good at French, but I struggled with it. They would make cake and coffee for us although they had very little food themselves.

While we were in Crutchen, the snow began to melt and it ran in streams off the mountains. The ground was frozen and the roads were solid ice. To walk from our house to the kitchen, about two hundred yards down the road, was a real ordeal. While we were there, we traded our combat boots and overshoes for shoepacs. They had finally arrived. Of course, it had stopped snowing by now!

The first morning we were there, Doc Bobb gave us a foot inspection. A lot of the men had trench foot and frozen feet. Doc Morris, my medic, had the worst swollen feet I'd ever seen. His feet were black and so swollen he could not get into his boots and had to be carried. Lieutenant Hartnett had it bad, too. We evacuated all our trench foot cases.

That night Kad and I gave Sergeant John Koors all the money we had and informed him he was going back to the States on furlough. He almost passed out he was so happy. We decided to make Sergeant Joe Pawlak the platoon sergeant.

Jerry Sheehan called for me about 8:00 one morning. When I got to his CP, he was putting on his shoes. Captain Charles Jones, Jerry's executive officer, and Capt. Tom Mattlock looked on. When he had finished putting on his shoes, Jerry opened a box, pulled out a little medal and pinned it on me. It was the Bronze Star. Captain Jones and Captain Mattlock stood at attention.

"I guess you know what this is for, Lieutenant Adkins?" asked Jerry.

I nodded. "Yes, sir."

"I'm proud of you, Andy. You know you're the first officer in the battalion to be decorated."

"Yes, Jerry, but remember, you and I are about the only ones left of the guys who landed with this battalion." He nodded his head slowly. They were sad words to think about.

APO 80, U. S. Army
GENERAL ORDERS)29 December 1944.
NUMBER 116) SECTION

AWARD OF BRONZE STAR:

By direction of the President, under the provision of Army Regulations 600-45, dated 22 September 1943, as amended, the Bronze Star Medal is awarded the following named Officers and Enlisted men:

ANDREW Z. ADKINS, JR. 0535891, 2d Lt, Inf, Army of the United States. For heroic achievement in France on 2 October 1944, in connection with military operations against an enemy of the United States. On 2 October 1944, Lt Adkins led a mortar section platoon in support of a rifle company in an attack on an enemy held town. The objective was successfully attained but the problem of supply was complicated by the fact that the enemy had perfect observation from the high ground behind the town. On his own initiative, Lt Adkins immediately organized a group from his platoon and set out to replenish ammunition stocks under the hazard of enemy artillery and mortar fire. Upon returning safely with the required supplies, he learned that the rifle company was urgently in need of ammunition and rations. With utter disregard for his personal safety and despite pain from a knee injury, Lt Adkins voluntarily, in the face of concentrated enemy fire, secured the supplies, and succeeded in returning safely with them. The outstanding courage, tireless efforts, and sincere devotion to duty displayed by Lt Adkins exemplify the finest traditions of the armed forces of the United States. Entered military service from Florida.

By command of Major General McBRIDE.

MAX S. JOHNSON
Colonel, GSC,
Chief of Staff.

* * *

I was proud of that little medal, but I couldn't help but think of Hank Walker, Ray Wadsinski, Bob Strutz, Doug Cox, and all the others who had done so much more than I had done. All they got was the Purple Heart—posthumously.

Jerry said there was a group of men going into Luxembourg City for the day, about 25 miles away. I could go with them if I wanted. I could hardly believe it. Lieutenant Rhodes and I went in together. We knew the quartermaster had showers there and we were really looking forward to just standing in the hot water until our skin turned red.

All the way in we talked about how nice the showers were going to be. When we got there, we learned that the quartermaster had no showers and the public baths of the city were closed due to a fuel shortage. In a final attempt to get clean, we went to the CP and told a lieutenant our troubles. He had been an infantryman in Africa and knew how much a bath meant. He showed us to his room and told us to enjoy the luxury of bathing in a bathtub! That tub looked like a swimming pool to me, it was so big. I hadn't had a shower since I left England in November.

After we had our baths, we went sightseeing. It was cold and drizzling rain, and none of the shops had anything to sell. We were disappointed, but we did find several stores offering real ice cream and hot, delicious pies. It was snowing outside, but we ate ice cream and pie until they almost had to run us out. I also found some candles for the men. We lunched in a place where they had roast beef, potatoes, and beer. We were in absolute heaven.

We met an ordnance lieutenant there who took it upon himself to tell us how rough he was having it "up at the front." When we were at the point of beating him, Rhodes reminded me that we didn't have enough money to pay for breaking up the joint, so we asked the lieutenant to excuse himself.

* * *

History now tells us the Battle of the Bulge began at 5:30 a.m. on December 16, 1944. None of the units at that time had any idea it would be the biggest battle in World War II for American forces. The Bulge lasted forty days and took place during the coldest winter in Europe in fifty years. More than 1,000,000 men—600,000 Americans, 50,000 British, and 500,000 Germans—fought in this battle. The Germans suffered 80,000 to 104,000 dead, wounded, or captured. There were almost 81,000 American casualties, including about 23,500 captured and 19,000 killed.

Chapter *11*
THE SIEGFRIED LINE

February 5, 1945–March 1, 1945

We left Cruchten, Luxembourg, at 10:30 a.m. on February 5 and marched nearly nine miles in cold rain to our regimental assembly area at Diekirch. We got there about 5:30 p.m. Before the war, Diekirch had been a very beautiful resort town situated in the mountains and was the summer residence of the Duchess of Luxembourg. Now it was nothing but a mass of ruins. The town was unoccupied, so we didn't have to fight for it. Our whole battalion moved into a big building that was once a college. Company H was in two large rooms and we had our kitchen with us.

On February 6, 2d Lt. Jack Burks joined the company and took over the 2d machine gun platoon. Tom Jennings left for the States, and Carl Carlson took over Tom's job as the 2d Battalion S-4.

We found some liquor in the college. Kad, Bill Butz, and I enjoyed ourselves as much as we could, because we were only a few miles from the German border. We knew our next mission would be to cross the Sauer and Our rivers and hit the Siegfried Line (known as the West Wall), and that wasn't going to be any picnic. Although we never talked about it, we had a pretty good idea what had to be done when the time came.

German engineers had constructed concrete "dragon's teeth" in parallel rows across hills and valleys. In some cases, the dragon's teeth were only heavy posts or steel beams embedded in the ground. More commonly, they were five rows of pyramid-shaped, reinforced concrete projections resting on a concrete mat, ten to thirty meters wide and sunk a meter or two into the ground. The approach side of the foundation was usually a few feet above ground rising to a meter or more in the rear.

The dragon's teeth were staggered and spaced in such a manner that a tank could not drive through. Interspersed among the teeth were minefields, barbed wire, and pillboxes that were virtually impregnable to artillery and set in such a way as to give the Germans interlocking fire across the entire front.[1]

While we were in regimental reserve, we constantly trained and were given instructions in demolitions—pole and satchel charges and a new putty-like explosive that could be used for breaching barbed wire and blowing holes in pillboxes—with special emphasis on squad assault teams. Every day, the Red Cross girls brought us coffee and doughnuts.

One night about 10:00 Red Bullard, one of our cooks, came in and said, "Lieutenant, will you and Lieutenant Kadison step into the kitchen a minute, please?" He surprised us with piles of pork chops and french-fried potatoes. Boy did they taste good. Kad and I ate a bellyful.

Max Kelly's Company F moved out the night of February 10 with Jack Burks's machine gun platoon to secure a bridgehead across the Sauer River and to protect the engineers while they tried to build a bridge. They were attached to the 318th Infantry Regiment. At 10:30 p.m. the rest of the 2d Battalion climbed aboard trucks and moved eight miles to Beaufort, where we arrived at 12:30 the next morning. It was cold and rainy, and there were only walls of houses remaining. Kad and I found a cellar full of potatoes and a can of lard. We took McCauley's helmet against his protest and fried up some of the potatoes.

That afternoon we went up to take a look at the place where we would have to cross the Sauer River into the Siegfried Line. The crossing site was in the vicinity of Dillingen. The other two regiments of the division had already crossed over at another place and were having a pretty rough time. Our self-propelled 105s and 155s had moved up and were keeping up a continuous shelling.

From our vantage point on the high ground, we looked down to our right front and could see the battered little town of Lellingen, where the engineers were going to try and build a Bailey Bridge. The surrounding ground was nothing but a pocket of shell craters, and the Krauts were still firing artillery. Our assistant division commander, General Summers, had gone down there earlier in the day. Division had to send a tank down to get him out.

The river was swollen many feet above its normal level and the current was very swift. It didn't look good at all. The river wasn't normally that wide, but an unusually early warm spell had thawed the snow, causing the river to swell to about twice its normal size and flow at about ten miles per hour.

Jerry Sheehan laid out the plan. We were going across in assault boats. Max Kelly was already over and had established a perimeter defense. The only things that would bother us were artillery and snipers. The Krauts were sending down combat patrols every now and then, but they didn't amount to much.

My mortar platoon was to be the last across. Carl Carlson, our new battalion S-4, had to get several days' supply of rations across before dawn. Kad and I weren't going across for several hours, so I told Carl I would help him. The night was black as tar. We went to the 1st Battalion, 318th to see the S-4 there.

While we were in the CP one of our men came in soaking wet. He had gone over on an engineer raft. The current was so strong it tore the raft to pieces and several of his men drowned. Carl and I went down to see the engineer captain who was in charge of the boats. He had a cable stretched across the river and had a system rigged up where the current would pull across the assault boats and rafts. The artillery was bothersome, but Carl managed to get some of his rations across.

About midnight, on my way back to rejoin the platoon, I met Kad bringing the platoon down the road. He had received orders to get them across right away. Someone else had priority on the engineer boats, so we had to find a phone and call Jerry Sheehan. A phone was in a cellar with a couple of engineers. Jerry said come across, but warned us that the current was very swift, and we could only put three men with their equipment, plus the engineer in charge, in each boat.

It was pitch black and we couldn't see a damn thing. Something didn't feel right, and I was getting nervous. We had crossed rivers before at night in assault boats and rafts, but this was different. I couldn't explain it. Mac, Sergeant Martin Roach, and I went across first. Kad was going to feed the men to us. We were going to assemble on the opposite bank, and then move west about half a mile to where Bill Butz was positioned.

Somebody wanted a jeep across, so Pvt. Slick Bannerman, one of my jeep drivers, got his jeep on a raft and took it across. About a third of the way across, it slid off the raft and stuck in the mud.

Two boatloads of my men made it across before the boats stopped running. There was no way we could get in touch with the other side to find out what was holding everything up. During this time our boys kept bringing in Kraut prisoners to be taken across the river. The enemy had had enough fighting; at least these Germans had. There were perhaps a hundred of them, and we had only two guards.

I went back to the wire cable, where I had left Sergeant Roach, but no one had come across. I sat down on the bank of the river with my hand on the cable. That way I could tell when a boat was coming across. The cable tightened. A boat was coming over. The cable grew tighter and tighter—and then it snapped.

It was an awful thing to witness. The night was so black we couldn't see our hands in front of our faces, and yet we could hear people yelling for help only a little way out in the river. We were helpless. If we tried to help them, we would surely have drowned ourselves. We didn't have any lights with us and, even if we had, we probably still couldn't see anything. I turned away from the water and felt like screaming.

When dawn came, we got the rest of the men across the river. I knew that Kad would see that all the men got across before he started, so I didn't ask anyone where he was until Sergeant Peck came across and asked me if Lieutenant Kadison was okay. I told him I hadn't seen him. Then Peck told me that after the boats broke down, Kad had crossed on a raft to tell me what the hold-up was. My heart fell into my boots. He was probably on the raft that had been torn apart in midstream.

It wasn't a pretty picture. Kad had on his overcoat and all his equipment. I could picture a flimsy raft tearing apart in midstream of a swollen river and the hundred boxes of heavy rations tumbling in every direction. It was so dark that visibility was impossible. Even an excellent swimmer could not have gotten out of that death trap.

I tried to believe that he had somehow escaped and had been swept somewhere downriver. Nothing could happen to my Kad. He had escaped death so many times that a little river could never hurt him. We had shared so much together. The snows were gone now and we would soon be through the Siegfried Line. The war would soon be over and we could relax and enjoy life together. He was a brilliant man and had so much to live for. I loved him as my own brother, and he meant so much to his men.

I did everything possible to find him. We asked everyone we saw. We checked every hospital and every aid station, asked every medic. Nothing—no one had seen him or heard from him. The 5th Infantry Division was crossing down the river a piece. We asked everyone there. Sometimes we got rumors. We traced each of them down, but they only ended in blind alleys. One man told us a dark-haired man who had been wearing a red scarf had been picked up out of the river. Kad wore a red scarf! I got my hopes up, but the tip led to nothing.

The Krauts had been sending combat patrols down to the river to try and get some of the prisoners back. For a while I convinced myself they had found and captured Kad. If that was the case, he was sure to be all right. But that was not the case. His body was found two months later, three miles below where we had crossed. Lieutenant Saul Kadison from Brooklyn, New York, my friend, my buddy, my brother, was dead.

* * *

We got the Kraut prisoners to pull Slick's jeep out of the mud, and I moved the platoon down the road about half a mile to where Bill Butz was waiting. Across the river from the site at which the engineers were trying to build a Bailey Bridge were the ruins of an old house. Lieutenant Jack Burks, who had the 2d machine gun platoon, had been killed the night before by an artillery shell that had dropped directly into his upstairs room facing the Kraut lines. Someone should have told him to go to the side of the house away from the Krauts.

Sergeant Joe Pawlak, my mortar platoon sergeant, spread the men out while I went to find out what was cooking. For the time being we were to just hold the high ground south of Rohrback while the engineers built their bridge. While we were waiting, the Krauts threw a barrage at the engineers. They had the end of the bridge sticking out over the water, and there were men swarming all over it. The barrage landed right in the middle of them. They didn't hear it coming and there was nowhere to go.

Later we started moving up the mountain. Part of the 318th was up there, and we were going to occupy part of their area. It was a tiresome job. There were a lot of dead around, ours and Krauts. The trees were torn up from air bursts.

There were a lot of dugouts and pillboxes in those woods along the Siegfried Line, and I found some nice ones for my men. Those Krauts really knew how to build dugouts. Mine was about twelve feet long and ten feet wide with bunks, tables, chairs, benches, and a window. Water from the melting of the snow kept seeping through our roof, but given what we had been through, it was like a five-star hotel.

* * *

On February 16, we moved up to the edge of the wooded mountain we were on. We were about three quarters of a mile south of a little town called Rohrback. The weather was clear and warming up. In addition to seeing small villages where we knew we might be able to find a few eggs and maybe a chicken or two, we could see more pillboxes all along the Siegfried Line. We dug in on the edge of the wooded slope. We knew that as soon as things became organized, we would take those little villages and those little pillboxes. We found a few dugouts and, of course, took advantage of them.

Just at the left edge of the woods was a little town. Jerry Sheehan sent a rifle platoon down to take it. They took it okay, but the Krauts wanted it back. Every now and then, they tried to send in a couple of tanks and a few infantrymen. Snipers were bad, too. Every so often the Krauts tried to send a small patrol into our area but we knocked them back. One afternoon, Lieutenant Rhodes came in with a bullet in his arm. He was happy. He told Jerry that he hated to leave, but he could use a couple of months in the hospital. Who could blame him?

We were in the woods. When artillery came in, it was mean. Every round was a tree burst. Fortunately, we were pretty well dug in and only suffered a few casualties.

Rohrback was the first little town to our front. It had only a couple of houses and a barn in it. The Krauts were in and around those few houses, and they kept picking at us. Our artillery tried to knock it down, but it was just one of those places where it seemed impossible to bracket my mortars on.

One afternoon I tried to burn it down with white phosphorous mortar rounds. I tried and I tried, but I still couldn't hit anything. I could hit on either side of one of the houses and I could shake the slate roof off, but I couldn't get a direct hit. Every now and then, a Kraut tried to do a little walking around. It was fun making him run instead of walk. During one of the artillery barrages, Corporal Hildebrandt was hit while in his hole. He didn't want to be evacuated, but I told him to go back anyway. He stayed away only a few days and then rejoined his buddies.

* * *

Major Samuel Williams took over the 2d Battalion about February 16. He looked pretty good from the start. On the afternoon of the seventeenth, he called in all his company commanders. It was the first time most of them had seen him. McDonells's Company E, Kelly's Company F, Hazel's Company G, and Butz's Company H were to attack the next morning with artillery support, and they were ordered to keep taking towns and hills until we reached Hill 407, the regimental objective. That hill was quite a distance away. This would take some time.

For the first time, my mortars were to stay in battery and give support from where they were dug in. The attack was ordered for dawn on February 18. We almost got lost trying to get to the OP. Everybody had a SCR300 radio. That was our only means of communication.

I fired more than 1,000 rounds that day. Up until that time, we could only shoot only what we could carry, about ninety rounds. But now we were in a position where jeeps could bring us ammunition, so instead of firing three rounds for effect, we could fire thirty.

Max Kelly was having a hell of a time getting into the second little town. The Krauts had a lot of machine guns, and Max had to cross a couple of hundred yards of open ground. The only way to do it was to go in with artillery and mortar support. I fired smoke to provide cover for our attacking troops, and the artillery fired high explosive shell. It was a pretty sight. Max and his boys charged with bayonets. It looked as if they hit the edge of the town the same time as the smoke and HE.

I moved the guns up right before dark. When I started to put them in a draw, I saw a small hill that looked as if it was covered with dugouts. Mac, my runner, and I walked over to take a look. The hill was indeed littered with dugouts that had once been a Kraut artillery battery position. Most of them had a foot or two of water in them, but it was excellent cover.

Mac and I went to check on the men. Sergeant Pawlak was sitting on a box reading an edition of *Stars and Stripes*. As we walked up, he said, "Did you read this damn paper?"

"No, why?"

"It says right here in black and white that General George S. Patton, Jr., Commanding General of the Third U.S. Army, swam the Sauer River with his assault troops," Pawlak replied. "Now Lieutenant, I want to ask you something. You are always braggin' about what a good swimmer you are. If you tell me that it was humanly possible for any living soul to swim those rushing cold waters, I will call you the biggest liar in this man's army."

As we later discovered, Patton had crossed the Sauer River on a partially submerged footbridge under a smoke screen, almost giving the impression of walking on water.[2]

We were still sweating out the bridge the engineers were building. We had no armor, because as soon as we got a toehold, the 4th Armored Division was to come through us. The second day out in the open a platoon of tanks joined us. Several of them were knocked out pretty quickly, and the rest of the crews weren't too anxious about losing more. Fortunately for us, the night was fairly quiet.

On the morning of February 19, Mac and I headed out to see what we could see. Max Kelly was in the only cellar in town. The rest of the few houses had been blown apart. Hazel and McDonell were already up to the next town, Nusbaum, Germany. When Mac, my runner, and I started back, a Kraut assault gun pulled up on the edge of town and started raising hell, so we decided to stay and visit with Max a little longer. We found him behind a chicken coop trying to go to the bathroom, when the assault gun opened up. He came rolling in the cellar holding his britches and cussing, "Damn those sons of bitches, they won't even let a man take a healthy crap!"

Every time we started back to our platoon, the damn assault gun let loose with a few rounds. Every time it hit the house, the plaster fell in the cup of coffee Max was trying to brew. Other than that nuisance, things were relatively quiet, so we decided to drop by the battalion CP on the way back.

We had about a hundred yards of open road to cross, and it seemed the Krauts were shooting at everything that moved. Mac and I decided to see who could cross the open stretch of the road the fastest. I won. Tom Moss, our artillery liaison officer, was frying chicken at the CP, so we stopped to pay him a little visit. Colonel Fisher, the regimental CO, came while we were there and asked if the chicken fell down and broke his leg. We told him no, it had stepped on a mine.

Bill Butz was out in the yard. Just as he picked off a good-sized turkey with his carbine, Major Jim Hayes, now the regimental S-3, came up and commenced to chew him out properly. "Why, Major, this bird attacked me," Bill explained with a straight face. "I had to shoot him in self defense." The major had no answer for that one, but I think a little later he enjoyed a leg or a wing himself.

Up the line a little piece were three little towns, all close together. Early on the morning of February 20, Mac and I went up find a place to relocate the guns. The major was in a house with George McDonell, who had just moved into one of the towns, Nusbaum, and had caught the Krauts in bed. They had no guards whatsoever and didn't seem to want to fight. Quite a contrast to the boys we used to run up against in France and in the Ardennes.

While we were there, Bellievue, a sergeant in the 1st machine gun platoon, came down the street with about thirty civilians. All of them had cows. The major yelled to ask him what the hell was going on. Bellievue, who hadn't seen Major Hayes before and thought he was just another GI, told him to blow it out his ass. Then he saw the little gold leaf on the major's helmet.

We brought the 81s up to Nusbaum and set them in the courtyard. While the men were moving up, Mac and I went to see how the machine gunners were coming along. Things were quiet now, and they were taking it easy, frying some delicious smelling ham. A couple of them were looking around for eggs.

One of the machine gunners, Sergeant Red Anderson, said he and his buddies were getting ready to go into a dark cellar when he spotted a Kraut running out of a house a hundred yards away. Red took a bead with his M-1 and let go with a couple of shots. While he was reloading, three Krauts came out of the cellar with a white flag. They thought he had been shooting down the cellar at them.

After the guns had been set up and we had laid them by map, Mac, Sergeant Pawlak, and I went up to the next little town. All kinds of troops were pouring into the area now. On the way up we passed a group of our boys taking a bunch of happy prisoners to the rear. Sergeant Pawlak rattled a little Polish off to the POWs. They seemed happy and laughingly answered him. I asked Pawlak if those guys were really Polish. "Sure, they're Polish," he replied. "They don't care who they're fighting for."

The 313th Field Artillery moved in near the dugouts where we had been a couple of nights ago, the 1st Battalion moved on our flank, and the 318th moved through our area. Things were fairly quiet. I could get used to this.

Lieutenant Meyers had his rifle platoon in the next little town, Freilingen. All of these towns joined one another, and all of them had been battered to a pulp by artillery. Hazel was in a cellar taking life easy in Freilingen.

* * *

The major had given each of the companies a town to take and he had given Max Kelly Hill 407, the regimental objective, to take. Max was having a rough time.

The hill had a strong pillbox on it that covered all of the surrounding terrain. The Krauts were very reluctant to give it up. Finally, Max got the pillbox, but that was as far as he could go. The hill was big enough for a regiment to dig in on, and Max had only a depleted company to take it.

On the hill to Max's right flank was a thick, scrubby wood. The Krauts had dug in there, but Max couldn't see to get them out. Our guns were laid, but the problem was to find a place from which we could observe in order to help Max. Every time Max and I tried to get on Hill 407, we were shot at big time.

There was another little hill to Max's right rear, so we set out for that with Sergeant Peck and a SCR536 radio. Max had radioed to us the position of his right flank so we could tell where not to shoot. While we were trying to get to the top of that little hill, the Krauts opened fire with either a tank or an antitank gun. I don't know whether they were shooting at us or not, but the bursts were close. Lieutenant Meyers was supposed to have a road block where those rounds were coming from. I spotted a 3/4-ton truck and a 57mm anti-tank gun through my glasses. Perhaps that was Meyers.

I also saw Krauts running around in the woods on the top of the hill above Meyers. I asked Peck and Mac if they wanted to go down and take a look. They agreed. On the way down a sniper threw a few rounds our way, so we had to double-time it.

The Krauts had set up a road block around the bend from where Meyers was supposed to have one. That was a good enough reason for Meyers to be where he was. We thought he was digging a hole under the road, and it was big enough to put a tank through.

"Meyers, what the hell are you doing here digging this hole?"

"Andy, I didn't dig the damn thing. The Krauts dug it and they piled up enough TNT to blow the whole road a mile high!"

Sure enough, he was right. "Keep your head down because when I get radio contact and find a place to observe, I am going to raise hell on the hill above you."

He nodded he understood. "When you see the major, please tell him that I'm still here and that every time I try to make a cup of coffee, these damn snipers start to get rowdy."

We had to run and crawl back. When I tried to borrow a radio, I found Major Williams and Colonel Fisher in a house. I told the major about Meyers. Peck and I tried to use the church steeple as an OP, but we couldn't see enough from there and, besides, a church steeple is usually a bad place to be.

Sergeant Peck pounded our SCR536 radio on the ground and it started working. We crawled about three hundred yards to the edge of the hill. Our radio worked perfectly, and after a few rounds we had all four mortars zeroed on the different patches of woods.

The Krauts were getting nervous now, and we could see them moving around a little. I asked for ten rounds from each gun. It was a beautiful sight. Every round was in the air before the first round hit. Max Kelly went in behind the mortars, and in a little while he had the whole hill. A little later, Mac and I went to see Max at his pillbox. When the Krauts started throwing artillery at us, I dove for the pillbox and tore my lip on a strand of barbed wire. It hurt like hell and bled some, but it could have been worse.

* * *

After Max took the hill, it became relatively quiet. We stayed in the area until February 25. Earlier in the month a new lieutenant had joined our company. He was to take over command of one of our machine gun platoons. The fire was too heavy for him to get to the platoon that was with Max on Hill 407, so Bill Butz kept him at the CP for a couple of days. When things quieted down enough, Bill sent him to the platoon.

Around the top of the hill were a number of German dead and their equipment. The new lieutenant had been there only a little while when he picked up one of the Kraut rifles with the intention of breaking it over a rock. "I've always wanted to do this," he told me. Before I could object, he lifted the rifle up and brought it down hard, whacking the weapon over a large rock. The weapon was loaded. It went off and the bullet went through the inside of the lieutenant's thigh and through the shoulder of a sergeant standing behind him.

* * *

Down the valley from Hill 407 was the relatively large town of Mettendorf. Part of the 318th was going to clear it and then we were going through them. On the morning of February 25, Mac and I went up to the forward edge of the hill with Max to look the situation over. Company F was going in from the right and Company G from the left. I was to follow Max Kelly in with my mortars. The artillery pounded the high ground around the town while our boys went in. Major Jim Hayes, the new regimental S-3, and the division G-3 were there to see how things were going.

Hayes was trying to impress the gentleman from Division. After the artillery had fired, he reported over the phone to Regiment that the rounds had been effective. The gentleman from Division eyed Major Hayes. "What the hell do you mean the artillery fire was effective?" he asked. The major just stared back. "Were you at the target? How do you know whether the rounds were effective—or not?" It did my heart good to see the West Pointer try and wriggle out of that one.

Mettendorf was taken the morning of February 25 without any trouble. Mac and I radioed back to our platoon on what to do next. We struck out cross-country into the town. On the way down we ran into a couple of knocked-out Kraut armored cars with dead crewmen lying around them in every conceivable position.

Right on the edge of the town was a river where the Krauts had blown out the bridges. As Mac and I got to the edge of the water, one of our medical jeeps came by us and went downstream to ford at a shallow spot. The Krauts had planted a mine field a hundred yards downstream from the bridge, and the medics crossed right where the mine field was. When they were halfway across, their jeep hit a mine. One of the medics was thrown to the opposite bank of the river, his body completely mangled. Two other medics sustained severe lacerations and shock. It made me sick to see things like that, and especially to hear the cries of the wounded.

The engineers moved in to build a bridge. Mac and I went on into town and found Bill Butz. After we saw Bill, we went a little further into town and found a nice house for the platoon. Major General Horace McBride, commanding general of the 80th Infantry Division, came down to see how things were going. It seemed as if everybody and his brother were moving into town.

Mac brought the mortar platoon in. We placed the guns, set up an OP, and waited for developments. No sooner had we gotten settled in than we received orders to move out. I think the general wanted the town for his CP. It looked like we had the Krauts on the run and we were going out after them.

We were ordered to take Berg, hold up there, and wait for further orders. We left Mettendorf just before dark and moved over some rough mountain roads to Berg. It was reported that the roads were mined, so we couldn't take our vehicles with us. We arrived about 9:00 p.m. on February 25 without firing a shot. We held up there and waited for orders. There was a cold wind blowing and everybody was shivering.

While we were there, our kitchens brought us hot chow. An old German civilian came walking down the road, mad as hell because the Americans were in his town. He was so old all we could do was laugh at him. We moved out of Berg two hours later with orders to take Mulback and a couple of other little towns.

We were moving at a pretty good clip now. Things were moving so fast we didn't know who was where. We had to move out on foot because the roads were supposed to be mined and there were supposedly no friendly troops in front of us. When we were about an hour out, we ran into a battery of our own medium artillery that was really banging away. A little farther on we ran into a recon outfit that had stopped for the night.

At 3:00 on the morning of February 26 we came to a sign that read, "Mulback ½ km." The major decided to go in with Company F and Company E, and send Company G onto some other town. We got the town without any trouble and took a few prisoners who were home on leave. While we were getting the town occupied and posted, Max Kelly, George McDonell, and I sat in a barn to enjoy a bottle of schnapps Max had found hidden away somewhere. Things looked quiet, so we settled down for the night.

When daylight on February 26 arrived it was raining and everything was muddy. The air stank because the manure piles around the town were flowing down the streets! We had a hot meal for noon and prepared to move out. Things were still moving fast. We left Mulback at 3:00 p.m. and walked cross-country to Wissmannsdorf, 3 ½ miles away. We arrived there about 5:00 p.m.

During our move we were able to see out across the hills and mountains, where our armored columns were scattered all over the place. Guides were already in Wissmannsdorf to take us right to our billets. This was the way I liked to fight a war! March a couple of miles and then have guides show you where to sleep. I got my whole mortar platoon into one house with plenty of comfort. The cellar was full of meat, eggs, bread, and potatoes, so everyone enjoyed a feast.

There was a good-looking girl in the house, but it was in everyone's best interest if she moved out for the night. It was not a popular decision with the men. One of the boys brought me in a nice plate of french-fried potatoes and some fancy sausages. We had a little champagne to go with it, so it was quite a feast. Things were quiet, and I went to bed early and enjoyed a good night's sleep on a soft feather bed.

We stayed in Wissmannsdorf until February 29. While we were there, we got haircuts, cleaned our weapons, and had hot chow. Lieutenant Edwin Heller joined Bill Butz and me there. We were glad to see him. Bill and I had been the only officers in the company for quite a while. It hadn't been bad at all, though, because we had some good sergeants as platoon leaders, and a good sergeant is worth two lieutenants any day in the week. Heller had a pint of Calvert's Reserve he had lugged all the way from the States, so we tapped that bottle hard and celebrated.

We moved out from Wissmannsdorf in a column of companies about 9:00 p.m. on February 29 with the mission of taking Ehlenz,

Schleid, and Hill 450. Ehlenz was our first stop. The major didn't think it was occupied, so he sent a jeep and our newly acquired half-track ahead to investigate. Bill Butz decided to go along. I think he was lazy and wanted to ride. Max Kelly was leading, so I decided to tag along with him.

We got into Ehlenz about 1:00 a.m. on March 1. Bill and a bottle of schnapps were waiting there for me. They hadn't met anything in town. McDonell went ahead to Hill 450, right on the edge of town, and Hazel went on into Schleid.

McDonell wanted some mortar fire while he was moving up, so we threw the guns up, laid them by map, and blasted away. He had a little town the other side of his hill, and that was what I was shooting at with my mortars. We were getting pretty good at shooting by maps, and the next morning McDonell told me that I'd done him quite a bit of good. He got his hill okay, but Hazel had a little trouble before he took his town.

By this time we were also taking a lot of prisoners in these towns. Every time somebody took prisoners, he would send a message over the radio: "Am sending back six supermen!" or "Am sending back fifteen of Hitler's elite."

Chapter 12
R&R IN PARIS

March 2, 1945–March 9, 1945

Things were pretty well under control in Ehlenz when daylight came on March 2. I was dog tired so I snoozed a little. Major Williams moved all of the civilians to one end of the town and Max Kelly and I occupied the other end with our men.

Sergeant Melcolm got the radios going and set us up a regular fire direction center. He put on his long antenna and set his radio up in the attic of our house. We had another radio at the OP with George McDonell. Every time I went to the OP to check on things, I had to bring back a load of prisoners with me that McDonell had captured. These prisoners were tired and didn't have any fight left in them. We were getting a lot of them now.

Lieutenant Emmett Taylor joined the company on March 2, and Bill Butz gave him to me. Bill also told me that I would be leaving the next day for a pass to Paris! I could hardly believe it. As terrible as it was at the front, I really hated to leave because I knew that we would probably be moving out again in a day or two. Sergeant Joe Pawlak, my mortar platoon sergeant, said he could break in the new lieutenant all right. Pawlak was a good soldier and good leader. I had all the confidence in the world in him.

Private Olson carried me back to the reinforcement company. When I got there, I saw Frank Caputo, who had just been made captain. I hadn't seen him since Colonel Boydstun was killed. Frank was on his way home.

Dave Morgan, from the 1st Battalion, and I were the only officers going to Paris. We had about twenty men with us. A truck carried us to Luxembourg City, where we were to catch a train to Paris. We stopped on the outskirts of Luxembourg at a place where the men had their duffel bags stored so they could get some clean clothes.

While we were there, Dave and I decided to look in our Val Packs. I hadn't seen mine for eight months, and I was just curious. We looked at our pinks, our blouses, and our low-quarter shoes, and then we looked at each other and decided we'd do the thing up right and go to Paris all dressed up. We had a few hours to wait in Luxembourg City, so we decided to try and get the men some passes. We had to go to Third Army Headquarters to get them.

A guard in a snappy uniform stopped us as we approached the grounds. After telling him what we wanted, he let us pass. As we walked toward the building, we could see that General Patton had done well for himself in choosing a CP. His headquarters was in a palace with long wide corridors and spacious rooms.

We stopped at a desk marked "Information." Behind the desk was a slick-haired lieutenant casually filing his fingernails. I almost vomited. He looked us over from head to foot and then with a disgusted grimace said, "What do you want?" It was all I could do to not jump over the desk and drag him outside. Dave said, "Say, Mac, is General Patton in?" To which the lieutenant replied in his sarcastic tone, "I can let you speak to one of his aids if you want to."

Dave turned red. "Lieutenant, we are on our way to Paris with a group of men. Some MPs stopped us near the railroad station and said that we were in a Third Army town, and that all troops had to wear helmet liners. Our men left their helmets and liners with the company when they left to go to Paris. We have only overseas caps and no weapons. Is there some way we could get permission to walk around in Luxembourg City without being stopped by the MPs because we don't have helmet liners?" With a brazen look, the lieutenant replied, "I don't think so, but you might ask the MPs. They have an office right down the hall."

We left Luxembourg City about 2:00 a.m. on March 4 via train, and arrived in Paris about 5:00 that afternoon. After we exchanged our money, Dave and I told the men that we would see them in a few days. A bus took us to our hotel, the Lafayette Club. As we checked in, the girl at the desk told us that they were now serving supper, and it would be best for us to eat now and clean up afterward.

As we started toward the dining hall, we had to stand aside to let "Air Corps" pass. He had thick black hair, tailored pinks, and a green tailored ETO jacket. Instead of a tie he had a white silk scarf folded around his neck. As he passed Dave said, "Doesn't he smell pretty. If you name it, you can have it." Another doughboy with us said it must be a fashion parade. They had an orchestra to play for us while we ate chow. "Air Corps" and some of his buddies passed by our table and dropped the remark, "What is it that stinks so about this place?" Those were clearly fighting words, but we remained calm. We were in Paris!

After supper, Dave and I enjoyed a hot bath, which we needed badly, climbed into our pinks, and set out to see the city. We headed for the Montmarte, went to a night club, and crashed the joint. A gorgeous brunette and a blonde took the table next to us soon after we sat down. We asked them to dance.

After a few dances Dave said to me, "Why in the hell can't you speak French, so we can get things started?" In front of us was a sergeant rattling in French with his girl. Dave punched him and said, "Say, Sarge, how about talking to our girls to see where we stand?" The sergeant rattled French to the brunette and blonde.

"What's the score, Sarge?" I asked.

"The girls seem to like you, but as far as anything else is concerned, they say that it all depends . . ."

We got back to our hotel at about 4:00 a.m. and decided to go into the Red Cross Club and have a cup of coffee before going to bed for a few hours. Who should be leaning against the doughnut counter but "Air Corps." Dave and I got our coffee and sat down at a table. "Air Corps," who looked as though he had had one too many, turned around to us with a grin that looked like a dog eating shit and said, "Well, if it ain't the dog-faced boys." He held a piece of doughnut out and said, "Here, doggie, have something to eat."

Dave was a big man with a hot tempered. He turned red, but said nothing in return. Then "Air Corps" whistled as if he was calling a dog.

"Be a good little doggie and fetch the doughnut" he said, throwing it. "Air Corps" shouldn't have done that. The doughnut bounced off Dave's blouse. Before it hit the floor Dave was on him like white on rice. The Red Cross girl called the MPs as another airman walked in to help his crony. I jumped up and the fists started flying. With Dave's help, we flattened both of them.

"Let's get the hell out of here," Dave yelled. "The gal has gone for the MPs! Give me your Combat Infantry Badge."

"What for?" I said as I headed for the side door.

"Don't ask questions and hurry," Dave cried. As he grabbed me, Dave laid the two airmen over the counter with their butts sticking up and pinned our badges on the seats of their pinks. We went out the side door as the MPs came in the front.

The next day, after we had seen most of the sights, Dave and I started wandering down the side streets of Paris to see what we could find. As we passed a bar, its doors were flung open and out ran a wide-eyed sergeant. He grabbed us both by the arms. From his breath we judged that he had been inside the bar for quite some time.

"I don't believe it, you have got to see for yourselves!" he told us breathlessly.

He led us inside. At the far side of the bar sat a beautiful blonde looking straight ahead with her hands folded in her lap. Her more than ample breasts were exposed and draped over the edge of the bar. My eyes nearly fell out of my head. Dave remarked that was one gal that would need no pins for a corsage.

The bartender was slowly wiping the bar with his towel. When he came to the huge breasts, he stopped and looked at the blonde. She didn't move. He gently lifted one tit up and wiped the bar, gently replaced it, and then proceeded to the other breast.

"I'll take a double cognac," stuttered Dave.

"Make that two," I said.

Chapter *13*
MARCHING ONWARD

March 9, 1945–March 26, 1945

I got back to the battalion on March 9, which was still in Ehlenz. Things were quiet and everybody was taking it easy. Times like this were usually devoted to conducting various types of training, equipment maintenance, and personnel rehabilitation. One afternoon I trained my men for a regimental gun drill. We won first place in the regiment and the prize for the men was a pass to Paris.

We were through the Siegfried Line now, and things were relatively quiet. Down south of us somebody had pinned about 15,000 Krauts and needed help cleaning them out of what had become the Ruhr Pocket. At 1:30 a.m. on March 11, we pulled off our division patches, covered up our jeep lettering to hide our identity, and headed south sixty-five miles to Gandren, France, which we reached about 10:00 that morning. There, we enjoyed hot cakes and cheese for dinner. That night my mortar men went to Paris on their pass.

We left Gandren at 12:30 p.m. on March 12 and traveled by truck thirty miles to a spot one mile northeast of Irsch, Germany, where we arrived at 3:00 in the afternoon. Then we marched two miles to a bivouac area. Major Williams was on pass to Paris, so Jerry Sheehan had assumed command of the 2d Battalion. Everybody and his brother were around us. It was muddy where we bunked down for the night.

We moved out of our bivouac area early on the morning of March 13 and held up for a little while about one and one-half miles west of Ober Zerf. The 3d Battalion was already in the town. There was a wide open space between the hill we were on and the town, and the Krauts threw stuff in every time anyone tried to go down into town.

Mac, my runner, was with me now. The 3d Battalion was moving out and we were to replace it. Butz, Bellievue, Mac, and I hopped on a jeep and barreled into town. Mac and I looked for a place to set up 81s.

We were walking down the middle of the street when it happened. I'd been under lots of fire, but this was the most concentrated and terrorizing I had encountered. We heard the artillery coming, and rockets followed right behind the artillery. I am not talking about screaming meemies, just rockets! The weird sound they made pierced your soul. We learned later that they were 150mm and 300mm rockets.

The barrage lasted for several minutes, and the whole town vibrated. Mac and I dove for what we thought was a cellar, but after we got in it we saw it was only a barn. Mac landed in a manure pile and right above him was a raking machine. The concussion bounced us all over the place, up and down, side to side. When Mac went up, he caught his face in the rake, and when he came down he would land in the manure pile.

Black smoke covered the entire town. Tom Moss, Bill Butz, and Bellievue were in a building across the street. One of the rockets hit their building and blew a hole in it big enough to drive a jeep through. Both Tom and Bellievue were hit. Tom was torn up pretty bad and had to be evacuated. While the rockets were still coming in, Doc Bobb went out on the street to care for the wounded. He was an inspiration to us all. Because he was out there amid all the fire, some of our men went out to help him bring the wounded back to cover. General McBride was also in the town. His jeep had so many holes in it that it looked like a sieve.

Once the firing ended, Bill Butz and I found a stone cellar full of potatoes and decided to await further developments there. Lieutenant Emmett Taylor had the mortar platoon back up on the hill and was to bring them down when things got a little quieter.

Every time someone in the cellar with us tried to go outside to the bathroom, the Krauts threw in more rockets. One guy who made a dive for the cellar left his britches outdoors. A little later Captain Walker and Captain McLarry, from Regiment, came tumbling in. They were looking for a regimental CP and decided to take over our cellar. I guess rank has its privileges. Butz found us another cellar.

The companies started moving into town that afternoon. Mac was pretty bruised and shaken up from all the artillery, so I left him in the cellar while I went back to meet Lieutenant Taylor and the rest of the platoon.

The rifle companies had to move on through to a hill on the far side of the town. The Krauts threw direct fire along the road leading into town and our boys had a hard time getting in. Lieutenant Taylor brought up the rear with the mortars. We got the men under cover and waited.

About 11:00 p.m. on March 13, I took the platoon and joined George McDonell up on the hill. We were going to move into Greimerath. It was pitch black. Mac and I left the platoon on the side of the road and went to find McDonell. He and his runner were taking it easy while the men were getting ready to move out. We dug under a blanket with them and lit a cigarette. Boy, it was cold. McDonell was in the lead, and Mac and I stayed with him.

Part of the 3d Battalion was in Greimerath, and I was to set the mortars up there. The rifle companies were going to move on to some high ground the other side of town.

Lieutenant Pheney, of M Company, was in town with his 81mm mortars. A tank occasionally threw a few rounds right down the center of the streets, so we had to be careful. Fitzpatrick, Lieutenant Pheney's communications sergeant, and his radio were with Mac and me. We finally found a place and waited for the rest of the battalion. We waited and waited, but still no platoon. We tried to call them on the radio, but the damn thing was broken. I borrowed another radio from Lieutenant Pheney and changed the channel, but still I couldn't get them. I walked a little way back up the hill and still could not find anyone. It was about 3:00 a.m., so Mac, Fitzpatrick, and I decided to take it easy until daylight. There wasn't much we could do except wait. Besides, my men knew how to take care of themselves.

About daylight, Company M's chow wagon came by, so we borrowed some pancakes and coffee from them. Right after daylight, Emmett Taylor came barreling down in a jeep and said that Jerry Sheehan had decided to keep the mortar platoon up on the hill. We went back up on the hill Things were quiet, so I dug a hole and went to sleep.

We moved into Greimerath late that afternoon. Things were still nice and quiet. We set the guns up and settled down for the night. I had a nice air raid cellar for a CP, and I slept well. The next morning, March 15, Sergeant Melcolm, as usual, was up bright and early to hunt for eggs to go with our K-rations. About 3:00 p.m. we moved up to join the rest of the battalion on the hill.

We were going to attack cross-country. The trees were thick among the rolling hills. Our objective was the town of Mitlosheim, five miles away. Artillery had been falling on our boys, and Lt. Edwin Heller had a couple of casualties. His runner was one of the killed.

While we were waiting to move out, Bill Butz introduced me to Lt. Caswell Higgs, who had just joined the company. Bill gave him to me. When darkness came it was really dark and the woods were really thick. We traveled single file and held onto the belt of the man in front of us to avoid getting lost in the dark. We also had to be quiet. A dog kept barking at us and snapping at our legs. Sergeant Bellievue caught the dog and silenced him. The last thing we needed was to let the Krauts know where we were.

We stopped about midnight, but Company E and Company F moved ahead. Mac and I went with them part way before Jerry Sheehan called us back. He wanted the mortars set up where we had stopped earlier. I looked for a hole in the trees, but there wasn't one. We had to move back several hundred yards. The ground was cold and hard, and it was so dark and quiet we couldn't dig in because we would make too much noise.

Major Williams got back from his Paris pass and joined us at daylight. We moved out about the middle of the morning and joined Company E and Company F, which were up the way about a mile. Then we started moving cross-country again over hills. It was a nice warm day. In the early part of the afternoon we ran into part of an armored column that was going the same way we were. We were really glad to see them.

We took Mitlosheim about 4:00 p.m. on March 16 without firing a shot. I was tired and my feet hurt. We had been walking for miles. We posted guards throughout the town and looked the joint over. It was a nice little farming community that hadn't been touched by the war. I got the men nice houses to stay in and selected a good CP myself. This was the way I liked to fight a war. There was an old couple in my house, and I moved them upstairs.

I went to see Bill Butz. He and Sergeant Bloodworth had a Kraut cooking potatoes, ham, and coffee for them. I joined them in their feast. They even had a nice bottle of schnapps. I told Bill that we should do this more often. He laughed.

When I got back, Taylor and Higgs had our Krauts cooking us fish and potatoes, so I ate again. Things were quiet and everybody was happy. We even had electric lights and hot water in our house. I took advantage of the opportunity and shaved. It made me feel better. It was March 16, 1945, my dad's sixty-eighth birthday and my mother and father's thirty-fourth wedding anniversary, so I wrote them a letter.

We left Mitlosheim at 3:00 a.m. in trucks on the morning of March 17 with the mission of pursuing the enemy. We rode six miles and arrived in Weierweiler at 5:30 a.m. We held up there a little while and heated up our K-rations. We left Weierweiler on foot about five hours later and marched two miles to Lochweiler. On March 18 and 19 we marched and rode approximately eighteen miles from Neunkirchen to Pfeffelback. The Kraut defenses were falling to pieces and we were moving almost at will.

On March 20, we piled into our jeeps and trucks to start out for the big town of Kusel. It seemed that everybody and his brother were trying to take that town. We ran into armored columns, 8-inch towed artillery pieces, and everything in the book. Three divisions were converging on the place. Bill Butz went in first and I brought in the rest of the company about dark. Bill had the kitchen ready to serve chow and had our billets all picked out. I had a whole block of luxurious apartment houses for my platoon, complete with drawing rooms, lounges, spacious bedrooms, and more. What a way to fight a war!

When Sergeant Joe Pawlak and I walked into the kitchen of our apartment, we found a nice, fat, juicy Kraut eating supper. He didn't seem to know about the war, so I told him to get out. He argued a little bit and said he would discuss it with me after he finished his meal. Pawlak grabbed him by the seat of his pants and the scruff of his collar and threw him out.

I walked into the bathroom, a large one with pink and green tiling. Just out of curiosity, I turned on the hot water spigot and what should come out but boiling hot water. I could hardly believe it. I just let it run and peeled off my clothes. I would have stayed in that tub all night, but Lieutenant Higgs rushed me out so he could take a bath, too. After supper, I censored mail with Taylor and Higgs and wrote to my mom.

Some of my men were having trouble with civilians in another apartment, so I went to have a look-see. There, I believe I encountered a typical Hitler youth. She was a pretty little blonde about fifteen or sixteen years old. She could speak a little English, but she was so high strung that it was hard to understand her. My men had politely told her to gather her things and get out. She was scared stiff and wouldn't let a soldier come near her.

My men certainly would not have been mistaken for pin-up boys at the time. They hadn't shaved in several days, their clothes had been on their backs for months, and they had a certain barnyard aroma about them. But they wouldn't have hurt a little girl like that. She calmed down a little bit after I told her that I was the "commandant" and that my men weren't going to hurt her. She told me that she thought she would be raped and that her mother and father, who were also there, would be murdered. That's what Hitler had taught the German youth about the Americans. She and her family reluctantly moved to the cellar, scared, but alive and unharmed.

The bed was so soft and comfortable that I had a hard time getting to sleep, but after I did I slept until late the next morning. When I finally got up, everybody was out in the town trying to see what they could "liberate."

That afternoon, I was out on the street taking in the sights when General McBride drove up and asked where my regimental CP was. I knew that things were moving fast and that Regiment had moved up the "axis of advance" some place. I told the general that. He asked me what I meant by the "axis of advance." I couldn't answer that, so the general drove off. A good-looking blonde and an elderly woman were waiting to see me when I went back inside my CP.

"Lieutenant, we're Americans," the girl said in perfect English. "My mother and I were stranded here when the war came and were unable to leave. Will you help us?"

I was dumbfounded. Here was a good-looking American blonde, in my own house, wanting me to help her. "Why were you stranded? You knew the war was coming. Why didn't you leave?"

"I was here taking dancing lessons, but was in the hospital with a broken leg when the United States entered the war." Her mother tried to say something. I gathered she had been in Germany quite a while, because her English was a little rusty. There was really little I could do, so I told Mac to take them to Battalion.

The afternoon of the March 20, we climbed aboard trucks and moved to Enkenbach. Everybody was happy. We were moving fast with very little resistance and hardly any fighting. I sure missed Kad.

The next day we moved thirty miles to Gundershein. During the last few days we had moved so fast that we slipped off one map and onto another, and I had quite a time trying to keep up. On March 24, we moved twenty miles to Oberndorf, where we stayed for two days. It was nice, quiet, and peaceful. We had a chance to clean ourselves, our guns, and our vehicles. We even cleaned out our jeep trailers. The junk and souvenirs that came out of those trailers was a sight to behold. We'd been "liberating" for quite some time.

The weather was warm and we had walked a long way. We were always conscious of our feet and our leg muscles. Although we could fight without proper clothing and food, it was a hard matter to keep going with tired and swollen feet. We were still wearing shoepacs and on this particular day, because of the warm weather and the long march, our feet were bothering us more than usual. Luckily a message came down from Battalion: Regiment is sending a truck up with our combat boots; assemble your men and have them turn in their shoepacs in exchange for combat boots. To add a little humor to the message, there was a P.S. "All those having two, turn in one."

My mortar platoon was stretched out in the spacious rooms of a large guest house. Mac and I were in a small room, cleaning our rifles when the door suddenly burst open. "We'll let the lieutenant settle this! By God you stole my whiskey!" It was Clarence Moss and John Windsor were going at it.

"Lieutenant, he said I stole his whiskey, and I didn't, and we want you to settle it for us," Moss said hotly.

"By God, Lieutenant, he stole my whiskey and I want it back!" exclaimed Windsor.

"Just a minute, now. Calm down and tell me what this is all about," I replied.

Moss spoke: "He says I stole his whiskey, and I didn't. I didn't know it was his."

"The hell you didn't. You saw me put it there. You know damn well it was my whiskey!"

"Just a minute, John. What whiskey? Where did you get it?" I asked.

John was breathing hard and getting madder by the minute. "Lieutenant, I found a bottle of whiskey next door. Good stuff too, not the rot gut these Krauts have. Good stuff I put it in the jeep while I changed my shoes, and when I came back it was gone. Moss took it. I saw him with the bottle, and by God, I want it back. He shouldn't have stolen it!" John said.

Moss was beginning to show his anger now. He was usually cool and calm, but when his temper was aroused ten horses couldn't hold him. "Now damn it, John, don't tell the Lieutenant I stole your whiskey. I'll get you another bottle," Moss said.

"I don't want another bottle. I want that bottle. That was good stuff, and if you want to make something of it, come outside," John retorted. "I can settle this without the lieutenant."

"That suits me!" shouted back Moss.

While this was going on, I tried to step in but couldn't. Clarence and John were boiling now, and I had to do something and I had to do it fast. Big John was afraid of nothing; when he got mad, it was always best to stay out of his way.

Along the Moselle several months ago, Windsor had stood in a foxhole with his shoulders exposed to shoot it out with SS men who were crouching just ten yards away. When one of his buddies told him to get down or he'd get hit, he replied, "I ain't scared of the sons of bitches!"

Among the men in the company, it was well known that Moss was the only man who could lick the first sergeant. The old timers in the company remembered well how he used to clean out the joints along the Mexican border when we were stationed in the desert.

I moved between them. "Clarence, John, cut this crap. We're supposed to be buddies and we are here to fight the Germans, not each other!" I shouted. "John, Clarence said he didn't steal your whiskey, and I'm sure he didn't. He didn't know it belonged to you. If he had known that it belonged to you, I'm sure he wouldn't have taken it." It looked like my words were working. "Now, John, if you don't want just any brand, tell Clarence and me what kind you want, and if he can't find it, I can. Now come on, damn it, end this nonsense and shake hands."

I was wrong. Moss wasn't cooling off. "Don't say I stole your whiskey, 'cause I didn't."

I had to do something. "Look, men, you two said I would settle this, right? I am telling you to shake hands and forget about this. I'd do anything in the world for you guys—you know that. So shake hands and forget it."

Moss said, "Lieutenant, I'd do anything for you, too, but I don't like John's saying I stole his whiskey."

They were calming down a little, but not enough. "John, Clarence," I pleaded, "I'm asking you as a personal favor to me to shake hands. I'd do anything for you two, and I know you'd do the same for me. So as a personal favor to me, let's shake hands and forget about this."

There was silence. Moss looked at John and stuck out a hand. A smile broke out on his face. Big John looked at Moss and looked at the extended hand. Slowly, Big John took it and said in a half-laughing sort of way, "Okay, Moss. But damn it, from now on watch whose whiskey you take."

Moss said, "Okay, John."

All the while, Mac had been sitting in the corner saying nothing. Now he moved to open the door as John and Clarence started out. I said, "Listen, you two, I don't want to hear of this drinking any more. You know you're not supposed to drink, and you'd better not let me hear of it. And don't let me catch you drinking, either. You know that we're moving out soon. I don't want you two with a belly full of liquor just when I need you, okay?"

"Okay," they said.

We had plenty of officers in the company now, so I officially took over the company executive officer's job. Bill Butz gave the mortar platoon to Lt. Edwin Heller, and Lt. Caswell Higgs got the 1st machine gun platoon.

On March 26, I managed to get Sergeants Wilber Peck and Joe Pawlak furloughs to the States. I hated to lose two such valuable men, but they had been through a lot and deserved it. I've never seen anyone as happy as Pawlak. I gave them all the money I had. Joe took home a pistol for me and promised to write the folks. Hazel and 1st Sergeant

Geste went home, too. I made Sergeant McQuain mortar platoon sergeant. The war was winding down.

That night Bill Butz was supposed to get a pass to the Riviera, but someone screwed up and he didn't get to go. We moved out about dark and headed to a little town near Mainz. Bill and I rode with Bellievue and drank champagne on the way.

Chapter *14*
CROSSING THE RHINE

March 27, 1945–March 31, 1945

The next morning Major Samuel Williams, our battalion CO, called for an officer from each company to go with him into Mainz to pick out billets. Mainz was on the Rhine River, so we knew what our next mission would be. Sergeants Lyles and Frank, both from Company G, had just received their battlefield promotions; they went along with us.

Mainz was battered to a pulp, but we managed to find decent sleeping quarters. When the rest of the companies came in that afternoon, we settled down and waited. Later in the afternoon the major called all of the officers to his CP. He had a big map spread out on his desk. "We are to make an assault crossing of the Rhine River at 1:00 in the morning," he told us. That really cheered us up.

The Rhine was by far the most formidable of the rivers we had to cross. It rose in the Alps and flowed generally north to Arnhem, Holland, where it made a sharp turn to the west. The river averaged between 200 and 500 yards wide and six to nine feet deep; it was swift and turbulent, with whirlpools and eddies.[1]

Following the meeting, the major took us all down to the river to look things over and review our crossing plans. We remained concealed and went down into a wine cellar located next to the river bank. From there small groups of officers crept up and looked at the river.

While we were sitting in that cellar, I could tell something was wrong. I suppose it was a premonition, and I wasn't the only one who felt it. A lot of us had been together for a long time. Somehow or another we could tell beforehand whether a job was going to be easy or hard. I was thirsty, but water couldn't quench my thirst. I wanted a cigarette, but every time I lit one up I didn't want it anymore. I tried to eat, but the food had no taste.

When I went up to take a look at the river, everything was calm and quiet; nothing could be seen and nothing could be heard. The only thing I saw was smoke coming from the chimney of a little house in the town across the river. A few hundred yards south of us was a blown bridge. One company was going to cross near it. Lieutenant Virgil McAlpin, the battalion S-2, walked out on the bridge and had driven his jeep along the river bank, but no one shot at him.

We went back to our billets. A few minutes later the major called and said the orders had been changed. We would have to cross south of where we had originally planned. We jumped in our jeeps again and drove to another spot along the river bank to evaluate our crossing. It still looked quiet. Plans soon changed yet again, and we went back to our billets. The kitchen had pancakes and coffee for us.

About nine that night we moved up to the bank of the river. Lieutenant George McDonell was away on a pass to England, so Lieutenant Meyers had Company E. Hazel had gone home, so Lt. Mike Damkowitch had Company G. Max Kelly was in the hospital, so Lieutenant Floyd had Company F. Company E was to cross near the bridge with Lt. Caswell Higgs's machine gun platoon, Company G was to cross about five hundred yards south of them with Ross's machine gun platoon, and Lieutenant Floyd put Company F in a huge air raid cellar as our reserve.

I placed the 81s in position on our side of the river and Lt. Emmett Taylor established an OP near the river bank. The artillery was in position on the outskirts of Mainz. The engineers were there with their wooden assault boats to put us across the river. The Navy was there, too, with huge landing craft to help us out. The 1st Battalion was to cross north of us a little piece, while the 318th and the 319th were to cross several miles south of us. Captain Tom Mattlock, the battalion S-3, was down at the position where Company E was set to cross.

About 9:00 p.m., Lieutenant McAlpin tried with some of his men to launch an assault boat to cross the river to have a look. The Krauts opened up on him every time he tried to leave the shore. They fired 20mm and 37mm antiaircraft guns as direct fire. McAlpin told Major Williams about it and said that he would try again if the major said so. The major said no, so we sat down and waited.

At about 1:00 a.m. on March 28, 1945, the 80th Division started the trek across the Rhine River. The first boats carrying Company E and Company G shoved off from slips and docks on the Mainz river front. The river was about 500 yards wide at the spot we had to cross. When the first wave reached the middle of the river, the Krauts opened up with their 20mm and 37mm antiaircraft guns and machine guns, small arms, and artillery. The men kept paddling.

The night was black as pitch. Two rifle platoons from Company G landed in the wrong place, on a small island off the opposite bank. We had no artillery support and no tank or TD support. Most of Company E and most of Higgs's machine gun platoon, including Lieutenant Higgs and Lieutenant Meyers, were either killed or wounded. What was left of Company E and Company G joined together to hold the bridgehead.

The Krauts counterattacked twice, throwing grenades and with bayonets fixed. Several of our boys were taken prisoners. Our lieutenants suffered particularly high casualties. Lieutenant Meyers was killed. Lieutenant Caswell Higgs, who had joined the company two weeks earlier, was also dead. Lieutenant Frank, who had just received his commission the day before, was also lost. Lieutenant Lyles, who had also received his commission the day before, was seriously wounded.

Right before daylight, things suddenly became quiet. The Krauts had pulled out, but they had left their mark. During the early morning hours between 1:00 and 5:00 a.m. on March 28, three companies of my battalion, E, G, and H, lost twenty-nine men killed and seventy-three wounded. That's a lot of casualties for four hours of fighting. Other elements of the 80th Infantry Division had crossed the river without a single casualty, with the exception of three men from the 1st Battalion who were wounded by a mine.

A few days later I read in Stars and Stripes that "Patton's Third Army had eased across the Rhine with very light casualties." That line made my stomach turn. Our dead lay scattered on both banks of the

Rhine, where they had been mowed down by the withering Kraut fire. All of us knew going in the war was winding down, and no one wanted to be killed or seriously wounded at any time—especially now.

The little town of Astel, which was directly across the Rhine from Mainz, had been heavily battered by our bombers. While we were there, we went to account for our men.

At 6:30 p.m. on March 28 we moved down the road to Biebrich, where we arrived at about two hours later. We had nice apartments to stay in for two days as division reserve, reorganizing and receiving replacements.

In crossing the Rhine River, the 317th Infantry Regiment also seized the town of Weisbaden which, among other things, included an airplane factory and airstrip with six planes, an ordnance depot, a military hospital, and a champagne factory filled with more than four thousand cases of bubbly. The German ordnance dump contained every kind of gun imaginable, many of them brand new. Everybody got all they wanted. We had our kitchens with us and we got some good hot chow. When the men were settled comfortably in their billets, Bill Butz finally got to go on his pass to the Riviera.

I thought long and hard about all the good men recently lost and wrote a long letter home to my mom.

Chapter 15
MOVING FAST

March 31, 1945–April 12, 1945

We were in division reserve and had a long way to go to catch up with the show. At 7:30 on the morning of March 31, we jumped aboard trucks and rode about 100 miles to Rorshain. We traveled on the autobahn, a very picturesque drive. That day we passed column after column and convoy after convoy of Kraut prisoners. They were giving up by the thousands. It was hard to believe our men had traveled so far after we had had such a bad time on the Rhine.

We left Rorshain in trucks at 8:00 p.m. on April 1 and arrived in Vorschuty shortly after midnight. Then we left Vorschuty early the next afternoon and marched two miles to Gunderisberg. It was cloudy and raining, but the roads were excellent. We made good time.

Two of our regiments had been fighting for Kassel for several days, but they still had not taken the whole town. On April 3 we took Wahlershausen, a suburb northwest of Kassel, without any trouble. Major Williams said we would hold up there for the night and put our men in houses. He assigned each of us a street. Mac and I went to get houses for our men.

The civilians were milling around on the streets, waiting to see what they were to do. "Can any of you speak English?" I asked. The

Germans grumbled among themselves. They looked scared when a burst of machine gun fire on the next street reached our ears. Mac laughed and said, "That must be Lieutenant McDonell opening a door."

I asked again, louder: "Can any of you people speak English?"

A female voice spoke from the crowd. "I can speak English. What do you want?" The voice belonged to a slight brunette barely five feet tall. Her right leg was crippled and she walked with a limp.

"Tell your neighbors they have thirty minutes to get what belongings they need for the night and go to their cellars. We are taking over your houses for the night. Tell them that under no circumstances are they to leave their houses between sundown and sunup. If any German civilians are seen out of their houses after dark, they will be shot on sight. If an emergency arises and they must come out, they are to call a guard who will be near their house." The lady translated my message. The Germans understood perfectly and complied.

Mac and I walked into our house. A short time later, the brunette came in and told me, "My father and I live here. Are you going to stay in our house?"

"Yes. You and your father take what you need and stay in the cellar."

She told me that my soldiers were in her neighbor's house and asked if her neighbors could stay in the cellar with her and her father. I said that it would be all right. I also told her I appreciated what she had done, and that if she wanted anything during the night, to let me know.

We settled down for the night. About midnight, Sergeant Bellievue woke me and said the brunette is here and wants to see Herr Commandant. She was pretty excited. There was a drunk American soldier down in the cellar with her and her father threatening to shoot the old couple from next door. "Take it easy, Lieutenant, it may be a trap," cautioned Bellievue.

I grabbed my rifle as the brunette led the way to her cellar. Sure enough, there was a drunk GI there, waving his pistol around. He was from Company A, and his buddies were up ahead fighting. I told Bellievue to take him to Battalion and put him under arrest. He did so without incident. The German in her late forties said something I did not understand.

"What did she say?" I asked the brunette.

"She has a soldier son and didn't want you to be too hard on this drunk American soldier."

That dumbfounded me, but women, no matter what their age or nationality, are always unpredictable.

As I started to leave, the brunette touched my arm. "Thank you very much."

She was smiling now, and her eyes looked rather exciting with the candle light dancing on them.

"Would you like to come upstairs and have a drink with me?" She smiled and I added, "It would probably help."

When we got upstairs, she said, "Come with me." She led me to a room I had not seen before and lit a candle. The room was furnished with nice comfortable sofas and chairs. She told me this was her music room. There were portraits of great musicians to go with the baby grand piano. The walls and ceilings were done in pale blue. The room made me homesick.

She sat by the piano and looked at it while I opened a bottle of champagne. I asked her to play for me, but she declined. "No. I'd rather not. I have not played much in the past few months." We talked a while. She was a concert pianist who had studied in England. When she learned I had been to London, she plied me with questions.

"Was the city damaged very much from the German bombs and rockets?"

"No," I lied. "Only a few had fallen on London." I paused. "When do you think the war will be over? She shook her head and shrugged. "Our troops have taken Kassel and are making good time driving into Germany.

"Our soldiers will be back," she retorted.

"It doesn't look that way by the number of Germans we are taking prisoner. They are surrendering by the thousands."

To that she replied, "You don't know the German people very well, do you? Our soldiers will come back."

Then we talked about Germany and the war. I tried to tell her that Germany didn't have to go to war. That it was one of the most beautiful countries in the world I had ever seen, and that the German people could concentrate on making many more useful products than war machinery. They could farm their lands and make farm machinery in Kassel instead of the famous Tiger tanks Kassel was noted for. Why, there were a million things Germany could do besides go to war.

Again she replied, "You don't know the German people very well."
"No, I guess not. Why don't you tell me about them?"

She tried to explain that after World War I and the worldwide depression, her people were hungry and Hitler promised them food and money if they would work in the armaments factories. I reminded her that Hitler had brought in thousands upon thousands of slave laborers against their will to work in the factories. She shrugged her shoulders and didn't seem to know or care very much about that. I asked her what she thought of the Nazi policy. She answered with a smile and a wink, "I am afraid that I will have to know you a little better before I can talk to you about my political views."

* * *

At 6:30 the next morning, April 4, we started moving through Kassel with the mission of taking Ihringshausen five miles distant. The weather was fair and things were easy, but I almost wore myself ragged trying to keep up with Major Williams. He would go through the front door of one building and come out the back. Every now and then he would take a shot with his .45 at something that looked like a Kraut. We stumbled across a factory where they made Tiger tanks. We found them in all stages of production. Boy, those were big babies. I'd never seen such thick armor in my life.

We left the factory and marched up a hill overlooking our objective. We had about a mile to go over open terrain. We went into a house from which we could see everything. Things looked peaceful and quiet, but the major wanted a smoke screen for his men. When he asked the artillery for smoke, they denied it. He really blew his top. He asked me about having the 81s fire some smoke, but we didn't have any. Then he started chewing butt and decided to go in anyway. Mike Damkowitch and George McDonell were to attack, each company with two rifle platoons abreast. It was one of the best attack formations I had ever seen, but we didn't fire a shot going in. On the outskirts of town we met a group of French prisoners who looted a Kraut warehouse for bread and food.

Sergeant Bellievue and I were with the command group. The good sergeant left us every few minutes to poke his nose in some house or barn as we passed. He had the curiosity of a virgin. As we were coming into town, Bellievue said, "I'll be back in a minute." In a few minutes he came running back out of breath and said, "Lieutenant, come help me out. I got a German general cornered in a house back here."

I ran with him into the home. Bellievue stuck his rifle down a stairway leading to a cellar and yelled "Come on out, you bastard." I almost fell over. Out walked a German dressed in a uniform that could only belong to a general. The blouse was field green and trimmed with gold braid. His shoulders shrugged from the weight of medals hanging on his chest.

Bellievue and I were as excited as two kids at a circus, for we knew the Kraut was at least an army commander, and maybe even a field marshal! We strutted up to the front of the column with our prisoner to show the major.

On the way up we could not decide between ourselves whether we would be awarded the Distinguished Service Cross or the Medal of Honor for capturing such a high-ranking officer. We reached the command group and excited voices described our deed to the major, who called his interpreter. Sergeant Black talked to our German general and then commenced laughing. We asked what was so funny. The sergeant was laughing so hard he was wiping tears from his eyes.

"This is the chief of the fire department!"

Mike Damkowitch turned left and headed up the main street with his platoon and had gone only a few hundred yards when the Krauts opened up on him with machine guns and burp guns. They were holding up in a hospital on the edge of town. Mike got his platoon organized and after a while, ran them out.

Lieutenant Taylor and Sergeant Melcolm set up an OP in the hospital and fired on a town across from the hospital. Taylor fired all afternoon. At one point he caught the head of a Kraut convoy trying to come into the town across the draw. My jeeps spent all afternoon bringing up mortar ammunition to him.

We had a few tanks with us. Major Williams decided to send one of Max Kelly's rifle platoons with two of the tanks down to clean out the draw. Max asked the major if he wanted him to lead the platoon. The major answered simply, "No." Max's platoon headed down and cleaned out the draw, but one of his men was killed and several others were wounded. They also took a few prisoners who told us that they had wanted to surrender, but their officers had shot several men who had tried to do so.

Mike Damkowitch was on the left side of town, Max Kelly in the middle, and George McDonell on the right. I put Company H's 2d machine gun platoon with Damkowitch and the 1st Platoon with McDonell. In front of us up on a hill was a Kraut garrison. Lieutenant McAlpin pointed an antitank gun toward it. Then he took one of my jeep drivers and, under a white flag, drove up to visit the garrison. He asked the men to surrender. They said no. McAlpin returned and fired a couple of rounds from the antitank gun. Two minutes later 450 Krauts came out with their hands up. We used all of my jeeps and every other vehicle we could find to carry them back. The night was quiet after that.

* * *

The next morning, April 5, we marched five miles to Bettenhausen, crossing the Fulda River. We were to follow the 3d Battalion, but it ran into a little trouble and was held up. The major got tired of his men standing around, so he put us in billets in Bettenhausen for the night.

My house had a great big buxom blonde in it. With her was a greasy little Italian who had guarded slave laborers the Germans had forced to work for them. I booted them both out.

Sergeant Christopher returned from a furlough to the States that day. It was hard to believe that a man from my company had been to the United States and back. We were all anxious to learn how things were back in the good old U.S.A. Chris said the girls were still pretty and that his mom still made the best apple pie in the whole world.

A little later our conversation turned to more serious subjects. I asked Chris if he told the people back home what we were going through. He said, "Oh yes, they all want to know what it's like over there. But when I tried to tell them what war is *really* like, what an artillery shell can do to a man's body, and how an American boy looks after he's been riddled with bullets and his body has laid out in the sun for a few days, or the feeling you get when you're told to attack, well, it just didn't seem to register with them. They looked at me as if I was a freak or some damn fool. Their faces would just go blank. They'd cluck their tongue a couple of times and either change the conversation or make some excuse to leave." I shook my head in disgust.

Chris paused a minute, laughed, and said, "I have got to tell you this. I got into a fight while I was home. I went out with some of my friends one night, and we happened to bump into an old boss of mine. He had turned his machine shop into a factory for manufacturing some gadget used on airplanes. After a while he turned to me and said in a tired sort of voice, 'Chris, when are you boys going to get this fighting over with? You've been over there long enough to have whipped those Germans. What's holding you up? Look at me,' my old boss said, 'I've got three shifts working at my plant and honestly I'm a physical wreck trying to keep going. I can't spend much time with my family and I can't get tires for my cars. God, the food we're getting! Now, don't misunderstand me, I don't mind eating the sorry food we are getting as long as you boys are getting the best beef, vegetables, and eggs. But I do wish you'd hurry and get this damn war over with so we could start living a normal life again.' I knocked hell out of the bastard, lieutenant."

A little later Chris said, "You know what, lieutenant? I had a girl when I left to come overseas the first time."

"I know what you mean, Chris. I guess she got tired of waiting for you and teamed up with some other guy," I replied.

"No," Chris said, "she didn't found another guy. When I first got home on my furlough, everything was swell for the first day or two. But after that she didn't show that old warmth she used to when I'd take her out. She got a little cool and mumbled something about how I had changed. I asked her in what way; I thought I was the same guy. She said, 'I don't know, Chris. You just seem different. You don't laugh as much as you used to, and you don't seem to enjoy going to the old places we used to go to.' It hurt when she told me that I had lines in my face and acted like a silly old man. She said that when I told her that I'd rather sit at home than go dancing.

I nodded at this because I understood. It would have been hard to be back home dancing with your buddies in Germany still fighting and dying.

"When I tried to tell her about what it was like over here, she smiled and said, 'Let's don't talk about the nasty old war. That's all I hear at the office all day long—war, war, war. Let's talk about something pleasant.' I thought if I told her what it was like she might understand a little better, but she wasn't interested in what I had to say. The climax came when she told me about her girlfriend's boyfriend coming home on furlough. She said, 'Chris, I can't understand you. Why can't you be like Mary's boyfriend? He just got back after being in Scotland for six months and all he wants to do is take her out dancing every night. He can carry on the cutest Scottish accent. He was overseas as long as you. He wrote Mary every day, but I was lucky if I got a letter from you once a month! How do you expect me to understand you when you act like that?' Lieutenant, what could I do?"

I didn't have an answer. This war had changed a lot of men, me included. I didn't have an idea what I'd be like when I returned to the States after this war.

* * *

Later that afternoon the major came around with a truck filled with whiskey. He gave me some and told me to give it to the men, but that he didn't want anybody drunk. Lieutenant Edwin Heller invited me in for a feast that night. He had doctored up a can of hash with tomato puree, onions, and everything else he had. It really tasted good. Later, Million made us some cheeseburgers with a can of cheese and a can of beef and pork loaf. I cleaned my carbine and pistol and went to bed.

Things were really moving fast now. The next morning, April 6, we climbed aboard trucks and moved forty-nine miles to Tungeda, the regimental assembly area. On April 7, we moved six miles to Pfulldendorf. We were in open terrain now, with little towns and villages scattered here and there. Sometimes we ran into a little bit of trouble and sometimes we just barreled on in with no resistance. Lieutenant McAlpin, our battalion S-2, did a swell job; he wasn't afraid of anything. He mounted a .30-caliber machine gun on one of my jeeps and drove on out ahead and to the side of us, trying to locate Germans. When he didn't encounter any resistance, he came back and told us, and we moved that much faster.

At 5:30 a.m. on April 9, we moved out and took Molschleben and some adjoining towns without any trouble. Sergeant Melcolm received a pass to Paris and Bill Butz returned from the French Riviera. I sent a couple guns home to dad and Bill and I took some pictures. On April 10, we marched four miles to Tiefthal. The war seemed to be winding down.

* * *

April 11, 1945, was quite an eventful day. We were nearing Erfurt, a city of flowers and 164,000 Germans. In addition to being the home of Protestant reformer Martin Luther, and the birthplace of the German Luger pistol, it was the present home of the remnants of an SS outfit, the Hermann Göring Division. Our objective was to take Hill 405 overlooking Erfurt.

The terrain was hilly with scattered woods and villages. We were attacking in a column of companies with Capt Tom "Matt" Mattlock's Company F in the lead. Matt had taken over the company after Max Kelly went home. We were only a little way from Tiefthal when Matt ran into trouble. As he was moving over open terrain the Krauts opened up on him from an old, medieval garrison that popped up out of nowhere. We had tank destroyers with us and they softened the place up while Mart's company moved in. Lieutenant Damkowitch, with Company G, cut around to the right of some woods that were to our front and took the little town of Bienstadt.

There were all kinds of women in that garrison, but we had to move on because the woods between us and Damkowitch had to be cleared of Krauts. The major gave the job to Matt. He was no fool and he was red hot because he had lost some of his men earlier in the day. He had to cross 500 yards of open terrain to get to the woods.

Matt placed two antitank guns and Sergeant Zane Turner's machine gun platoon to give him preparatory and covering fire. In addition, he got the tank destroyers to help him out. As his troops fixed bayonets, my mortars fired a barrage. We had to be careful because Mike Damkowitch was on the other side of the woods.

Matt moved in with two platoons abreast. The supporting fire preceded him. When they got to the edge of the woods, the TDs rushed up. About thirty Krauts ran out of the woods with their hands up. Lieutenant Hoffman, the artillery observer with Matt, spoke fluent German. He formed the Krauts in a column of twos and marched them down to where Damkowitch was already holding about 100 more prisoners. It was quite a sight to see Hoffman marching those Krauts. I almost split my sides laughing.

We were in Mike Damkowitch's town only a little while before we were ordered to attack Gispersleben-kiliani, a suburb of Erfurt. One of our other regiments was getting ready to take Erfurt itself. Bill Butz and I went with the major to a little hill on the edge of Mike's town to case the next place we had to take.

After Bill and the major went ahead, the regimental CO, who was sitting in his jeep behind a house, asked me what was going on. I told him that Company E and Company G were attacking in a few minutes. I was going to a little hill overlooking our objective and didn't he want to come along.

"How far is it?" he asked.

"About a mile up a little hill," I replied.

"No, they probably won't need me."

I thought to myself, "You old bastard, these men of yours have walked all the way from Utah Beach, and the walk wasn't easy, but you're too damn lazy to walk a mile to let them see that you're at least interested in what they are doing."

Our objective was about a mile away over rolling terrain. Company E and Company G would attack abreast with Company E on the right and Company G on the left. Company E also had a couple of tanks with it. Both our 81s and some 4.2-inch mortars were set up to give supporting fires.

The attack started off beautifully. Both companies were well spread out. When they were halfway to town, the Krauts opened up on the men with machine guns, small arms, and 20mm and 37mm antiaircraft guns, and on the tanks with antitank guns.

First Sergeant Bloodworth, Bill Butz, Emmett Taylor, and I were up on the hill with Major Williams. As a couple of tanks rumbled by us, I hugged the ground as close as I could, but that stuff was still coming too close. I got tangled up in a barbed wire fence and almost ripped all of my clothes off trying to get loose.

Our boys were down on the ground now, but they kept moving. The major had good radio control and he kept both Damkowitch and McDonell abreast of one another's progress. They captured the town about twilight. I learned that Lieutenant McAlpin had been hit pretty badly. Part of his shoulder had been torn off from a round that had hit a tank he was standing by.

The rest of the battalion finally got into the town right after dark. We knew nothing about the town and it was hard as hell to set up a defense at night. Company E was on the side of town facing Erfurt, Company F was to its right, and Company G wrapped around the back end.

The major sent for the burgermeister and, with the help of an interpreter, told him that he wanted the same old thing: all civilians indoors and all weapons turned in. If any of the Kraut civilians helped the Kraut soldiers or hindered the American soldiers, they would be shot. I told Jerry Sheehan that I didn't like this setup at all: it was dark and we couldn't see just exactly what we had. Sergeant Walstad's machine gun platoon was with Company E, Sergeant Ross's machine gun platoon was with Mike Damkowitch, and the mortars set up near the center of town. I was right to be worried.

At 6:00 a.m. on April 12, some 300 SS troops accompanied by four tanks attacked us. The brunt of the attack hit Company E and Walstad's machine guns. A new lieutenant with Company E pulled his platoon out and left Walstad's gunners with only one squad of riflemen. I don't know why, but that single rifle squad refused to pull out when they saw that the machine gunners were not going to pull out. I guess they weren't going to leave their buddies.

Some of the Krauts and two of the tanks got through our lines. One of the tanks was poking its nose around the corner of a building on the street when a Sherman tank sneaked around the corner to get it. As the Sherman was creeping up the street, a Kraut civilian poked a Panzerfaust out the window and knocked off one of the tank's tracks. The boys nailed the bastard a little later. One of our tank destroyers bypassed the Sherman and got the tank and its crew. Machine guns, both ours and theirs, were zooming up and down all of the streets and it was dangerous business to stick your head around a corner. A woman up the street came running out of her house frantically pointed to her cellar. Mike Damkowitch and I got some of his men to investigate. A Kraut was hiding in there. The boys killed him. I guess the woman was afraid she'd be shot if she was caught harboring an enemy soldier. If so, she was right; we would have.

We lost contact with Company E and both machine gun sections that were bearing the blunt of the attack. The major told Mike Damkowitch to send one of his rifle platoons to find out what was happening. Bill Butz went with one part of the platoon to look for one section of machine guns, and I went with the other. The long lanky sergeant who was the tank destroyer platoon leader said that he would take one of his tank destroyers with us. I decided to walk along with him.

Things were fairly quiet now, but I was still scared as hell. We were down the street a few blocks when the sergeant and I saw some movement in a house. We thought that was where our boys should be. Since we did not particularly care to be out on the street, we ran to the house and flung open the door. About six Krauts were standing in the hallway. They were as surprised to see us as we were to see them!

I never knew I could run so fast. I even outran the long-legged sergeant. The gunner in the tank destroyer figured out what had happened and was swinging his turret around as the sergeant and I skidded around the protective sides of the tank destroyer. One of the Krauts tossed a grenade at us. The damn thing went off just as we rounded the TD, and a piece of it hit my wrist. I thought right then and there that I had lost my hand. About that time the turret gunner was spraying the house with his .50-caliber machine gun. I was scared as hell. Mike Damkowitch was behind a stone fence across the street. He yelled for me to come over. I didn't waste any time getting there. Mike's men were closing in on the house now. It didn't take them long to get what was left of the Krauts after the .50-caliber got through with them.

When I finally had a chance to look at my hand, I was happy as hell to see it was still there. It was numb and I couldn't move it. The shrapnel had cut the band of my wrist watch and I was about to lose it. My hand and arm had no feeling in them, and I couldn't move them. "It's a damn shame it wasn't a little deeper and a little more serious, Andy. You could have been evacuated!" said Mike. It would have been nice to go back to the hospital for a little rest.

We finally got to the machine gunners. They had a field day. They had their guns in the upstairs windows of houses on the outskirts of the town. Between our town and the city of Erfurt was about 800 yards of open ground. The Krauts had come right across the open ground into the range of the machine guns, and were mowed down.

Later, we got the whole story from our prisoners. The Germans were ordered to attack before daylight, but for some reason they hadn't. One body of the attackers was supposed to come straight in from Erfurt, and another body was to skirt around the left flank. The Krauts on the left flank, the ones who were supposed to come around our rear, had run into the 1st Battalion as it was moving into our town with us.

Sergeant Walstad and his gunners had let the Krauts come in close before they opened up on them. In fact, they let them come in too close, because some of them were able to get through. The Krauts put a couple of Panzerfaust shots through the window of one of the sergeant's houses, and that really pissed him off.

All of it had not been a bed of roses, though. Some of our boys had been hit, some of them captured, and some of them murdered. Not killed in action—*murdered*. Part of a squad from Company E had been caught in a house sitting out in the open. The circumstance was a bad one, and they had the choice of surrendering or being killed. They chose to surrender and came out with their hands up. Three of them had Lugers strapped to their belts; they had taken them from Kraut prisoners captured a few days earlier. Their SS captors didn't even question them. Instead, they put a bullet through each of their heads. I saw their bodies and what was left of their heads.

Two of their buddies who managed to get away from the Krauts a few days later told us what happened. These SS were part of the Hermann Göring Division. They were mean customers to deal with. We hadn't taken many SS prisoners, but we decided from now on that no SS troops would be taken alive.

Sergeant Red Anderson, one of our machine gunners, had spotted a sniper who had sneaked around behind his squad and was picking at his boys. He went out to get him. On the way out he was hit pretty bad in the hip and leg. Themuda and Huston were covering Sergeant Anderson as he went out. When they saw he had been hit, both of them went out to bring him back to cover. When they reached him, a Kraut hiding in the bushes near Anderson threw a grenade that exploded close by, wounding Huston pretty badly. Themuda shot the Kraut with his pistol. Huston was too badly hit to help bring Anderson in, so Themuda told him to go back by himself while he brought Sergeant Anderson in. Huston's buddies kept him covered. Anderson got the Silver Star and Themuda and Huston each got the Bronze Star. Sergeant Walstad was hit twice in the leg by a sniper who had sneaked around to his rear.

By noon, things were fairly quiet in our sector, but the 318th Regiment was having a hard time trying to get into Erfurt. The rest of the 1st Battalion moved on through us.

We started moving out about the middle of the afternoon. As we were leaving, the Krauts started throwing in artillery and mortars. Some of the men were wounded by the shrapnel. We had to hold it up for a little while one combat team of the 4th Armored Division came through us. The armor boys were bypassing Erfurt and fanning out. It was always a comfortable feeling to have the 4th Armored around us. Our mission was to move way the hell out and take a little town. We didn't think we'd run into much, but you could never tell.

Lieutenant George McDonell had a lot of casualties that morning, and he was mad as hell about it. While we were walking down the road, he picked up a civilian and made him march with him. I asked him what the score was, and he said that this old bastard had two sons in the service, and "I'm going to make him walk until his feet hurt as much as mine do."

On the way, we passed a dummy airfield the Krauts had fixed up. It was even decorated with dummy planes. We had been moving fast for the past few weeks and, as usual, our column was too close together. We had jeeps mixed in with our foot troops. As the head of our column entered the town, the Krauts opened up on us from the left with antiaircraft guns. It didn't take long for everybody to get into town and under cover.

Our town was on the side of a sloping open hill and we were way out by ourselves. Major Williams ordered a perimeter defense and said, "We may be way out here on a limb by ourselves, but we've got three day's rations, so if anything happens we'll dig in and hold on until they send us help."

Two Krauts cut around the far edge of town. I took a shot at one of them but missed him by a mile.

We had a radio contact and every half hour would check in. In the middle of the night Captain Mattlock ran into trouble. He had lost contact with one of his outposts, and one of his boys came in and told him the outpost had been overrun and the men in it killed. Matt called the major over the radio and told him that he was going out, and that things may not be cooking when he got there but that would soon change.

It turned out later that the soldier had been suffering from hysteria and that everything was all right. The only problem was that the telephone line to the outpost had been cut.

Chapter *16*

BUCHENWALD

―――――――――――――――――――――――――――――――――

April 13, 1945–April 15, 1945

The next morning, April 13, we took another little town without any trouble. It was near Weimar, the birthplace of the German Republic in 1919. The division had been given the mission of taking it and the Buchenwald concentration camp, located about three miles to the northwest. My battalion was to take and hold a little town on the flank of Weimar while the 319th Regiment took Weimar itself. We had been hearing rumors about atrocities for many weeks, but had no idea of what we were about to encounter.

On the outskirts of town was a little hill. Bill Butz and I went with Major Williams to the top of the hill for a look-see. We had been there only a little while when we saw six men, formed as skirmishers, coming toward us with their rifles at their hips. Naturally we spread out and took cover. This would have been a hell of a time for the Krauts to attack us, as all of our men were just moving into town.

We looked through our glasses. The men heading toward us were not wearing helmets. When they came closer, we saw their striped pants and shirts and realized they were escapees from the concentration camp. Soon enough we found out they were Russians. Then they told us what had happened.

Fifteen thousand of them had overpowered their SS guards at Buchenwald. They had taken their weapons and spread out to find and kill Krauts—particularly SS. Major Williams was a little skeptical. About that time, one of Company G's scouts brought up an SS soldier he had caught in the woods. The major pointed to the Kraut and told the Russians, "Him SS." One of the Russians said, "Give him to me." Then he kicked the SS man and told him to start running. The Russian took aim and let him have it. Before he had covered twenty yards he had more holes in him than a sieve.

We later became more acquainted with the Russian escapees and learned a lot about daily life in the concentration camp. Two of them were infantry lieutenants who had been captured at Stalingrad. They wanted to stay with us and fight with the Americans until we met up with the Russians. When we got to Weimar, the major put them into GI uniforms. They were happy to take care of any SS troops for us. And they did.

* * *

We moved to the flank town of Weimar, a city of 50,000, but we didn't even stop there. We were on the outskirts when the major received word that two battalions of the 319th were getting ready to attack Weimar and the mayor of the city had ridden out on his bicycle and surrendered the town unconditionally. The 319th moved in without firing a shot, tramping through streets lined with cheering civilians. We were then ordered into Weimar.

My feet were killing me, but as we moved into Weimar I forgot all about them. It was like a circus in that city. There were several hundred Kraut troops stationed and on leave in Weimar. The mayor ordered all Kraut soldiers, as well as civilians to turn in their arms; the Kraut soldiers had to turn themselves in by dark.

It was the strangest sight I'd ever seen. As we were marching down the street we passed a Kraut army hospital. Hundreds of Krauts stuck their heads out of the windows and looked at us. A little German boy, about nine years old, came running down the street with his hands over his head. Somebody had scared him. I calmed him down and let him walk with me to show him that we weren't going to kill him. Hitler surely had stuffed the heads of his youth with wild tales about the Americans.

When we got to the center of town, the sights were even stranger. Kraut policemen, still armed, were directing traffic and Kraut soldiers were walking everywhere. It reminded me of a big army town back home. Only the uniforms were different colors.

Civilians were taking all sorts of arms and swords to the major's office and turning them in. Pretty girls were turning in their husband's war trophies. Old men were taking in their collection of old swords and muzzle loaders. Men and women were pulling carts loaded with guns and swords.

When we got to our area, Mac and I went looking for billets while the men sat around marveling at what was going on around them. Two good- looking girls walked down the street carrying a bag between them. Mac said, "There's Lugers in that bag." We both started running. Mac grabbed the bag. I reached first. I came out with two horse pistols. Mac took his time and came out with two Lugers. I tried to pull rank on him and we made a deal. I traded him a watch that I had gotten earlier in the morning for a Luger.

We got settled in our billets and Sergeant Bloodworth and I proceeded to warm up a K-ration. It seemed as if these city folks didn't have as much in their cellars as the country folks, so we didn't have anything to supplement our meal. There was a young professor and his wife in our apartment (or we were in their apartment). I proceeded to tell them what a wonderful country America was, and what big corn and strawberries we grew there, and how rotten Nazism had made Germany. They agreed with me one hundred percent. It's funny how none of the people I talked to were Nazis or had voted Hitler into power, but they always told me that their neighbors had.

About the middle of the afternoon, the 319th moved out of Weimar and the rest of my regiment moved in. We were given the mission of maintaining law and order in the city. The 2d Battalion concentrated in the middle of town. Company H was given the mission of patrolling the town with its machine gun jeeps. I checked the patrols occasionally. People were still turning in their arms and wives were walking with their soldier husbands while they turned themselves in. Looters were breaking into stores and taking food and clothing. German civilians were helping themselves. It's funny how Krauts will rob their brothers. We had a hard job trying to stop them.

The next day, April 14, Bill Butz left for the States. I hated to see him go. We had gone to OCS together, had joined the same company on the same day, and had fought our way across Europe side by side. Somehow we had managed to survive. This war was about over and we were getting where we could enjoy life a little with beds to sleep in instead of snow- filled foxholes. We were getting hot chow occasionally instead of frozen K-rations, and we were getting champagne by the barrel and things to go with champagne. Bill and a machine gun platoon leader from the 318th Regiment were the only line officers who came overseas with the division who had not missed a single day of combat. Of course, it was past due for him to get a break like going home, but I still hated to see him go. I took over as commanding officer of Company H.

We stayed in Weimar for three days, taking advantage of the attractions that can be found in a city. Major Williams was promoted to lieutenant colonel, which called for a celebration. He had his CP in the best hotel in town, filled with plush suites, a dining room and an orchestra. We decided to have a banquet in style. That is, with certain limitations.

I only had one pair of pants to my name, and they were as stiff as a board from the dirt, but my apartment had a bath and I found a girl to make my pants presentable. Our newly minted colonel had the hotel staff make the arrangements. We had everything from pink champagne to liquor. During the course of the evening, toasts were proposed.

Soon it was Tom Moss's turn. He was our artillery liaison officer. "I've been fighting with you infantry birds for a long time," he said, "and all I ever hear is 'Infantry, Infantry, Infantry,' and I'm getting tired of it." Everyone stopped laughing and looked at Tom. "I propose a toast," he continued. "The Infantry may be Queen of Battle, but the artillery is King of Battle." Tom let out a big grin. "Because the King places his balls where it makes the Queen happy." Everybody roared.

The party broke up about midnight. Some of us thought it was still a little early, so we proceeded to take in the night life of the city. Lieutenant Hoffman, my German-speaking artilleryman, had a nice quiet little apartment off by itself. Lieutenant Hartnett and I decided to join him in a private little party there.

* * *

Lieutenant George McDonell, Company E's CO, and one of my machine gun platoons were guarding and maintaining order at the Buchenwald concentration camp. The place was horrible beyond description. There were thousands of prisoners composed of every nationality, creed, and color in the world. Twenty different languages were spoken there.

I walked into a prisoner barracks with McDonell. Perhaps 100 men could have arranged themselves comfortably in there, but the Krauts had crowded in more than 1,000. There were wooden bunks from the floor to the ceiling, just like shelves. Once a man got on his "shelf" he didn't even have enough room to turn over.

Some of the prisoners had a thin, stinking blanket. Others had none. Some were too weak to get up, and they looked at us with dull eyes, not realizing who we were or what was going on. To say that they were nothing but skin and bones is not enough. They had ugly looking running sores, swollen ankles, and their minds were often deranged.

Everything stank. General McBride came out and inspected Buchenwald. He ordered all the windows broken out and said he would send several truckloads of blankets down. Of course, higher echelons were sending medical staffs and food. There were more than 20,000 prisoners still in Buchenwald by the time the 80th Division arrived. This was the first major German concentration camp to fall into Allied hands while it still had a full population of prisoners.[1]

Outside were what looked to be thousands of naked bundles of dead skin and bones, their torsos and faces twisted in all sorts of grotesque designs. Bodies were stacked on top of bodies, neatly arranged, and stacked like cords of wood. The stack was about five or six feet high and extended for about fifty feet. All were dead, all were naked, and all were face up. It was a sickening sight because beyond this stack of bodies were more stacks of bodies. And more beyond that.

And then we discovered the crematorium. Set in the brick walls were small openings with iron doors about two feet wide and two feet high. There were several sets of these doors. Most were closed, but we found one wide open. Inside were heavy metal trays with partially burned bodies. It looked like each tray could hold three corpses at one time.

It was later estimated that during the last part of the war, about 5,000 prisoners died each month at Buchenwald. We found one huge hole where thousands of naked bodies had been dumped. The Krauts had tried to burn the bodies to hide the evidence, but we had gotten there too soon. The smell of death stayed in my nostrils for days.

From the day it opened to the day we closed it, 32,887 prisoners died at Buchenwald—not including those who were quickly executed, sent on death transports to extermination camps, or those in the worst condition who were transferred to other camps. An estimated death toll of 55,000 in seven and one-half years—an average of 7,300 per year—would not be too high.[2]

A day or two later, the mayor of Weimar, his wife, and citizens of Weimar were brought to see the sights of Buchenwald. They were met at the gates of the concentration camp by an interpreter and were given a tour. In fact, because of a problem of citizens returning to Weimar after the tour, they were brought back and given another slower, more "detailed" tour of all the facilities at the camp. The mayor of the town of Ohrdruf committed suicide, along with his wife, after General Eisenhower ordered the townspeople to visit one of Buchenwald's satellite camps near Ohrdruf.

The internees had their former SS guards safely stowed away in a cellar. We took a look at them. They looked the part: animals with no souls and no hearts. Even the SS women who managed the women prisoners looked utterly evil. Everyone had the same question on their minds: *How could a human being do this to another human being, let alone thousands of men, women, and children?*

One of the men showed us something he had found. It seems the wife of the commandant of Buchenwald, Ilse Koch, was quite a collector. She collected tattoos and had several boards of tattoos. Any prisoner who had tattoo marks on his body would have his skin peeled off for the lady's collection. We later learned that she rode her horse through the camp, looking for prisoners with tattoos. When she found one, she tapped him with her riding whip and the Kraut guards would haul him away to the infirmary. Whether the prisoners were skinned alive or not, I don't know. Because of her "experiments," she was known as the "Bitch of Buchenwald." She had a beautiful, but grotesque, collection. There were works of art there from tattoo artists from all over the world. She was later arrested and sentenced to life in prison, and killed herself while in prison in 1967.

Later, we visited the SS Officer's quarters. There we found lamp shades made from tanned human skin with tattoos on them. Some of the men took them for souvenirs. That made me sick. At the Nuremberg war crimes trial for Ilse Koch, exhibits included a piece of tattooed skin tanned at Buchenwald especially for her.

One of the men showed us some photos he found. Two of them were very disturbing and I have never forgotten them. The first showed a naked man who had a rope with a hook on one end of it fixed through his testicles. The other end of the rope was tied to the limb of a tree, suspending the man above the snow-covered ground. His organs were stretched hideously out of proportion and he was drawn up in utter agony. The prisoners we had taken told us that the picture had been taken while the man was still alive.

In the second picture, his body was limp in death.

Chapter 17

NUREMBERG

April 15, 1945–April 28, 1945

We left Weimar on the morning of April 15 and moved forty-five miles to Hermsdorf. Colonel Williams had been given the mission of cleaning out a stretch of woods eight miles deep that lay between Hermsdorf and Bad Kostritz. An autobahn ran along the edge of the woods and small bands of snipers had been picking at convoys as well as mining the road and occasionally pulling a raid.

The colonel didn't lose any time getting started. We were to attack the minute we piled off the trucks. Company G and Company E attacked through the woods, each with a machine gun platoon from Company H. Company F guided along a road that ran through the woods. The mortars displaced forward, one section at a time, and we had five tanks with us.

When we were about halfway through the woods, Lt. Mike Damkowitch ran into snipers and a Kraut killed one of his sergeants. The German ran out of ammunition and came out with his hands up. He took about two steps and had enough lead in him to make him weigh a ton. That was the dirtiest thing a Kraut could do: kill your men until he ran out of ammunition and then come out with a grin like it was all in fun and try to give himself up.

We passed through a couple of little towns and rounded up a few Krauts who were home on leave. We looked at the papers of some of the civilians. Two men dressed in civilian clothes had Wehrmacht identification papers. Lieutenant Colonel Fisher, the 317th commanding officer, was up to see how things were coming along, and one of the Krauts gave him a "Heil Hitler" salute. Colonel Williams kicked him in the ass to teach him a little respect for his superior officers. He didn't pull that "Heil Hitler" crap again.

One of my mortar jeeps came speeding down the road with six men in it. The regimental CO barked, "Adkins, is that your jeep?"

I answered, "Yes, Sir. They're displacing a section of mortars forward so they can give close support to Company G."

"Damn it," the CO said. "Didn't you know there was an order out saying that only five men were to ride in a jeep?"

"Yes, Sir," I replied, "but we need those mortars up fast."

"That makes no difference," the CO snorted. "Don't you ever let me catch you with more than five men on a jeep again."

"Yes, Sir." I said, thinking, *Why is it that we never saw your sorry ass back in the Ardennes or the Moselle River, when it was so cold? You could really chew butt the way we were violating uniform regulations, wearing anything we could lay our hands on, while trying to keep from freezing to death.*

We were nearing the edge of the woods when a burp gun opened up on us from the right flank. It scared the hell out of me. I never did like fighting in woods; you couldn't see anything. Thankfully, no one was hit. We all hugged the ground while Company G took care of the burp gunner. He didn't give us any more trouble.

We got into Bad Kostritz about five in the afternoon. Company G came strolling in with a large number of prisoners. First Sergeant Smith was as mad as hell, and he had the Krauts, about thirty of them, marching in step at rigid attention.

We stayed in Bad Kostritz for five days. It was a nice little town, untouched by war. First Sergeant Bloodworth was getting ready to go home on furlough, so I brought Sgt. Ed Turner, our assistant supply sergeant, to learn a little about first sergeant work.

As always when we had a break, we cleaned ourselves, our jeeps, and our guns, and carried on a little training. My machine guns were in bad shape. If we were to take all of the haywire and solder out of them, they would have fallen apart. I tried for a long time to get them replaced with new ones, but the battalion S-4 couldn't help me because, as he said, they were still striking back home. The tank captain had a brand-new one on his jeep that he had picked up somewhere, so I made a deal with him. He wanted a light .30-caliber machine gun, so I got one from Carl Carlson, our battalion S-4, and traded it to him.

The colonel called a company commanders' meeting. When we were done with business, he served us champagne. We were sitting around in a bull session when a runner came in and told us that Lieutenant McAlpin had died in the hospital. He has been torn apart outside Erfurt by a chunk of steel that had ricocheted off a tank. Colonel Williams bowed his head a minute, then stood up, raised his glass, and said, "Gentlemen, to Lt. Virgil McAlpin." McAlpin was quite a guy. He was a brave man and afraid of nothing. He was the battalion S-2 who often took one of my machine gun jeeps out ahead of us to looks for Krauts.

One day while we were in Bad Kostritz we had a parade. A little while before the parade I saw Sergeant Pollectcus, the regimental sergeant major, who probably knew more about the regiment than any other man in it. I told him that John Windsor had been awarded the Silver Star for a deed he had done along the Moselle eight months earlier, but had never received the medal. The good sergeant major told me that he would take care of it, and he hurried off to Regiment. I rounded up Windsor, and pretty soon Colonel Fisher came back with Pollectcus. Windsor and another man from Company G reviewed the parade and, afterward, Colonel Fisher pinned their Silver Stars on them.

We had more champagne than we knew what to do with. We were even getting particular about what brand we drank. If it wasn't pink champagne, we threw it away. I wish I could have gotten a couple of truckloads of it home.

We left Bad Kostritz early in the morning of April 20 and moved 150 miles by truck. Our destination was Burglesan, a farm town composed of about twelve buildings, three fourths of which were barns. Our job was to maintain law and order and patrol the place. The war was about over now, but we did not know just when it would fold up completely. While we were there, we had a clothing and equipment check.

In my house were an old farmer, his wife, and two daughters. The farmer was a harmless old soul who hadn't paid much attention to the war. He had one weakness, though, and that was schnapps. He hadn't been getting much lately, and he sure missed it. Some of the men decided to please him and gave him some schnapps. He was just like a kid at a circus. I've never seen a more jovial drunk in my life. I laughed with him until I thought my sides would split.

Lieutenant Edwin Heller and his machine gun platoon were in a country guest house across the street. The cellar was full of beer, so he set up a club for the company. The men really enjoyed themselves.

We left Burglesan on the morning of April 23 and moved to Nuremberg to relieve the 3d Infantry Division. Nuremberg had been beaten to a pulp. It had formerly been a walled city with a moat around it—a medieval jewel no longer, courtesy of Mr. Hitler.

I relieved a heavy weapons company of the 3d Division and was given the mission of furnishing 24-hour motorized patrols with radios throughout the city. The riflemen had walking patrols through the city and my boys coordinated with them. The 3d and 45th Infantry Divisions had a hard time taking Nuremberg, and the civilians were hostile. Snipers were raising hell and our boys had to be very careful. Our job was to maintain law and order, enforce military law, prevent looting, and continue our training. Most important, though, was to give the men a much-needed rest and time to clean and repair their weapons.

We arrived there in the morning and my patrols were working by noon. About the middle of the afternoon, one of my jeeps brought in two German civilians who had shot at my troops. One shot went through the windshield and another through the hood. The boys had just missed getting hit.

These Krauts were little dried-up men in their late thirties. My battalion hadn't gotten settled yet, so I took them around to 3d Division Intelligence. I didn't want to bloody up my place. There were two Poles there who still bore the scars of concentration camp life. They could speak German, so the Intelligence Officer and I told them to get some information out of these guys.

These Krauts were died-in-the-wool Nazis. They wouldn't say a word, even though they knew that they would probably die for trying to kill my men. We searched them. One of them had a cat-o-nine-tails whip. One of the Poles grabbed it and told the Kraut to talk. There was a gang of snipers on the loose in Nuremberg dressed in civilian clothes, and we wanted to know about them. The Kraut refused. The

Pole started beating him, but the Kraut still didn't talk. The other Pole joined in, but the Kraut still didn't talk. He just whimpered like a rat caught in a trap. I left eventually. I don't know if the Krauts talked before they died or not, but I don't think they did.

Nuremberg was dangerous at night. All that was left of the town was a pile of rubbish. At night, the ruins silhouetted against the sky looked like death. At all hours of the day, civilians could be seen digging out their dead from the ruins and carrying the limp forms away in sheets and blankets. It was like Hell. There was only one water point in our section of the city, and all day long civilians lined up with their buckets and pitchers to get some.

My CP was in a bakery. It was warm there. We let the people run their bakery, but we borrowed a few of their rooms. When I first walked in, I went into the bathroom. Out of habit I turned on the hot water spigot of the tub to see if it worked. Sure enough, hot water came out, so I just let it run, pulled off my clothes, and took a bath. We had hot water the whole time we were there. Those were the advantages of living in a bakery—plenty of hot water and plenty of heat.

The couple who ran the bakery had an anemic little daughter named Nellie. She took a fancy to me, and pretty soon we became close friends. She reminded me of a Dali painting of a bean pole. I don't know why she liked me so much. Maybe I looked like an anemic bean pole to her, and she liked anemic bean poles.

Anyway, she took it upon herself to look after my clothes. I had just one pair of trousers, so I had to stay indoors while she cleaned and pressed them. I also had an old torn trench coat I had bought in London the previous November, and had worn it all through the winter without taking it off. It was now every color in the rainbow. It had everything on it from blood to K-ration stains. Nellie thought she could make it presentable. I didn't believe it possible, especially since the coat weighed more than she did. But she scrubbed and scrubbed and sewed up holes, and when she finished, it looked pretty good.

Across from my area were the repair shops and headquarters for the communication system of Nuremberg. I had guards posted on it with orders that no one was to enter. One day this major came to me with credentials that authorized him to take over the installation. He told me that for the last year he had done nothing but study the communication setup of the city of Nuremberg so that when American troops took the city, he would come in and take over the system. He had even studied the German language. Boy, what a racket. Why couldn't I have gotten a job like that? Can you imagine doing nothing for a year but sitting around some headquarters reading books and waiting for the infantry to take some town?

Nuremberg had been the seat of Nazism. The city was full of stadiums, a sportzplatz, and parade fields where Hitler and his buddies gathered thousands of their followers together for a real Nazi pow-wow.

Things were going pretty easy so Colonel Williams challenged the 1st Battalion to a ball game, complete with a band and Red Cross girls. We had two games, one played by the enlisted men and one played by the officers. The 1st Battalion won both games.

I had three men, Private First Class Terribilini, Sergeant McQuain, and Private Ford, who had Bronze Stars coming to them. The colonel decided to have a parade, complete with marching music over a PA system, right where Hitler used to parade his would-be world conquerors. I always did like a parade, especially when we could march to the tune of "What do they do in the Infantry?"

After the ball game, the colonel thought it was about time we had a little party, so that night we all went around to the CP. George McDonell was promoted to captain there. We had a two-and-one-half ton truck whose sole mission was to carry the beverages we had picked up here and there. Whenever the opportunity presented itself, the colonel would send the truck around to each of his companies and give the men a liquor ration. He didn't mind how much his men drank as long as they drank it like a man. (No one I knew drank during battle.) Things got dull at the party, so I called up John DePauw, my runner, and asked him to come up and play for us.

John was nineteen. He had left college to come into the army. He could speak German, and he could play the piano like Eddie Duchin. Man, that boy knew how to play a piano. He could change from boogie woogie to Chopin without missing a beat. The officers almost went wild when they heard him play. As a reward, the colonel gave him a pass to Paris. John had a doctor brother stationed there, and that pass suited him just fine.

The colonel called me around to his CP the next morning. When I got there, he asked me if I had looked at my kitchen lately. I told him that I hadn't looked at it too closely. He said, "Don't you think it would be a good idea if you looked it over now and then?" I agreed that it was a good idea, then he handed me a piece of paper. He had inspected the kitchens of his battalion that morning and everybody had been rated excellent but Company H. Mine was rated "unsatisfactory." That's what I liked about the colonel—he was always frank with you and, if you were wrong, he would chew your pants out from stem to stern. But when he finished, he'd offer you a drink, and that was all that was said about the matter. I left the colonel and went to look at my kitchen. After what we had been through—crapping and eating out of the same helmet came to mind—it didn't seem too bad to me, but I admit it did not resemble my mother's kitchen. I turned the colonel's tactics on Sergeant Benifield, Company H's mess sergeant. It wasn't long before the kitchen looked more like mom's.

Tom Moss, our artillery liaison officer, invited Damkowitch, McDonell, Carlson, and me to go out to the airport with him and take a ride over Nuremberg in one of the 313th's observation planes. It was quite a thrill to see Nuremberg from the air. Boy, that town had been splattered by our bombers and our artillery. I got some good pictures.

There was a German doctor living next door to me who had been to America and who spoke English. I went over to see him my first day there. He didn't seem to like Hitler (but few admitted it anyway). He had an edition of *Stars and Stripes* that someone had left there, and in it was an editorial suggesting the Nazi leaders had withheld the truth from their people. The doctor agreed with the editorial.

He was listening to a German newscast over his radio when I got there. He was laughing at it. "What is the guy on the radio saying?" I asked.

"The newscaster is telling his audience that the American troops are suffering heavy casualties trying to take Nuremberg, and it looks as if the Americans will give it up as hopeless because of our stubborn defense!"

Our troops had been in Nuremberg for three days.

Chapter *18*
THE END OF THE WAR

April 29, 1945–May 8, 1945

The war was a rat race now. It looked as if the dough boys' job was about over. Armored columns were shooting out from everywhere. All we could do was to pile into our jeeps and trucks and drive like hell to catch up. Occasionally, we ran into some die-hard Nazis who refused to surrender. We accommodated them accordingly.

When we took these long jaunts along the autobahns or other roads, we didn't even bother with prisoners. There were too many of them. They were giving up by the thousands. All along the road were Krauts in a column of twos marching to the rear. Sometimes they carried white flags and sometimes they didn't. Wives were walking with their husbands while they were going to turn themselves in. Sometimes they carried the baby along. No one was paying any attention to the Krauts. We just told them to keep moving to the rear.

German equipment was everywhere. I wished that some of my buddies were still alive to witness these sights. What a contrast these people were to the SS troops we had fought a few months earlier. We never took an objective without being counterattacked, and those counterattacks were of the first order, too. The Krauts came in until it was hand-to-hand combat, and somebody was always hurt.

In addition to its original personnel of approximately 1,000 men and officers, the 2d Battalion had 3,334 reinforcements come to it during its nine months of combat. My company landed in France with 152 men and 7 officers. During its time in the ETO, Company H, 2d Battalion, 317th Infantry Regiment, had 608 men and 31 officers come in as replacements. Thirty-six of them were killed in action. Hundreds of others were wounded. Of course, there were other outfits that had experiences that made ours look like a walk in the park. But there were also outfits that hadn't seen as much of this war. When the Germans surrendered 274 days after we landed at Utah Beach, 187 men of Company H were still in the hospital.

* * *

We left Nuremberg early on the morning of April 29 and moved to the little town of Alteglofsheim. My CP was in a school house. I opened a door of a bedroom. In bed was a dreamy-eyed brunette with her hair spread out on the pillow. I didn't know what to think. She was pale. I brought Million in to do a little interrogating. A plane had strafed her house and she had been hit in the arm. She had no doctor to look at her. Her arm was swollen and black. It looked like gangrene. I asked Doc Price to drop around. He dressed her arm and the next day we sent her to Regensburg in an ambulance. I never learned what happened to her.

There was an old-maid school teacher living there who could speak a little English. I tried to get her views on the war and German's pending defeat. I've never seen a woman so scared of men. If I tried to move within ten feet of her, she would raise her screechy voice to such a high pitch that I thought the windows would break.

On April 30 we moved to a little town on the north bank of the Isar River. Across the river from us was the town of Dingolfing, Germany. We were approaching the Austrian border. Two of our battalions had already crossed the river to the west of us and were getting ready to move into Dingolfing. Our mission was to secure the north bank opposite Dingolfing while the other battalions moved in.

Lieutenant Edwin Heller set up the mortars and I sent Sergeant Ross and Sergeant Christopher with their machine gun platoons with Company E and Company G to the river bank. Right before dark the Krauts pulled out of Dingolfing and our other battalion moved in. We settled down for the night. There were two pretty girls in my house, but Colonel Williams kept me busy all the time. I didn't have the chance to get to know the frauleins. The weather was cold and rainy and we had frosty mornings.

The next day, May 1, 1st Sergeant Bloodworth left for the States. He had been with the company a long time and had seen his share of fighting. I was sorry to see him go.

Around noon, we crossed the Isar River to Dingolfing in assault boats. Even though we had intermittent rain and snow, this was the way I liked to cross rivers: in assault boats with no one shooting at us!

After changing positions and outposts a few times we settled down to enjoy the advantages of Dingolfing. It was a beautiful little town scattered over several hills. Most of the homes were new and modern. George McDonell and Company E were in the center of town down by the river. He had setup in a hotel. It was quite a scene. He took over a restaurant for his men and had a blonde vocalist and a guitarist to entertain them while they sat around and drank beer. The men had it easy.

We just had a few outposts and changed them frequently. Some of my men liberated quite a few boxes of silk stockings, sweaters, and gloves. Everybody got all they wanted, and we stowed the rest away on our jeeps to save them for men going to Paris or the Riviera. The women there would be quite appreciative.

* * *

We received word on May 1 that Adolf Hitler was dead. He had committed suicide. All kinds of thoughts went through my mind, including what I would have done had I gotten my hands on him. I'm sure the other men had similar thoughts. Fighting Krauts for months in the cold, living in rain-filled holes, and seeing so much death gets to a guy after a while. If Hitler was dead and the Krauts were retreating, then the surrender couldn't be far off, could it?

One day, while one of the runners and I were walking down the street, two good-looking girls passed us, gave us the eye, and made some remark in French. I knew a little French, so I tried out my line to see if it was rusty or not. The girls were French and had been brought to Germany as workers. I had a quiet little house up on the hill. The girls were hungry and liked my silk stockings. I always did have a warm place in my heart for the French.

We hadn't seen our kitchens for quite some time. While we were in Dingolfing, I ate eggs and french-fried potatoes. I had been eating so many eggs lately that I began to cackle. Our kitchens finally caught up with us the day before we moved out.

* * *

On May 4 we moved a hundred miles to Vochlabruck, Austria. We crossed a few rivers that day, including the mighty Danube. We also crossed the Inn River that divides Austria from Germany. There was a sign on the bridge that we crossed: "You are now leaving Germany through the courtesy of the Engineers."

We took a break soon after we had crossed the Inn River. I saw a little puppy dog, just a few weeks old, playing on the grass. He was solid white with the exception of a black spot on the tip of his tail. The minute I saw him I knew he was mine and that his name would be Slingshot, after my good buddy Captain Mattlock. "Slingshot" was a name applied by Mattlock to anybody or anything he did not know. Often I had seen some Kraut come up to Mattlock and start rattling off in German. Mattlock would let the Kraut rattle his head off and nod his head occasionally, even though he didn't speak a word of German. Then Mattlock would say in his slow Arkansas brogue, "Now look, Slingshot . . ."

Slingshot and I came to be good buddies. He ate and slept with me, and after a while he became an old hand at the game of jeep riding. He was careless about his personal habits though, and would relieve himself at the most inopportune times and in the most inappropriate places.

* * *

May 5 was a day I never forgot. Everything and everybody was going wild. We moved sixty miles to Steinbach, Austria, even though we got tangled up with convoys of tanks, tank destroyers, artillery, engineers, and everything else. Everybody was chasing Krauts. Colonel Williams got two of my machine gun jeeps and led our column. Our troops were so thick that one time the colonel tried to cut cross-country. We got to the top of the hill, and spotted several hundred Krauts down in the valley. They didn't know which way to turn. The men threw their machine guns on them and they scattered like rats. Things were too congested to move, so we settled down for the night a mile and a half east of Steinbach.

The next morning, May 6, we moved two miles back across the river to Unt Grunburg. The 3d Battalion was there, but it moved out so we took over their area. I hated to kick that woman out of her nice room, but Slingshot and I had to have a place to sleep.

That afternoon Sergeant Christopher came to tell me that he and some of his men had met this girl who worked in a large small arms factory out from town about ten miles. He wanted to go out and look the joint over. I told him to take two machine guns with him and take a look, but not to stay more than an hour. A few minutes after Sergeant Christopher left, Colonel Williams called me up and told me that he saw my men with a civilian in their jeep. I told him what happened. He didn't like the idea much.

About an hour later Christopher came back with two British soldiers he had found at the factory. I took them to the colonel and they told us about the two small factories. The Brits had been prisoners of war working in the factory. They were mighty glad to see us Yanks. They told us that there were several hundred German and Hungarian troops in the valley around the building, and they thought they would surrender if the Americans would come after them.

The colonel wanted to go fishing out that way, so he arranged to take a rifle platoon, a machine gun platoon, and a section of 81mm mortars with him. On the way out to the factory we passed through a little town. The civilians stopped us and told us that there was an SS trooper dressed in civilian clothes who was threatening to kill the civilians if they didn't fight the Americans. We found him cowering in a house. He wasn't so tough when there was someone there who could kick his ass. The colonel brought him along with us.

We went to the first factory and met the British prisoners. Man, were they glad to see us. Down the valley, across the bridge about a mile, were the Kraut and Hungarian garrisons. Two of the British boys went over to tell them to come out in thirty minutes in a column of twos. While the British boys were gone, a liaison plane flew over. We were undecided whether it was Russian or German. Our Kraut SS man told us that it was German. I grabbed one of the machine guns on the jeep and let go with a belt. It was pretty seeing those tracers shooting up. I came close, but am pretty sure I never hit the plane.

The British boys came back and said the Krauts and Hungarians wanted three hours to get ready. Sergeant Christopher took one jeep and I took the other, and he went after them. The Hungarians were sitting around outside their barracks and it looked as if their first sergeant was having a little trouble getting them to fall out. Christopher fired a few rounds from his machine gun and they came out a little faster.

Down the way a piece was a group of Krauts. They didn't want to march with the Hungarians. Van Court was driving me. He drove that jeep around like he was herding cattle. We backed up a little way and fired a few rounds. The Krauts decided the Hungarians weren't so bad after all.

The British boys said they would destroy the weapons and take care of the stragglers. We went back. The colonel had gone to look the gun factory over. He didn't seem to think there was much to this business, so he had left me to hold the bag.

About that time a Kraut officer came up. He wanted to know what the score was. The British boys were doing the interpreting for me.

"How many men do you have?" I asked.

"I have about one-hundred twenty-five," he answered.

"You have one hour to gather them, lay down your arms, and come down to us in a column of twos."

He looked mad. "I need two hours."

"You have one hour, that's it." I stared at him with hard, cold look.

He was getting red around the gills. "I require two hours!"

"Let me make it clear, buddy. If you are not out in one hour," I said, holding up my forefinger, "I am going to call up for artillery and the tanks waiting down the road, and I'll come in and get your men for you. And they won't be walking out." If he had known all we had were two jeeps, he would probably have scalped me. The British boy made it sound authentic about the tanks and artillery, and the Kraut officer took it all, hook, line and sinker.

Within the hour he came out with his men in a motorized column composed of everything from convertibles to trucks. Frankly, I was scared as hell. He stopped his convoy and his men pitched everything from Lugers to machine guns over the sides of the trucks.

About that time, a Hungarian SS trooper came down out of the hills. His commanding officer had sent him down to find out what was going on. I told him the same thing. "Come out or we're coming in after you" He came back a little later with a message from his commanding officer: come and get us. I decided that then and there it was time to get the hell out.

I led the motorized patrol back while the riflemen took care of the foot column. All the way back to Unt Grunburg the Kraut officer kept looking for our tanks and artillery that were supposed to be there. The farther we went, the redder his face got.

When we reached the POW cage, we compared notes. He had been in command of a tank unit in Normandy and had fought around Argentan the same time we had. He had three tanks knocked out from under him and had been unable to get a replacement as the war wound toward a close.

Colonel Williams came in ahead of the foot column and went fishing with Tom Moss in a little stream on the edge of town. I told him that I would appreciate it if he would not ask me to go on any more fishing trips with him. He laughed and praised the men for bringing in 850 Krauts and Hungarians.

Slingshot and I were staying in a guest house. When we came in that night, the old lady who ran the joint had supper for us. She had made a lettuce salad. Those were the first fresh vegetables I had in quite some time. She called me Herr Kommandant. I liked the sound of that.

The next day, May 7, we moved to Hofern where we arrived at 10:30 p.m. Nothing much happened, so the men took it easy.

During the middle of the morning on May 8 we held up in a little country town in the vicinity of Spital, Austria, and got the men into billets. It was a beautiful day and the grass in my yard was green and soft. Slingshot and I were sitting under a tree and I was cleaning my rifle. Slingshot had oil all over him. I took my shoes off. It really felt good to wiggle my toes in the grass.

Sergeant Albert Melcolm came out and said there was a conference called for all COs. He read a message to us and said that an order would be down in a few minutes. I prayed to God. I asked 1st Sgt. Ed Turner to assemble the company. When the men came in, I told them to sit down and read General Eisenhower's order announcing the end of the war.

Supreme Headquarters Allied Expeditionary Forces

Eisenhower's General Order

1. A representative of the German High Command signed the unconditional surrender of all German land, sea, and air forces in Europe to the Allied Expeditionary Force, and simultaneously to the Soviet High Command at 0141 Hours, Central European Time, 7 May 1945, under which all forces will cease active operations at 0001 Hours, 9 May 1945.

2. Effective immediately all offensive operations by Allied Expeditionary Forces will cease and troops will remain in their present positions. Moves involved in occupational duties will continue. Due to the difficulties of communication there may be some delay in similar orders reaching the enemy troops, so full defensive precautions will be taken.

3. All informed, down to and including Divisions, Tactical Air Commands, and Group and Base Sections and Equivalent. No release will be made to the press pending an announcement by the heads of the three Governments.

Eisenhower

No one said a word for some time. Then, one of my men got up and said, "Lieutenant, read us that again, please."

* * *

Austria 8
May 1945

Dearest Mom & Dad,

Shortly after I wrote to you day before yesterday I received the cease fire order. At that particular time I had my shoes & shirt off & was playing with a little dog on the grass of some Austrian's yard.

My men were all in houses taking it easy. My battalion had momentarily stopped in a little mountain village. I told the first sergeant to assemble the company. As my men came marching up a big lump formed itself in my throat because many familiar faces were missing from the files of men who were to hear me read to them General Eisenhower's order that hostilities had ceased. I told my men to sit down & take it easy & that I had something to tell them. Then I read to them General Eisenhower's order about the unconditional surrender. When I finished no one said a word. Finally, one man said, "Lieutenant, read that again please."

The day that we had died & bled for so long had finally arrived. No one knows what the word "peace" means except those who have been at war. As yet I feel no great emotional change. But gradually I am beginning to realize that there will be no more suffering & no more dying & the sensation is truly wonderful.

Tonight I am in another mountain village high in the Bavarian Alps. I have a radio & can listen to the celebrations that the people in England & America are having. Here, we are having a different type of celebration. Ours is a quiet celebration. We still have to maintain order, but we are so happy & it's hard for us to realize this mess is over.

I love you both dearly.

Devotedly,

Andy

Appendix 1

THE 80TH INFANTRY DIVISION

World War I

The 80th Division was first organized August 5, 1917, in the National Army and headquartered at Camp Lee (now known as Fort Lee), Virginia. The division originally consisted of men mostly from Pennsylvania, Virginia, and West Virginia, and was nicknamed the "Blue Ridge Division." The unit's distinctive insignia was adopted in 1918, and consists of three blue mountain peaks representing the Blue Ridge Mountains in Pennsylvania, Virginia and West Virginia. The division also adopted the Latin Motto *Vis Montium* or "Strength of the Mountains."

In World War I, the 80th Division reached full strength with 23,000 soldiers and sailed to France, landing on June 8, 1918. The 80th Division trained with the British Third Army and joined forces on the front lines near the Artois sector and saw heavy action in the Somme Offensive of 1918 and in the Meuse-Argonne. The 80th returned to the States in May 1919 and was inactivated at Camp Lee on June 26, 1919.

World War II

Twenty three years later, on July 15, 1942, the 80th Division was again ordered into active service. Major General Joseph Dorch Patch, the division's commander, issued General Order No. 1 to reactivate the 80th Division. Initially, soldiers reported to Camp Forrest, Tennessee, named for General

Nathan Bedford Forrest, a famous Confederate calvary commander in the Civil War. The division later moved for training at Camp Phillips, near Salina, Kansas, and in the California-Arizona Desert Training Center (known today as Fort Irwin).

The 80th Division set sail aboard the SS *Queen Mary* on July 4, 1944, landing a few days later on July 7 at Greenock, Firth of Clyde, Scotland. The arrival of the 80th Division in England brought the European Theater of Operations total of U.S. Divisions to 22: 14 infantry, 6 armored, and 2 airborne. By the end of the campaign, there would be a total of 46 divisions in Europe.

The division proceeded south to Northwich, England, via trains for additional training. Training included learning how to waterproof equipment for the upcoming channel crossing. The division crossed the English Channel in LSTs and Liberty Ships, landing in Normandy on Utah Beach shortly after noon on August 3, 1944—D-Day + 58. The division assembled near St. Jores, France. A few days later on August 8, 1944, the 80th was initiated into battle when it took over the LeMans bridgehead in the XX Corps area.

The war ended on May 7, 1945. The 80th Division remained in Europe for several months to help restore and keep peace, and finally returned to the States in January 1946. The division was one of the stalwarts of Patton's Third Army, and had participated in the following campaigns: Northern France, Ardennes, Rhineland, and Central Europe. All the fighting cost the division dearly. During its 277 days of combat, the 80th Division captured 212,295 enemy soldiers, and suffered 17,097 casualties:

Killed in Action: 3,038
Wounded: 12,484
Missing: 488
Captured: 1,077
Total Casualties: 17,097

According to official reports, the 80th Division's "bloodiest day" was October 8, 1944, when approximately 115 men lost their lives. The "bloodiest month" was September, 1944.

Many officers and enlisted men of the 80th Infantry Division received battle honors, including four who received the Medal of Honor:

Sgt. Day G. Turner, Company B, 319th Infantry Regiment, Dahl, Luxembourg, January 8, 1945. Posthumously awarded;

1st Lt. Edgar H. Lloyd, 319th Infantry Regiment, near Pompey, France, September 14, 1944 (KIA). Posthumously awarded;

2d Lt. Harry J. Michael, Company L, 318th Infantry Regiment, Neiderzerf, Germany, March 14, 1945 (KIA). Posthumously awarded;

Pvt. Paul J. Wiedorfer, Company G, 318th Infantry Regiment, near Chaumont, Belgium, December 25, 1944.

Other honors awarded officers and enlisted men of the 80th Infantry Division include:

Distinguished Unit Citations: 6
Distinguished Service Crosses: 48
Silver Stars: 671
Bronze Stars: 3,357

80th Infantry Division: Table of Organization

317th Infantry Regiment
318th Infantry Regiment
319th Infantry Regiment
80th Reconnaissance Troop (Mechanized)
305th Engineer Combat Battalion
305th Medical Battalion

80th Division Artillery

313th Field Artillery Battalion (105mm Howitzer)
314th Field Artillery Battalion (105mm Howitzer)
315th Field Artillery Battalion (155mm Howitzer)
905th Field Artillery Battalion (105mm Howitzer)

Special Troops

780th Ordnance Light Maintenance Company
80th Quartermaster Company
80th Signal Company
Military Police Platoon
Headquarters Company
Band

Attachments

Unit / Dates / Notes

633d AAA AW Bn (Mbl) / 9 AUG 44-13 MAY 45 / Anti-aircraft Artillery

702d Tk Bn (Co D) / 8 AUG 44-27 FEB 45 / Armored

Co D, 702d Tk Bn / 8 AUG 44-1 MAR 45 / Armored

CC B (4th Armored Div) / 29 JAN 45-4 FEB 45 / Armored

CC B (4th Armored Div) / 21 FEB 45-24 FEB 45 / Armored

702d Tk Bn / 11 MAR 45-7 JUL 45 / Armored

42nd Recon Sq (2d Cav Group) / 23 NOV 44-6 DEC 44 / Cavalry

2d Cavalry Recon Sq (2d Cav Group) / 1 DEC 44-6 DEC 44 / Cavalry

16th Cavalry Group / 27 MAR 45-31 MAR 45 / Cavalry

Co A, 91st Chemical Mort Bn / 5 JAN 45-12 JAN 45 / Chemical

Co B, 91st Chemical Mort Bn / 5 JAN 45-28 JAN 45 / Chemical

Co A, 91st Chemical Mort Bn / 28 JAN 45-10 MAR 45 / Chemical

Co A, 81st Chemical Mort Bn / 11 MAR 45-18 APR 45 / Chemical

Co B, 81st Chemical Mort Bn / 27 MAR 45-12 APR 45 / Chemical

Co A, 94th Chemical Mort Bn / 29 APR 45-1 MAY 45 / Chemical

94th Chemical Mort Bn (Co A) / 29 APR 45-11 MAY 45 / Chemical

328th Infantry (26th Div) / 4 OCT 44-14 OCT 44 / Infantry

53d Armored Inf Bn (4th Armored Div) / 4 FEB 45-9 FEB 45 / Infantry

51st Armored Inf Bn (4th Armored Div) / 4 FEB 45-18 FEB 45 / Infantry

53d Armored Inf Bn (4th Armored Div) / 20 FEB 45-21 FEB 45 / Infantry

610th TD Bn (SP) / 9 AUG 44-25 SEP 44 / Tank Destroyer

691st TD Bn (T) / 16 SEP 44-18 SEP 44 / Tank Destroyer

808th TD Bn (SP) / 25 SEP 44-21 DEC 44 / Tank Destroyer

Co C, 602d TD Bn (SP) / 4 OCT 44-14 OCT 44 / Tank Destroyer

610th TD Bn (SP) / 23 NOV 44-6 DEC 44 / Tank Destroyer

610th TD Bn (SP) / 21 DEC 44-28 JAN 45 / Tank Destroyer

Co A, 631st TD Bn (T) / 7 JAN 45-20 JAN 45 / Tank Destroyer

802d TD Bn (T) / 28 JAN 45-4 FEB 45 / Tank Destroyer

811th TD Bn(SP) / 3 FEB 45-4 JUL 45 / Tank Destroyer

Co B, 603d TD Bn (SP) / 4 APR 45-9 APR 45 / Tank Destroyer

Detachments

Detachments / Dates / Notes

319th Infantry / 10 AUG 44-15 AUG 44/XX Corps

319th Infantry / 16 AUG 44-21 AUG 44 / VIII Corps

319th Infantry / 22 AUG 44-27 AUG 44 / XII Corps

319th Infantry / 11 SEP 44-15 SEP 44 / 4th Armored Div

1st Bn, 318th Infantry / 12 SEP 44-15 SEP 44 / 4th Armored Div

1st Bn, 2nd Bn, 318th Infantry / 24 DEC 44-28 DEC 44 / 4th Armored Div

319th Infantry / 26 JAN 45-28 JAN 45 / 4th Div

3d Bn, 317th Infantry / 26 JAN 45-25 FEB 45 / 4th Div

2d Bn, 3d Bn, 318th Infantry / 26 JAN 45-25 FEB 45 / 4th Div

319th Infantry / 29 JAN 45-4 FEB 45 / 4th Armored Div

318th Infantry / 1 MAR 45-3 MAR 45 / 76th Div

319th Infantry / 8 MAR 45-9 MAR 45 / 46th Div

318th Infantry / 16 MAR 45-18 MAR 45 / 10th Armored Div

1st Bn, 3d Bn, 318th Infantry / 19 MAR 45-22 MAR 45 / 10th Armored Div

318th Infantry / 30 MAR 45-1 APR 45 / 6th Armored Div

WWII COMMAND POSTS			
DATE	TOWN	REGION	COUNTRY
13 JUN 44	Liverpool (Adv)	Lancashire	England
14 JUN 44	Sandiway (H mi SW; Pettypool Hall) (Adv)	Cheshire	England
7 JUL 44	Sandiway (H mi SW; Pettypool Hall) (Main Body) (Entire division arrived in ETO 7 JUL 44)	Cheshire	England
31 JUL 44	Salisbury (marshalling area V-1)	Wiltshire	England
3 AUG 44	St-Jores (3 mi. NE)	Manche	France
9 AUG 44	Montsuer	Mayenne	France
11 AUG 44	Amne (vic SW)	Sarthe	France
13 AUG 44	St-Mars	Sarthe	France
15 AUG 44	Jublains	Mayenne	France
17 AUG 44	Alencon	Orne	France
26 AUG 44	Valetien (3 mi. NE)	Aube	France
27 AUG 44	St-Flavy (2 mi. E)	Aube	France
28 AUG 44	Villeseneux (11 mi. NE)	Meuse	France
30 AUG 44	La Veuve (1 mi. E)	Meuse	France
1 SEP 44	Vignot (2 mi. E)	Meuse	France
3 SEP 44	Girauvoisin (1 mi. E)	Meuse	France
4 SEP 44	Limey (1 mi. SW)	Meurthe-et-Moselle	France
12 SEP 44	Mamey (2 mi. E)	Meurthe-et-Moselle	France
18 SEP 44	Dieulouard (1 mi. N)	Meurthe-et-Moselle	France

WWII COMMAND POSTS (continued)			
DATE	**TOWN**	**REGION**	**COUNTRY**
19 SEP 44	Dieulouard	Meurthe-et-Moselle	France
25 SEP 44	Dieulouard (2 mi S)	Meurthe-et-Moselle	France
27 SEP 44	Dieulouard (2 mi N)	Meurthe-et-Moselle	France
29 SEP 44	Belleville	Meurthe-et-Moselle	France
13 OCT 44	Ville-au-Val	Meurthe-et-Moselle	France
10 NOV 44	Mailly	Moselle	France
11 NOV 44	Liocourt	Moselle	France
13 NOV 44	St-Epvre	Moselle	France
16 NOV 44	Lesse	Moselle	France
24 NOV 44	Charbonnages	Moselle	France
28 NOV 44	St-Avold	Moselle	France
18 DEC 44	Bining	Moselle	France
20 DEC 44	Luxembourg		Luxembourg
21 DEC 44	Dommeldange		Luxembourg
22 DEC 44	Reckange les Mersch		Luxembourg
6 JAN 45	Oberfeulen		Luxembourg
24 JAN 45	Wiltz		Luxembourg
28 JAN 45	Fels		Luxembourg
18 FEB 45	Bettendorf		Luxembourg
26 FEB 45	Mettendorf	Rhineland	Germany
6 MAR 45	Rittersdorf	Rhineland	Germany
11 MAR 45	Mondorf	Rhineland	Germany

WWII COMMAND POSTS (continued)			
DATE	TOWN	REGION	COUNTRY
13 MAR 45	Beurig	Rhineland	Germany
17 MAR 45	Losheim	Rhineland	Germany
19 MAR 45	St Wendel	Rhineland	Germany
20 MAR 45	Glen-Munchweiler	Pfalz	Germany
21 MAR 45	Kaiserslautern	Pfalz	Germany
21 MAR 45	Bad Durkheim	Pfalz	Germany
24 MAR 45	Rockenhausen	Pfalz	Germany
27 MAR 45	Mainz	Hessen-Nassau	Germany
29 MAR 45	Wiesbaden	Hessen	Germany
30 MAR 45	Lich	Oberhessen	Germany
31 MAR 45	Neukirchen	Hessen-Nassau	Germany
1 APR 45	Homburg	Hessen-Nassau	Germany
4 APR 45	Oberzwehren	Hessen-Nassau	Germany
7 APR 45	Gotha	Thuringia	Germany
12 APR 45	Dietendorf	Thuringia	Germany
13 APR 45	Weimar	Thuringia	Germany
14 APR 45	Gera	Thuringia	Germany
16 APR 45	Limbach	Saxony	Germany
19 APR 45	Schesslitz	Bavaria	Germany
22 APR 45	Nurnberg	Bavaria	Germany
29 APR 45	Ziegelsdorf	Bavaria	Germany
30 APR 45	Ergoldsbach	Bavaria	Germany

WWII COMMAND POSTS (continued)			
DATE	TOWN	REGION	COUNTRY
2 MAY 45	Frontenhausen	Bavaria	Germany
3 MAY 45	Simbach	Bavaria	Germany

80TH INFANTRY DIVISION STATISTICS		
Chronology	Date	Location
Activated	15 July 1942	Camp Forrest, Tennessee
Arrived ETO	7 July 1944	Greenock, Firth of Clyde, Scotland
5 MAY 45	Vocklabruck	Austria
Arrived Continent (D+58)	3 August 1944	Utah Beach, Normandy, France
Entered Combat	8 August 1944	LeMans Bridgehead
Days in Combat	277	
V-E Day	8 May 1945	
Return to States	January 1946	
Deactivated	10 January 1946	Camp Kilmer, NJ

TYPES OF CASUALTIES	NUMBERS
Killed	3,038
Wounded	12,484
Missing	488
Captured	1,077
Battle Casualties	14,460
Non-Battle Casualties	11,012
Total Casualties	25,472
Percent of T/O Strength	181

INDIVIDUAL AWARDS	NUMBER
Distinguished Service Cross	48
Legion of Merit	13
Silver Star	671
Soldiers Medal	30
Bronze Star	3,357
Air Medal	121
DFC	5

Appendix 2

INFANTRY ORGANIZATIONS

By the end of World War II, the United States Army numbered about 8,300,000. A few short years earlier in 1939, the total strength of the U.S. Army was only about 174,000.[1] The fact that he United States was able to build such a powerful army in such a short time is a testament to its organizational and industrial capabilities.

As Adolf Hitler and the Third Reich began overrunning Europe, many of the leaders of the United States recognized the threat Germany would eventually pose. The threat to the security of the United States could no longer be disregarded; public opinion rallied and demanded Congress take action. The Selective Service Act was signed by President Franklin D. Roosevelt on September 16, 1940, authorizing the U.S. Army to raise its manpower to 1,400,000 from an estimated 210,000.[2]

On December 7, 1941, Japan bombed Pearl Harbor, an act that brought the United States into what would be forever after known as World War II, effectively declaring war on the United States. Four days later, Germany and Italy declared war as well.

During the early weeks of the war, the United States was primarily on the defensive, organizing its forces and preparing to strike the enemy. Men had to be inducted and trained for combat, industrial capacity had to be expanded to properly supply the troops, and the number and size of our military facilities, both at home and abroad, needed to be increased.[3]

It took the United States, in collaboration with her allies, about eight months to train men, build and accumulate required weapons, and transport them to the various theaters of war to begin the initial offensive. The end of this phase was marked by their first successful assault in August 1942 against the Japanese at Guadalcanal and Tulagi in the Solomons.[4]

The structure of United States Army units is detailed in a formal document called the "Table of Organization & Equipment." The "T/O&E" details the number of men in each unit, the ranks and positions for every size unit, and the weapons and equipment assigned to each man and each unit. Knowing how these various units were organized makes it easier to understand each man's assignment, how each man was supplied, and how attacks were planned.

In the early 1940s, the army adopted a new divisional organization. It was called the "Triangular Division" because of the use of three Infantry Regiments as the base. The infantry division was intended to be simple and mobile, and included only essential troops and equipment. This new division included three infantry regiments and a variety of combat and combat support troops at the division level.

The following table provides a simple "top-down" understanding of the organization within the infantry.

U.S. ARMY TABLE OF ORGANIZATION, 1943

Unit	#Men	Example	Description
Army		3rd Army	Several Corps and Divisions; commanded by Lt. General or Full General
Corps		XX CORPS	3 - 6 Divisions; commanded by Major Generals
Division	13,412	80th Infantry Division	3 Regiments; commanded by Major Generals
Regiment	3,118	317th Infantry Regiment	3 Battalions; commanded by Colonels
Battalion	871	2d Battalion	3 Rifle Companies, 1 Heavy Weapons Company; commanded by Lt. Colonels
Rifle Company	193	E Company	3 - 4 Platoons; commanded by Captains

U.S. ARMY TABLE OF ORGANIZATION, 1943 (continued)			
Heavy Weapons Company	166	H Company	3 - 4 Platoons; commanded by Captains
Platoon	40 - 45	1st Platoon	3 - 4 Squads; commanded by Lieutenants
Squad	12	2d Squad	Ten men armed with M1 rifles, one with BAR, one Sniper armed with M1903 Springfield rifle; commanded by Jr. Sergeant or Corporal

The World War II Infantry Division

The division was the largest ground combat formation and normally included infantry, artillery, and armored components. A division was usually commanded by a major general. Divisions were fixed combined arms organizations of eight to eleven maneuver battalions, three to four field artillery battalions, and other combat, combat support, and combat service support units. They were self-sustaining and flexible units capable of performing any tactical mission.

Divisions were (and still are) the basic units of maneuver at the strategic and tactical level. There are six types of divisions in various armies: infantry, light infantry, mechanized infantry, armored, airborne, and air assault.

The U.S. Army had a peak strength of eighty-nine divisions during World War II—sixty-six infantry, sixteen armored, five airborne, one mountain, and one cavalry. For a brief time there were ninety divisions, but the 2nd Cavalry Division was deactivated in May 1944.

The size of divisions varied during the war. Under the Table of Organization in June 1941 a U.S. infantry division had 15,245 officers and enlisted men; by June 1943 the number was reduced to 13,412 men; in January 1945 an infantry division was authorized to have 14,037 men.

The World War II Infantry Regiment

The regiment was a major army formation and the principal component of U.S. infantry and airborne divisions. They were normally commanded by colonels. Regiments were the largest U.S. Army units with infantry, artillery, and armored components. The standard infantry regiment consisted of three infantry battalions (1st, 2d, and 3d Battalions), an anti-tank company (with nine 57mm AT guns), a cannon company (with six 105mm Howitzers), a headquarters company, a service company, and a medical detachment.

The infantry regiment of World War II was a powerful and flexible organization of units and was considered the core of the infantry division. Unfortunately, poor planning for replacements in the early part of the war meant that the infantry regiment was chronically understrength. For example, on December 1, 1944, the Third Army was understrength by some fifty-five rifle companies. On average, each of the Third Army's infantry divisions was operating at about two-thirds its strength in rifle companies.

The World War II Infantry Battalion

The battalion consisted of three or four companies and a headquarters, and was normally commanded by a lieutenant colonel. Infantry, artillery, and armored battalions were normally subordinate to regiments or divisions, although these and special-purpose battalions (e.g., signal, reconnaissance) were sometimes attached to higher formations or could serve as independent units. Battalions attacked, defended, delayed, or moved to assume new positions. Battalions were numbered sequentially: 1st, 2d, and 3d Battalions.

In the 1943, U.S. Army Tables of Organizations for an infantry battalion provided for 871 officers and enlisted men, a tank battalion 729 men, and an infantry (airborne) parachute battalion 530 men. The Infantry Battalion consisted of three rifle companies, each with its own support weapons (60mm mortars and air-cooled .30-caliber light machine guns); a heavy weapons company (with both 81mm mortars and water-cooled. 30-caliber heavy machine guns); and a headquarters company. The 1st Battalion consisted of rifle companies A, B, and C, with heavy weapons company D. The 2d Battalion consisted of rifle companies E, F, and G with heavy weapons company H. The 3d Battalion consisted of rifle companies I, K, and L, with heavy weapons company M.

The specialized battalions of an infantry division in 1943 consisted of a medical battalion, with an authorized strength of 465 men; an engineer battalion, with 647 men. The 1943 armored division had an engineer battalion of 693 men, a medical battalion of 417 men, and an ordnance (maintenance) battalion of 762 men.

The World War II Company

The company consisted of three or four platoons: three Infantry platoons, a weapons platoon, and a Company HQ, for an official total of 193 men: six officers and 187 enlisted men. Combat companies were normally subordinate to battalions and were the smallest military organization that provided mess, supply, and other support functions to troops. Companies were normally commanded by captains.

Infantry companies were lettered sequentially through the infantry regiment: "A Company," "B Company," "C Company," and so on, through "M Company." The letter "J" was omitted so it would not be confused with "I" Company. Three rifle companies and one heavy weapons company were assigned to a Battalion. Companies were also given nicknames, depending on their letter designation. Note that these nicknames were the designated phonetic alphabet in 1944-45. The phonetic alphabet has since changed since World War II:

A: Able Company
B: Baker Company
C: Charlie Company
D: Dog Company
E: Easy Company
F: Fox Company
G: George Company
H: How Company
I: Item Company
K: King Company
L: Love Company
M: Mike Company

Rifle Company. The rifle company consisted of a small headquarters (HQ) section, three rifle platoons, and a weapons platoon. Rifle companies were usually commanded by captains. The infantry rifle company men were the close-in fighters around whom the rest of the division was built. A rifle company HQ comprised of the following personnel:

Company Commander: Captain, armed with an M1 Carbine;
Executive Officer: 1st Lieutenant, armed with an M1 Carbine;
First Sgt: Sergeant, armed with an M1 Carbine;
Mess Sgt: Sergeant, armed with an M1 Garand;
Supply Sgt: Sergeant, armed with an M1 Garand;
Communications Sgt: Sergeant, armed with an M1 Carbine;

Company Clerk: Corporal, armed with an M1 Garand;
28 assorted privates, armed with M1 Garands.

All five of the company's bazooka anti-tank rocket launchers, six BARs, and six submachine guns were allocated as needed by the company commander.

A rifle platoon consisted of a small Platoon HQ and three squads, each numbered sequentially (1st, 2d, and 3d). Each rifle platoon consisted of 41 men. A rifle platoon HQ was composed of the following personnel:

Platoon Leader: 2d Lieutenant, armed with an M1 Carbine;
Platoon Sgt: First Sergeant, armed with an M1 Garand;
Guide Staff Sgt: Staff Sergeant, armed with an M1903 Springfield;
Two Messengers, armed with M1 Garands.

Each rifle squad consisted of twelve armed men with ten M1 Garand rifles, one Browning Automatic Rifle (or BAR, pronounced B-A-R, not "bar"), and one M1903 bolt-action Springfield rifle. Rifle Squads were composed of the following personnel:

Squad Leader: Staff Sergeant, armed with an M1 Garand;
Assistant Squad Leader: Sergeant, armed with an M1 Garand;
Automatic Rifleman, armed with a BAR;
Assistant Automatic Rifleman, armed with an M1 Garand;
Ammunition Bearer, armed with an M1 Garand;
Seven Riflemen, armed with M1 Garands.

The weapons platoon of a rifle company consisted of a small platoon HQ and two sections: a 60mm mortar section and a light machine gun section. The weapons platoon HQ was equipped with two jeeps; one with a mounted .50 caliber MG and another with a 1/4 ton trailer. In addition, the weapons platoon was equipped with three 2.36-inch bazookas. Weapons Platoon HQ was composed of the following personnel;

Platoon Commander: 1st Lieutenant, armed with an M1 Carbine;
Platoon Sergeant: Sergeant, armed with an M1 Carbine;
Two jeep drivers, armed with M1 Garands;
Two messengers, armed with M1 Garands.

The 60mm mortar section consisted of three squads, each with its own 60mm Mortar and a small HQ. 60mm Mortar Section HQ consisted of the following personnel:

Section Leader: Sergeant, armed with an M1 Garand;
Messenger: armed with an M1 Garand;
Two Privates, each armed with an M1 Garand.

Each squad in the 60mm mortar section consisted of the following personnel:

#1 Gunner: Corporal, armed with an Colt automatic pistol;
Assistant Gunner: armed with a Colt automatic pistol;
Three Ammunition Bearers, each armed with an M1 Carbine.

The light MG section consisted of two squads, each with its own .30-caliber air-cooled light machine gun, and a small HQ. A Light MG section HQ consisted of the following personnel:

Section Leader: Sergeant, armed with an M1 Garand;
Messenger, armed with an M1 Garand;
Two privates, each armed with an M1 Garand.

Each squad in the light MG section consisted of the following personnel:

Squad Leader: Corporal, armed with an M1 Carbine;
#1 Gunner, armed with a Colt Automatic Pistol;
Assistant Machine Gunner, armed with a Colt automatic pistol;
Two Ammunition Bearers, each armed with an M1 Carbine.

Heavy Weapons Company. The heavy weapons company was equipped with 81mm mortars and water-cooled .30-caliber machine guns. The chief duty of a heavy weapons company was to provide support to the three rifle companies in the battalion. There were three platoons in a heavy weapons company and a HQ. The heavy weapons company was also equipped with two jeeps, one with a mounted .50-caliber machine gun. The company was also provided with a weapons carrier. A Heavy weapons company HQ consisted of the following personnel:

Company Commander: Captain, armed with an M1 Carbine;
Executive Officer: 1st Lieutenant, armed with an M1 Carbine;
First Sergeant: Sergeant, armed with an M1 Carbine;
Staff Sergeant: Sergeant, armed with an M1 Carbine;
Supply Sergeant: Sergeant, armed with an M1 Carbine;
Communications Sergeant: Sergeant, armed with an M1 Carbine;
Recon Sergeant: Sergeant, armed with an M1 Carbine;

Transport Sergeant: Sergeant, armed with an M1 Garand;
Company Clerk: Corporal, armed with an M1 Garand;
Three Cooks, armed with an M1 Garand;
Two Cook's Helpers, armed with an M1 Garand;
Armorer, armed with an M1 Garand;
Auto Mechanic, Truck Driver, armed with an M1 Garand;
Bugler, armed with an M1 Carbine;
Two Messengers, jeep drivers, armed with an M1 Carbine;
Messenger, armed with an M1 Carbine;
Fourteen Privates, armed with M1 Garands.

The 81mm mortar platoon consisted of a small HQ and three sections of two squads each. The 81mm mortar platoon was also equipped with a jeep carrying two bazookas. The 81mm mortar platoon HQ consisted of the following personnel:

Platoon Commander: 1st Lieutenant, armed with an M1 Carbine;
Platoon Sergeant: Technical Sergeant, armed with an M1 Carbine;
Instrument: Corporal, armed with an M1 Garand;
Transport: Corporal, armed with an M1 Carbine;
Messenger, Jeep Driver, armed with M1 Carbines;
Messenger, armed with an M1 Carbine.

Each Squad in the 81mm mortar platoon was equipped with an 81mm mortar and consisted of the following personnel:

Squad Leader: Staff Sergeant, armed with an M1 Garand;
#1 Gunner: Corporal, armed with a Colt automatic pistol;
Assistant Gunner, armed with a Colt automatic pistol;
Ammunition Bearer, Jeep Driver, armed with M1 Carbines;
Four Ammunition Bearers, armed with M1 Carbines.

The machine gun (MG) platoon consisted of a small HQ and two sections of two squads each. The MG platoon was also equipped with a jeep carrying two bazookas. The MG platoon provided heavier sustained fire capability than the light MGs in the rifle companies' weapons platoons. Being water-cooled and having stronger crews, the heavy MGs could maintain sustained fire for long periods of time, denying an area to the enemy or supressing the defense before an attack. The MG platoon HQ consisted of the following personnel:

Platoon Commander: 1st Lieutenant, armed with an M1 Carbine;
Platoon Sergeant: Technical Sergeant, armed with an M1 Carbine;

Instrument: Corporal, armed with an M1 Garand;
Transportation: Corporal, armed with an M1 Garand;
Messenger, Jeep Driver, armed with M1 Carbines.

Each section of a MG platoon consisted of two squads each. The MG platoon section leader was a staff sergeant armed with an M1 Garand.

Each squad of a MG Section handled one .30-caliber water-cooled machine gun. The squad was also equipped with a jeep and a 1/4-ton trailer. The squad consisted of the following personnel:

Squad Leader: Sergeant, armed with an M1 Garand;
#1 Machine Gunner, armed with a Colt automatic pistol;
Assistant Machine Gunner, armed with a Colt automatic pistol;
Ammunition Bearer, Jeep Driver, armed with M1 Carbines;
Three Ammunition Bearers, armed with M1 Carbines.

The World War II Platoon

The platoon was (and still is) the smallest military unit led by an officer in the U.S. Army. Platoons are found in most types of military organizations and are normally a component of companies. They consist of three squads. Infantry platoons had some forty to forty-five men and were normally commanded by lieutenants.

The infantry platoon was composed of three rifle squads, as well as an HQ section. The HQ consisted of a platoon leader, usually a lieutenant, a platoon sergeant, a tech sergeant, a platoon guide, usually a staff sergeant, and two messengers. Everyone in the platoon was armed with the M1 rifle except for the BAR men (armed with Browning Automatic Rifles) and the platoon leader, who carried an M1 Carbine.

The World War II Squad

The squad was the smallest infantry unit. In the U.S. Army and Marine Corps, squads were normally commanded by junior sergeants or corporals. Three rifle squads generally comprised a rifle platoon.

During World War II, U.S. Army squads generally consisted of twelve men, ten of whom, including the squad leader, were armed with M1 Garand semi-automatic rifles, one with a Browning Automatic Rifle (BAR), and one with an M1903 Springfield rifle fitted with a sniper scope.

Each squad operated as a BAR team, a grenadier team, and a scout and command team under the squad leader. The squad generally operated as a two-man scout section and a four-man maneuver and assault section. The squad leader customarily advanced with the scout section.

A BAR team comprised three men: the BAR gunner, the BAR assistant, and the ammo bearer. Two riflemen were considered scouts; the rest of the squad (five men) were the rifle team. During combat, the scouts were supposed to locate the enemy, the BAR team was supposed to lay down a base of fire, while the rifle team maneuvered to eliminate the enemy.

You'll hear a lot about the "S-3", the "G-2" and other similar names. The "Gx" designation is the principal staff officer for the division level. The "Sx" designation is the principal staff officer for the regiment or group level. The following table provides an overview of these positions and their duties.

DIVISION LEVEL		
	Officer	Description
G-1	Personnel	Personnel and administration section of the general staff or principal staff officer heading that activity in a division or higher command.
G-2	Intelligence	Intelligence section of the general staff or principal staff officer heading that activity in a division or higher command. G-2 is responsible for the Production of Intelligence; Counterintelligence; Intelligence Training for all Staff Members.
G-3	Operations and Training	Operations and training section of the general staff or principal staff officer heading that activity in a division or higher command.
G-4	Logistics, Supply, Construction	Supply and maintenance section of the general staff or principal staff officer heading that activity in a division or higher command.
G-5	Civil Affairs, Military Gov't	Civilian Affairs section of the general staff or principal staff officer heading that activity in a division or higher command.

REGIMENT LEVEL		
	Level	Description
S-1	Personnel	S-1 is the regiment's principal staff officer for all personnel matters, including planning and supervision of matters of procurement, classification, assignment, pay, promotion, transfer, retirement and discharge, decorations, citations, honors, awards, religious, recreational, welfare, postal service, morale, stragglers, and collection and disposition of POWs.
S-2	Intelligence	S-2 is the regiment's principal staff officer for all matters dealing with military intelligence, including collection, evaluation, interpretation, and distribution of information about the enemy.
S-3	Operations	S-3 is the regiment's principal staff officer for all matters dealing with operations and training, including organization, training, and combat operations.
S-4	Logistics	S-4 is the regiment's principal staff officer for all matters dealing with logistics, including supply support.
S-5	Civil Affairs, Military Gov't	S-5 is the regiment's principal staff officer for all matters dealing with civilian affairs.

During wartime, it is the rare individual unit that operates at full strength. Casualties and disease whittle away at a unit's manpower from the day it is formed. With higher than expected casualties, the U.S. Army adopted a "spare parts" approach to infantry replacements, throwing new arrivals straight into combat. The original idea was to continuously replenish men daily—this way, entire divisions could remain in combat for a longer period of time. Replacements would join veteran soldiers in companies, platoons, and squads. They would be integrated into the fighting unit and be taught how to fight and survive in combat. About half of the 3,000,000-plus men who served in the U.S.

Army in the ETO arrived as replacements.[5] More than one-half of the replacements moved into combat and were killed or wounded within a short time. If a replacement survived his first few days, he had become a combat veteran, even though there was still a lot to learn—and his chance of surviving increased substantially.

The 80th Division entered the ETO on 3 August 1944. It suffered more than 25,450 casualties during its 277 days of combat, a 180.8% turnover.

GLOSSARY

AA: Antiaircraft Artillery
AEF: Allied Expeditionary Force
AT: Antitank
CO: Commanding Officer
CP: Command Post
CT: Combat Team
DSC: Distinguished Service Cross
ETO: European Theater of Operations
FA: Field Artillery
FFI: French Forces of the Interior
FM: Field Manual
GI: Government Issue
HE: High Explosive
I&R: Intelligence and Reconnaissance
KIA: Killed in action
LD: Line of Departure
MG: Machine Gun
MP: Military Police
NCO: Noncommissioned officer
OD's: Olive Drab uniform of the U.S. Army
OP: Observation post

POM: Preparations for Overseas Movement
Pvt: Private
Pfc: Private First Class
POW: Prisoner of war
S-1: Personnel
S-2: Intelligence
S-3: Operations/Training
S-4: Logistics/Supply
S-5: Civilian Affairs
SS: Schutzstaffel ("Protection Detachment")
SHAEF Supreme Headquarters, Allied Expeditionary Force
TD: Tank destroyer
TO: Table of Organization
TO/E: Table of Organization and Equipment

ENDNOTES

Chapter 1

Blumenson, Martin, *The Duel for France, 1944. The Men and Battles that Changed the Fate of Europe*, (Da Capo Press, 2000), p. 17.

Chapter 2

1. Murrell, Robert T., *History 317th Infantry Regiment, 80th Infantry Division*, p. 2.
2. Ibid, p. 3.
3. "317th Infantry Crushes Foe in Victorious Drive through France, Luxembourg, Germany, Austria." *The Thundering Herd*, Published in Fussen, Germany by 317th Infantry, 80th Infantry Division, September 26, 1945, p. 1.
4. Hayes, Col. James. *The Valiant Die Once*. Personal memoirs, 1998.
5. *80th Infantry "Blue Ridge" Division*. (Paducah, Kentucky: Turner Publishing Company, 2nd Edition, 1999), p. 21.
6. Murrell, Robert T., *History 317th Infantry Regiment, 80th Infantry Division*, p. 8.
7. *80th Infantry "Blue Ridge" Division*, pp. 17-18.

Chapter 3

1. Doubler, Michael D., *Closing with the Enemy - How GIs Fought the War in Europe, 1944–1945* (University Press of Kansas, 1994), p. 142.

2. Ibid.

3. Cole, Hugh M. *The Lorraine Campaign.* United States Army in World War II. (Washington, D.C.: U.S. Army, Office of the Chief of Military History, 1965), 65.

Chapter 9

1. Murrell, Robert T., *Stories of the Men of the 80th Infantry Division World War Two: Relief of the Besieged U.S. Troops in Bastogne by Richard Radock, 319th Inf Medic Bn Company C 8th Division* (Oakmont, PA, 2001), p. 26.

2. Ambrose, Stephen E., *Citizen Soldiers* (New York, Touchstone, 1997), pp. 233-234.

3. Doubler, Michael D., *Closing with the Enemy,* (Lawrence, KS, University of Kansas Press, 1994), p. 201.

Chapter 11

1. Ambrose, *Citizen Soldier,* p. 144.
2. Ibid., p. 412.

Chapter 14

1. Ambrose, *Citizen Soldiers,* p. 418.

Chapter 16

1. The Buchenwald Report (*Bericht über das Konzentrationslager Buchenwald bei Weimar*), prepared April and May of 1945 by an intelligence team from the Psychological Warfare Division, SHAEF, assisted by a committee of Buchenwald prisoners. (Westview Press, Inc., Boulder, Colorado, 1995).
2. Ibid.

Appendix 2

1. Forty, George. *US Army Handbook 1939-1945.* Sutton Publishing Limited, 1995, p. 1.
2. Ibid., p. 5.
3. Ibid., p. 6.
4. Ibid., p. 7.
5. Ambrose, *Citizen Soldiers.*

BIBLIOGRAPHY

In addition to Lieutenant Adkins's own detailed journals and recollections, the following books and materials were used to help produce this book.

The Buchenwald Report, translation of Bericht über das Konzentrationslager Buchenwald bei Weimar, prepared in April and May of 1945 by a special intelligence team from the Psychological Warfare Division, SHAEF, assisted by a committee of Buchenwald prisoners. Published in 1995 in the U.S. by Westview Press, Inc., Boulder, Colorado.

80th Infantry "Blue Ridge" Division. Paducah, Kentucky: Turner Publishing Company, 2nd Edition, 1999.

The Thundering Herd, September 26, 1945, No. 12. 317th Infantry, 80th Infantry Division.

Ambrose, Stephen E. *Citizen Soldiers: The U.S. Army from the Normandy Beaches to the Bulge to the Surrender of Germany. June 7, 1944 to May 7, 1945.* New York: Simon & Schuster, 1997.

Anderson, Rich. "The United States Army in World War II." Military History Online: www.militaryhistoryonline.com.

Blumenson, Martin. *The Battle of the Generals: The Untold Story of the Falaise Pocket—The Campaign That Should Have Won World War II.* New York: William Monrow and Company, Inc., 1993.

Blumenson, Martin. *Breakout and Pursuit United States Army in World War II.* Washington, D.C.: U.S. Army, Office of the Chief of Military History, 1961.

——. *The Duel for France, 1944: The Men and Battles that Changes the Fate of Europe.* Da Capo Press, 2000.

Bradley, Omar N. *A Soldier's Story.* New York: Rand McNally, 1951; reprint edition, New York, 1978.

Cole, Hugh M. *The Ardennes: The Battle of the Bulge. United States Army in World War II*. Washington, D.C.: U.S. Army, Office of the Chief of Military History, 1965.

Doubler, Michael D. *Closing with the Enemy: How GIs Fought the War in Europe, 1944–1945*. Lawrence: University Press of Kansas, 1994.

Featherston, Alwyn. *Saving the Breakout: The 30th Division's Heroic Stand at Mortain, August 7-12, 1944*. Novato: Presidio Press, 1993.

Forty, George. *US Army Handbook 1939-1945*. Sutton Publishing Limited, 1995.

Hayes, James H. *The Valiant Die Once*. Privately Printed. N.D.

Murrell, Robert T. *317th Infantry Regiment History*. Privately Printed, Oakridge, Pennsylvania. N.D.

———. *Operational History of the 80th Infantry Division. August 1944 to May 1945*. Privately Printed, Oakridge, Pennsylvania. N.D.

———, compiler. *Stories of the Men of the 80th Infantry Division World War II*. Company M 318th Regiment, 2001. Privately Printed, Oakridge, Pennsylvania, 2001.

Polmar, Norman and Allen, Thomas B. *World War II: America at War*. New York: Random House, 1991.

Weigley, Russell F. *Eisenhower's Lieutenants: The Campaigns of France and Germany, 1944-1945*. Bloomington: Indiana University Press, 1981.

INDEX